# THE HEART OF THE

# NEW TESTAMENT

# THE HEART OF THE
# NEW TESTAMENT

*By* H. I. HESTER

*Head of the Department of Religion, William Jewell College, 1926-1961*
*Vice President, Midwestern Baptist Theological Seminary, 1961-1965*

**BROADMAN PRESS**
**Nashville, Tennessee**

*Fifth Printing, 2000*

DEWEY DECIMAL CLASSIFICATION: 225.95
SUBJECT HEADING: BIBLE. N.T.—
HISTORY OF BIBLICAL EVENTS

# A FOREWORD BY THE AUTHOR

*The Heart of the New Testament* is the second and final volume in the series of college textbooks on the Bible sponsored by the Education Commission of the Southern Baptist Convention. This volume, like the one on the Old Testament *(The Heart of Hebrew History)*, was prepared for college students on the freshman and sophomore level. It has been produced to meet a need for an acceptable guide to the study of the New Testament.

The contents of the book are arranged in three sections. Part One is intended to introduce the student to the New Testament. Part Two is the story of the earthly life of Jesus Christ as it is recorded in the Gospels. Part Three deals with the growth of the Christian movement as given in the book of Acts and later books in the New Testament.

The book is not designed to take the place of the New Testament. It is an effort to arrange in narrative form the contents of the New Testament in chronological order so that the student may get an intelligent view of the origin and development of Christianity. With the purpose of letting the New Testament speak for itself the author has made frequent use of direct quotations from the scriptures. To encourage the student in the use of the New Testament as his text, specific scripture assignments are given with each topic.

The author is indebted to a number of friends who have given generous assistance in producing the book. Dr. Charles D. Johnson, Chairman of the Education Commission, has given constant encouragement and help. Mr. John Nowell, Manager of the Quality Press, Inc., and his staff have done excellent work in putting the manuscript in book form. To these and all others who have assisted in this undertaking the author hereby expresses his sincere appreciation.

REVISED EDITION

The first edition of *The Heart of the New Testament* came from the press in September, 1950. The book met with immediate favor both in colleges and with the public. Consequently it has been necessary to issue other printings each succeeding year. From time to time corrections and slight changes have been made. But after twelve years it is time for a more extensive and thorough revision. Accordingly each chapter has been read carefully and various changes have been made both in language and in content. In some chapters we have condensed the material without loss in meaning. The closing chapter has been expanded considerably so as to do justice to the important material under discussion. Each scripture reference has been checked and where necessary has been corrected. We hereby express appreciation to all who have assisted in this revision.

H. I. HESTER

# CONTENTS

Crucifixion. 18. Via Dolorosa. 19. The First Three Hours on the Cross. 20. The Three Hours of Darkness. 21. All Nature Speaks. 22. The Burial of His Body.

# MAPS

# PART ONE

*Introducing the New Testament*

*Chapter 1*

## WHY WE STUDY THE NEW TESTAMENT

1. Significance of the Christian Movement. 2. The Greatness of Jesus. 3. Effects on History. 4. The New Testament in Modern Life. 5. Plan of Study.

# Why We Study the New Testament

## 1. Significance of the Christian Movement.

The most amazing movement in all history is the one which arose with Jesus Christ and his disciples. This movement was launched by Jesus during the "days of his flesh" in Palestine more than nineteen hundred years ago and has been carried on by his disciples since his death. The most meaningful book in all literature is the New Testament, our only authentic record of this historic enterprise.

The story contained in the New Testament is known to more people than any other ever written. While more than half the people of the world know something of this story our knowledge of it is often fragmentary and incomplete. To obtain accurate knowledge of all the facts in the record will require long and diligent study. To understand fully the exhaustless meaning of the truths contained in this story is an accomplishment which no one man in all history could claim. Each new generation will continue to discover new truths which hitherto have been unobserved. Human minds will never outreach the truth incorporated in this story; indeed, we may never completely understand all that is contained therein. This fact, however, should inspire the student to enter this field of study with enthusiasm. A well planned course of study in the New Testament will be an enjoyable and rewarding experience. An understanding of the basic facts of historic Christianity introduces the student to a field which will become increasingly rich and satisfying.

## 2. The Greatness of Jesus.

By any and all standards Jesus Christ has always been regarded as the greatest figure in human history. As we enter upon the second half of the twentieth century a number of men have prepared lists of the greatest men of these fifty years. While we recognize the great achievements of men selected in these lists none of us could think of comparing any of them to Jesus Christ. On any list of the world's greatest men we always find at its head Jesus of Nazareth. Regardless of whether or not men acknowledge him as Saviour and Lord they must pay tribute to him as the world's outstanding man.

In many volumes one may find the greatness of Jesus extolled. "It was reserved for Christianity to present to the world an ideal character, which, through all the changes of eighteen centuries, has inspired the hearts of men with an impassioned love; has shown itself capable of acting on all ages, nations, temperaments, and conditions; has been not only the highest pattern of virtue, but the strongest incentive to its practice, and has exercised so deep an influence that it may be truly said that the simple record of his three short years of active life has done more to regenerate and to soften mankind than all the disquisitions of philosophers and all the exhortations of moralists. This has, indeed, been the well-spring of whatever is best and purest in Christian life. Amid all the sins and failings, amid all the priest-craft and persecution and fanaticism that have defaced the church, it has preserved, in the character of its Founder, an enduring principle of regeneration."[1]

In his book, *The Character of Jesus,* Dr. Charles Jefferson says of him: "More lives of Jesus have been written within the last fifty years than of any other historic character. More pages are printed about him every week than about any hundred of the world's greatest men. He exerts a power which is so phenomenal that many feel he must be more than man, linked in some way or other with the Eternal. He must be — men say — the Son of God. In this land alone men contribute several hundred million dollars every year to support the institutions which bear his name. They are not compelled to do this. They do it voluntarily because they want to do it, and because he so works upon them that they count such giving a privilege and pleasure. As Napoleon Bonaparte once said, 'This man vanished for eighteen hundred years still holds the characters of men as in a vise.' The little Corsican sat dumfounded as he compared his greatness with the greatness of the Man of Galilee. Napoleon's last biographer devotes two volumes to the rise of his hero and two volumes to his decline and fall. All the volumes of the life of Jesus record the story of his ascent. He goes on and on from victory to victory, from glory to glory, and as men's eyes become cleansed and their hearts purified they see with increasing certainty that God has indeed so highly exalted him and some day every knee shall bend to him and every tongue confess that he is King indeed.

"His greatness is full-orbed. He was complete, and in his completeness we find an explanation of his beauty. Men who stood nearest to him were charmed and swayed by his loveliness. He was full of grace and truth. He had a charm about him which wooed and fascinated. Children liked him, boys sang for him, publicans hung upon him. He had the heart of a child, the tenderness of a woman, the strength of a man. The three dimensions of his life were complete. He had eyes which looked along extended lines running into eternity; he had sympathies wide enough to cover humanity to its outermost edge; he had a purpose which included all lands and ages, his kingdom is to be universal and it shall have no end. He is at every point complete. His virtues are all full-statured, his graces are all in fullest bloom. You can no more add anything to him than you can add something to the sky. He pushed every good trait of human character to its utmost limit. His forgiveness was unbounded, his generosity was untiring, his patience was inexhaustible, his mercy was immeasurable, his courage was illimitable, his wisdom was unfathomable, his kindness was interminable, his faith removed mountains, his hope had no shadow in it, his love was infinite. And so it is impossible to go beyond him. We can never outgrow him. He will be always ahead of us. We shall always hear him saying, 'Follow me!' He is the ideal of the heart. He is the goal of humanity. It is this completeness of his character which accounts not only for his beauty but for his perennial and increasing power. He is the lily of the valley, the fairest of ten thousand, and one altogether lovely. He is the image of God!"[2]

A more recent writer, Dr. Walter Bell Denny, pays his tribute to Jesus. "And this perfect character is no mere formal pattern, but a living force, a radiant, contagious personality, whose spirit flows out into the lives of those who attach themselves to him, like living water from an endless spring. From this dynamic center has continued to flow through nineteen centuries a stream of vitalizing energy that has quickened and set in motion the spiritual life of the world. Where the life of men has sent its roots down to that undercurrent, all the noblest and most creative impulses of human nature have been released. The beauty of his life has set free in men the noblest creations of art and music. The unselfishness of his character has inspired our finest public service and philanthropy. The profoundness of his insight has quickened all our search for truth. The loftiness of his spiritual vision has carried us above the sordidness of earthly satisfactions. The perfectness of his love has shamed us with its purity and wooed us with its gentleness from stained lives to holiness of heart. The greatness of his faith has caught us in its spell until we, too, have shared with him the assurance of the life immortal. His greatness is not only that he made us know that we are sons of God. He showed us, in himself, what a real, complete Son of God is like."[3]

"And still Christ is not yet expelled from the earth either by the ravages of time or by the efforts of men. His memory is everywhere: on the walls of the churches and the schools, on the tops of bell-towers and of mountains, in street-shrines, at the heads of beds and over tombs, thousands of crosses bring to mind the death of the Crucified One. Take away the frescoes from the churches, carry off the pictures from the altars and from the houses, and the life of Christ fills museums and picture-galleries. Throw away breviaries and missals, and you find His name and His words in all the books of literature."[4]

### 3. Effects on History.

During his lifetime no one understood or even dreamed of the influence which the work of Jesus would have on the history of the world. It is possible now, however, for the student of history to look back upon these two thousand years and understand to some degree the revolutionary, beneficent and far-reaching influence which the teachings of Jesus have had upon the races of mankind. Indeed, many books have been written to demonstrate this fact.

These effects are to be seen in every area of human life. Christianity at the start revolutionized the life of the Roman world. It has been the saving influence of every generation and century since its beginning. It has inspired men to their highest endeavors in intellectual areas. It has profoundly affected all the arts. Its contribution to painting, sculpture, architecture, music, education and literature has been immeasurable.

In no realm have the teachings of Jesus produced such beneficent results as in the field of human welfare or social progress. From him we have learned the true ideals and values of the social order. From him we have learned the dignity and worth of personality. He first gave to the world the idea of the brotherhood of man. His teachings have contributed immeasurably to the uplift of women. Because of him womanhood and childhood have been emancipated. The inspiration for every piece of humane legislation has come from the Man of Nazareth. His teachings have done more to eradicate human slavery than all other agencies combined. Because of the truth which Jesus lived and taught all the charitable institutions which minister to underprivileged and needy people have come into existence. His teachings have been the source of the inspiration and passion for the social reforms of recent centuries.

The influence of Jesus on the religious life of the peoples of the world has been incalculable. He came into a world already filled with religious institutions. Slowly and yet surely his truths triumphed over the false teachings of other systems. That triumph has continued through the centuries. Despite temporary and discouraging delays it is steadily moving ahead and ultimately will reach the degree of complete and final victory predicted for it.

"Here is a man who was born in an obscure village, the child of a woman who, to her peasant neighbors, was just one of them and one with them. He grew up in another village. He worked in a carpenter shop until he was thirty, and then, for three years, he was an itinerant preacher. He never wrote a book. He never held an office. He never owned a home. He never had a family. He never went to college. He never put his feet inside a big city. He never traveled two hundred miles from the place where he was born. He never did one of the things that usually accompany greatness. He had no credentials but himself.

"While still a young man the tide of private opinion turned against him. His friends ran away. One of them denied him. He was turned over to his enimies. He went through the mockery of a trial. He was nailed to a cross between two thieves. As he was dying, his executioners gambled for the only piece of property he had on earth, and that was his coat. When he was dead he was taken down and laid in a borrowed grave through the pity of a friend.

"Nineteen wide centuries have come and gone and today, He is the centerpiece of the human race and the leader of the column of progress.

"I am far within the mark when I say that all the armies that ever marched, and all the navies that were ever built, and all the parliaments that ever sat, and all the kings that ever reigned, put together have not affected the life of man upon this earth as has that One Solitary Life!"[5]

Because of the greatness of Jesus as a person and because of the ever-enlarging effects of his teachings upon the lives of men, it is imperative that every intelligent person be acquainted with the origin and early development of the Christian enterprise.

*4. The New Testament in Modern Life.*

What has been said up to this point should convince one that Christianity has vitally affected the life of the world during the past 1900 years. Thoughtful people naturally wonder will this be true in the future. Will Christianity continue to live and to affect the lives of individuals and society tomorrow? Frankly there are some who say no. These are bold to affirm that we have outgrown Christ in the present progressive period of history; he has lost his appeal to men, and the future can never be influenced by him and his teachings like past centuries have been. According to those who hold this view the place of Jesus in the lives of men is steadily diminishing and will continue to decrease in the future.

Naturally no one can tell just what place Jesus Christ will have in the lives of men in the future. However, before concluding that Christianity has already reached its zenith of power and is declining, it will be well to examine some aspects of life today with a view to discovering how they are influenced by him.

At the outset we may admit that Jesus Christ does not have the place in the world which he should have. The degree to which his teachings are accepted and followed is far less than ideal. His kingdom has not yet come. He does not reign in the lives of men as he should. However this is the failure of his followers and not Jesus. Without making any exaggerated claims, we may be surprised to discover how deeply and vitally his teachings are affecting the lives of people in our own time.

The church is the one organization of which we naturally think first. What is its place and influence today? To begin with we may note that reliable statistics show that in the United States there has been a steady increase in church membership for many years. This growth persists through periods of peace and war. It is worthy of note also that in every community the best citizens are those who proudly claim membership in some Christian church. The critics of the church assert that church attendance is steadily decreasing; that its members do not often support the services with their presence. Admitting that church attendance is far from ideal, the fact remains that there are still millions of people who gather in their churches for worship services every Sunday. No other institution continues to command the support and devotion which multitudes of people gladly give to their church. A study of the budgets of churches for their work at home and abroad will reveal a steady increase in gifts which reaches an amazing total each year.

According to the report of the Stewardship Department of the National Council of Churches, made in November 1962, the total gifts of the forty-six Protestant denominations in the United States for all objects in 1961 was well over two and one half billion dollars. Were the gifts of Catholic churches included the amount would probably be doubled.

The influence of Jesus Christ in the educational life of our country is vast and far-reaching. Every denomination has a program of education designed for the needs of every age group from infants to adults. This program involves the spending of millions of dollars for teaching materials and equipment. It involves the labor of tens of thousands of men and women who voluntarily prepare themselves to teach each Sunday a total number of some fifty million people in church schools. One should not forget the thousands of Vacation Bible Schools held each summer; the hundreds of week-day church schools; the inumerable young people's organizations with their programs of study; the great hosts of devout women who study missions and promote the missionary activities of their churches. In addition to these educational activities in the churches we may mention the place of religion in the field of higher education. There are in our country today approximately five hundred church-related colleges which are providing educational opportunities for nearly one-half of the 3,000,000 young people in colleges and universities. An indication of the growing significance of Christianity in higher education in America is the emphasis which large universities are giving to it by the establishing of Schools of Religion. Finally, one should remember that there are two hundred or more seminaries or divinity schools where many thousands of young men are being given professional training for their work as ministers and missionaries.

The first book to be printed from moveable type was the Bible. Since that date, some five hundred years ago, religious forces have employed printed materials in ever increasing volume. No statistician would be able to calculate the thousands of tons of paper used in teaching materials — books, tracts, magazines and journals. The annual output of some of the great religious publishing houses would fill the cars of several long freight trains. The secular press gives much space in one manner or another to religious subjects. More than four hundred newspapers print each day a verse or a text from the Bible. Almost every secular magazine publishes some articles on religious subjects at regular intervals. In the field of fiction religion is always prominent. Books of a wholesome religious character, with literary worth, are usually popular. A number of "best sellers" in fiction in recent years have been of a religious nature. The fact that the Bible itself continues year after year to be the "best seller" among all books is known to every intelligent person. It is estimated that the total sales of

Bible reaches more than forty million copies each year. It is further estimated that there are more than 950 million Bibles now in use.

The teachings of Jesus are brought to the attention of the public by various other means in America today. On the legitimate stage and in motion pictures, plays of a religious nature have great appeal to audiences, and often prove to be top "box-office" attractions. Sermons, addresses, plays, music and other types of religious programs are broadcast to millions of people by means of radio week by week. No one can evaluate the effect of these religious presentations, but all know that they bring the claims of religion to many millions of people. Television, the newest medium of communication, is already being used by various Christian bodies.

There is but one reason for the tremendous emphasis on religion as indicated by these agencies mentioned above. People are interested in it; they need it and respond to it. It is not forced upon them but is provided because of public demand.

The New Testament is not an obsolete book which no longer attracts or challenges scholars. On the contrary there are good reasons why it receives today a measure of study and serious consideration from great scholars beyond that of any other time in history. Certainly no other writings have been subjected to such continued and diligent study as the New Testament.

Leaders in all fields of thought must face it and examine its teachings since its truth enters every area of life. One can not be an authority in philosophy without a knowledge of what Jesus taught. In psychology, psychiatry and all related fields scholars are amazed to discover the authority of Jesus. His truth and his technique in presenting it are in harmony with the best research in this field. Jesus has invaded the field of sociology, or to state the case more accurately, modern sociologists are learning from him. Even in the field of economics teachers must reckon with his ideals. In government and politics his influence is felt through the voice of Christian statesmen who discern the weakness of the present order by comparing it with the standards of the Man of Galilee.

The New Testament still exerts its authority in the lives of individuals. In his earthly ministry Jesus dealt with men as individuals. He still meets them in this way. In various ways people in countless numbers are challenged by the inescapable Christ who lives in his world today. He is not dead; he lives among men; he speaks and men are arrested, challenged, and transformed.

Because Jesus Christ still lives, because his teachings touch all areas of life, and because of his place in modern life no person can claim to be educated without an acquaintance with the New Testament.

5. *Plan of study.*

In this study we shall treat the materials involved under three general headings. Part one will give consideration to some important introductory matters. Part two will be devoted to the earthly life of Jesus Christ as found in the gospels. Part three will be concerned with tracing the main events in the expansion of Christianity from the ascension of Jesus to the close of the first Christian century.

[1]Lecky, *History of European Morals,* II, p. 9.
[2]Jefferson, *The Character of Jesus,* pp. 350-352.
[3]Denny, *The Career and Significance of Jesus,* pp. 385-386.
[4]Papini, *Life of Christ,* p. 5.
[5]Phillips Brooks.

*Chapter II*

## THE HISTORICAL BACKGROUND

1. The Old Testament Related to the New. 2. Importance of Old Testament History. 3. Resume of Old Testament History. (1) Period of Beginnings. (2) Hebrew Patriarchs. (3) Slavery and Deliverance. (4) Conquest and Settlement in Canaan. (5) The Hebrew Kingdom. (6) Captivity and Restoration. 4. The Inter-Biblical Period. 5. Sources of Study. 6. Divisions of the Period. 7. The Jews Under Persia. 8. The Rise of Greece. 9. Philip of Macedon. 10. Alexander. 11. The Jews Under Alexander. 12. Division of Alexander's Empire. 13. The Jews Under the Ptolemies. 14. The Septuagint. 15. Significance of Hellenism. 16. The Jews Under the Seleucids. 17. Antiochus Epiphanes. 18. Maccabean Dynasty. 19. Mattathias at Modein. 20. Achievements of Judas. 21. Worship Restored. 22. Jewish Independence. 23. Successors to Judas. 24. Pharisees and Sadducees. 25. The Roman Empire. 26. Pompey Conquers Palestine. 27. Struggles for Power. 28. Antipater in Palestine. 29. Herod the Great. 30. The Birth of Christ.

CHAPTER II

# The Historical Background

*1. The Old Testament Related to the New.*

Even to the casual student of the Bible there is a very obvious relation between the Old Testament and the New. In the words of Dr. W. O. Carver: "Without the Old Testament the New Testament could never have been. Given the Old Testament, if its apparent source, significance, and claim were true and genuine, the New Testament had to be. They supplement and explain each other. The Old anticipates the New: the New presupposes and uses the Old. Each in part explains and interprets the other."[1]

It is obvious that the leaders and teachers in the New Testament story considered themselves the heirs of a rich heritage. They felt that what they were experiencing and saying was a fulfillment of what was begun in Old Testament times. Jesus himself was master of the Old Testament and wherever there was occasion he related his work to that of Old Testament leaders. He and the apostles accepted the teachings of the Jewish Scriptures and considered their work as the completion of God's revelation of himself to the Jewish people.

*2. Importance of Old Testament History.*

Because of this vital relation the importance of the Old Testament record is understandable. Without a knowledge of God's dealings with his people in the long centuries prior to the coming of Christ one is not prepared to appreciate and interpret the work and the teachings of Jesus. It is well therefore, for the student entering upon the study of the New Testament to get at least a brief resume of Hebrew history.

*3. Resume of Old Testament History.*

In the briefest form we shall present a summary of this history arranged by the main periods in chronological order.

(1) *Period of Beginnings* — The first eleven chapters of Genesis cover the period from the time of creation to the time of Abraham. This period is concerned with beginnings. The Genesis account tells of the creation of the world and is climaxed by the creation of man and the institution of the home and the Sabbath. Then follows the story of the Temptation and Fall of man, with its consequent punishment. This is followed by the story of Cain's slaying of Abel, and the birth of Seth.

The story of the wickedness of the race, the building of the Ark, and the Flood is then related. The accounts of the new start after Noah, the building of the Tower of Babel and the confusion of tongues are then given.

(2) *Hebrew Patriarchs* — The second period begins with Abraham, approximately 1850 B.C. and goes to the time of Moses about 1250 B.C. This history is recorded in Genesis 12-50. The contents of this period may be summarized as follows: The call of Abraham and the record of some of his experiences, the career of his son Isaac, the stirring stories of Jacob and his twelve sons, the heroic struggles and achievements of Joseph in Egypt, and finally the account of the coming of the sons of Jacob (Israel) to Egypt and their experiences there up to the death of Joseph.

(3) *Egyptian Slavery and Deliverance* — This period begins with the work of Moses and goes to the time of the conquest of Palestine by the children of Israel. There is some difference of opinion as to the time of Moses' work. While the exact date has not been finally determined there seems just now to be a turning to the date of approximately 1250 B.C. Be that as it may, this period in the history of the Hebrews is full of interesting and important history. These events are recorded in the books of Exodus, Leviticus, Numbers and Deuteronomy. Moses is the chief figure in this era. He was born and reared in Egypt, adopted by the daughter of Pharoah and trained in the best Egyptian learning and culture. He fled to the land of Midian and there, after a residence of some forty years, was called to be the deliverer of the Hebrews from Egyptian slavery. He organized the Hebrews and led them forth from Egypt to Palestine through a period of some forty years. They were led first to Sinai where they received the Law. From there they went to Kadesh-Barnea about eighteen months after their departure from Pharoah's land. Upon their failure to exercise faith and enter the "Land of Promise" they were forced to wander for nearly forty years. Moses led them through many trying experiences to the land of Moab east of the Jordan, where he relinquished his leadership, commissioned Joshua to be his successor and then bade farewell to his people before his mysterious death in the silent hills of Moab.

(4) *Conquest and Organization in Canaan* — The period begins with Joshua's work as leader in crossing the Jordan river to capture Jericho and includes his further conquests. After the so-called conquest of the land of their fathers (Abraham, Isaac and Jacob) Palestine was

divided among the twelve tribes. Joshua finished his labors and the
people were left without an outstanding leader. The period that follows
is called the period of the Judges and was a time of apostasy, decline
and failure. These Judges, who really were only military deliverers,
were not great national figures. The last and the greatest of these was
Samuel who bridged over the chasm between the period of the Judges
and the establishment of the Kingdom (1,100 B.C.).

(5) *Hebrew Kingdom* — This period is the most glorious one, from
a material point of view, in all Hebrew history. It began about 1,100 B.C.
and closed in 587 B.C. Samuel anointed Saul as the first king who started
auspiciously, but ended his career in disaster. His reign of forty years
left the Hebrew people in a weak state, harassed by their enemies, and
discouraged. David assumed leadership now and was the greatest of
all the kings of the Jews. He reigned for seven and a half years at
Hebron in southern Palestine and then became king over all twelve
tribes. He captured the ancient city of the Jebusites (Jerusalem) and
made it the capital of his kingdom. He rapidly organized his forces,
and in brilliant military movements soon subdued his enemies and gave
to his people the greatest reign of all the kings. He died as an old man,
after forty years' reign, and was succeeded by his son Solomon. Solomon
inherited this strong kingdom and then inaugurated his great building
program including fortresses, his palaces, and the Temple of Jehovah
in Jerusalem. Solomon's reign marked the climax of the golden age of
Israel's history. The splendor and the fame of his reign were the pride
of the Hebrews and the envy of the world. But he ended his career,
after forty years' reign, almost as a failure. The seed of rebellion had
been sown as a result of Solomon's lavish expenditure of money and
the consequent imposition of very heavy taxes, and immediately after
his death this rebellion broke out. His son Rehoboam succeeded him
and then the ten northern tribes revolted and established the Kingdom
of Israel which existed for about 250 years as a rival to the southern
kingdom, Judah. The northern tribes finally established a capital at
Samaria. In 722 B.C. Samaria fell, after a siege of several years, and the
best people of these ten tribes were taken into Assyria as captives. With
this event the record of the ten tribes came to an end. Judah, the
southern kingdom, continued to exist as a small but mostly independent
nation after the fall of Samaria until 587 B.C. when their beloved city
was finally captured and destroyed. Then the last group of Hebrews
was taken into captivity in the land of Babylonia near the ancient city of

Ur, the original home of Abraham their forefather. Thus the kingdom of the Hebrews came to an end.

(6) *Captivity and Restoration* — The next period, 587-400 B.C., closes the record in the Old Testament. This includes the Captivity and the Restoration. These captive Hebrews remained in Babylonian exile, not as slaves but as colonists, for about seventy years. Three distinct groups made the long journey back to the old homeland of Palestine after the famous decree of Cyrus the Great, king of the Persians and sovereign of the Jews. Under the leadership of Nehemiah the walls of ancient Jerusalem were rebuilt, and Zerubbabel was successful in rebuilding the temple. Ezra was the great reformer and teacher of the Jews in this restored kingdom. It was only a small kingdom, subject to the king of Persia, but it was distinctly spiritual in nature. About 400 B.C. the Old Testament closes with the Hebrews back in Palestine, but not as an independent kingdom.

### 4. *The Inter-Biblical Period.*

For various reasons it will be well to give more detailed consideration to the period just before the birth of Jesus. While many students have a general idea of the course of Old Testament history, there are very few who have any acquaintance with the important events in the Inter-Biblical period, because we have no record of these events in our Bible. This period, sometimes called "Between the Testaments," is nevertheless of unique significance to the student. Such far-reaching changes in the political, economic, social and religious life of the Jewish people took place that one unacquainted with these events is wholly unprepared to understand the New Testament. The student who finishes the reading of Malachi and turns immediately to Matthew finds himself in a new world. The Jews, while still living in Palestine, were under a new regime. New officials and new institutions, political and religious, had arisen. Life in every area was different. We can best acquaint ourselves with these developments by a brief study of these eventful four hundred years.

### 5. *Sources of Study.*

The Bible itself contains none of the history of these four hundred years. Secular history, the works of Josephus and the Apocryphal writings, furnish source material for this period.

The history of Persia, Greece and Rome supplies a great deal of information. The eminent Jewish historian, Josephus, while not always reliable, gives full consideration to the history of the Jewish people during this period.

There are fourteen books of Jewish writings which belong to this general period and are known as the Apocryphal ("secret" or "hidden") books. These writings, historical and religious in nature, are not included as a part of our canon of the Bible, though there has been frequent debate and difference of opinion on this matter. Even though they are not included in the list of inspired books they have remarkable value and significance in the understanding of Jewish history and life at this period. Because of their value we are giving the list of these books at this point in our study. They are: I Esdras, II Esdras, Tobit, Judith, Esther (additions), The Wisdom of Solomon, Ecclesiasticus, Baruch, The Song of the Three Holy Children, The History of Susanna, The History of the Destruction of Bel and Dragon, The Prayer of Manasseh, I Maccabees and II Maccabees.

6. *Divisions of the Period.*

This history between the Testaments is made up of four distinct divisions which we shall consider in proper order in this chapter. These are: (1) Persian, 538 (400)-332 B.C. (2) Greek, 332-167 B.C. (3) Hebrew Independence, 167-63 B.C. (4) Roman 63 B.C.-70 A.D.

7. *The Jews Under Persia.*

We need not give here the details of the story of Persia's gaining control over the Jews by their conquest of Babylon in 538 B.C. The Jews, being captives of Babylon, naturally became the subjects of Cyrus the Great. Under Cyrus and succeeding rulers the Jews were given many privileges and were accorded many favors. Cyrus not only permitted them to return to their homeland but gave them great assistance in these undertakings. Protection in travel and special monetary grants were provided for them. So far as the record goes the Jews were treated fairly by the Persian rulers, both in Persian territory and in Palestine. Naturally they were not free but so long as they recognized the supremacy of Persia and observed the laws governing them they were not molested or abused.

When the Old Testament closed about 400 B.C. the Jewish people in Judah were still the subjects of Persia. This continued, apparently without any outspoken resentment on the part of the Jews, until the Persian power began to wane and finally came to an end with the swift conquests of Alexander the Great of Greece.

## 8. Rise of Greece.

It is not necessary here to recount the story of Persia's expansion after the time of Cyrus into a great world power. Suffice it to say that under vigorous leadership her armies advanced ever further westward until they reached the Aegean Sea, the western boundary of Asia. Not content with this they even crossed the sea to enter Europe (Greece) where they maintained a slight foothold for a little time. However, here they met their strongest opponent, the Greeks, who challenged them and drove them out of Europe and ultimately conquered all of the territory once held by the proud Persian forces. This contest between the powerful Persian empire of the Orient and Greece, the dynamic new power in the West, was one of the most far-reaching in all history. Had Persia won in this contest the course of history for centuries might have been different.

The Greeks who were to affect so deeply the course of history, began to emerge as a nation several centuries before Alexander the Great. They occupied the southeastern fringe of Europe and some of the Aegean isles—the territory still called Greece. The very mention of the word Greek brings to mind some of the glorious achievements of this remarkable race. They excelled in almost every area of human activity. Ancient Athens was the intellectual center of pre-Christian history. Here all the arts flourished and reached the heights of attainment. They developed the most effective language the world has known. In philosophy, literature, sculpture, architecture and other liberal arts they made a contribution unequalled by any other people. They gave to the world such men as Thucydides, Aristophanes, Xenophon, Socrates, Plato, Aristotle, Diogenes, Alexander, Demosthenes and many others. In the fourth century before Christ their culture was to be taken by zealous apostles far east into the Orient itself.

## 9. Philip of Macedon.

Macedonia was one of the chief states of Greece. Philip, the father of Alexander, was king of Macedonia until the time of his death in 334 B.C. His two great ambitions were to see Greece attain a place of leadership in the world, and to prepare his son to realize this dream. Both these ambitions were to a remarkable degree attained.

## 10. Alexander

This man, destined to affect the lives of millions of people and scores of nations, began his career in vigorous fashion after his accession in

335-34 B.C. In his brief reign of twelve years he accomplished more in conquest than any man before him.

He defeated the Thebans in several decisive battles. Crossing into Asia, he met and defeated the forces of Darius in the two famous battles of Granicus and Issus. He then moved through Syria and Palestine to Egypt. Tyre defied his armies for several months before falling. On his way to Egypt he approached Jerusalem, which he took apparently without difficulty. There is a tradition that he was met outside Jerusalem by a company of Jewish priests who impressed him so favorably that he granted them very favorable terms for their holy city. One story has it that among these priests who met him, Alexander recognized one who had previously told him that he should conquer the world.

From Jerusalem he went to Egypt which soon fell completely into his hands. On the northern shore of this ancient country he founded a great city to which he gave the name Alexandria. This city still stands after having played a prominent role in world events during these twenty-three centuries.

Not yet satisfied, he led his army back through Palestine and Syria to meet the forces of Darius at Arbela on the plains of Assyria. This battle was decisive and brought to its end the empire of Persia. All Persian territory now belonged to Alexander but this ambitious conquerer was not yet content. The fabulous wealth of far eastern countries beckoned to him. He continued his march eastward finally moving into India itself. Here his soldiers rebelled and his career of conquest came to an end.

Intoxicated by his phenomenal achievements, Alexander surrendered his ideals so that his character underwent a complete change in his last years in the Orient. He became vain and unreasonable and yielded to the temptations by which he was surrounded. He drank to excess and contracted a fever which brought on his death in Babylon in 323 B.C. He died at a very young age, but in a few short years he had "made history."

We may not agree that Alexander deserved the appellation "the great," but we must admit that he was an unusual man. While he was not without fault, at the same time his character was far above that of most conquerors. As a student of the philosopher Aristotle, he became a passionate disciple of Greek culture and believed that he was under obligation to spread this culture over the ancient world.

*11. The Jews Under Alexander.*

Throughout his career Alexander seemed to be partial to the Jews. He admired their excellent qualities and granted to them in Alexandria and in other cities the privileges of citizenship. Apparently they were never the victims of discrimination as long as he lived. No doubt he would insist on their accepting Hellenistic philosophy but there is no record of his forcing them to renounce their faith in order to do this. After his death, however, the Jews entered upon an era of the bitterest suffering in their long history.

*12. Division of Alexander's Empire.*

When Alexander died in 323 B.C. there was no man strong enough to succeed him and to hold together this vast empire he had molded. Accordingly the kingdom was divided in 323 B.C. among four of his generals — Ptolemy, Lysimachus, Cassander and Seleucus. These divisions are usually called: the western or Greece proper; the northern or Armenian; the eastern or Syrian; and the southern or Egyptian. We need not give attention in this connection to the western or the northern divisions since the Jews were not involved in either of these. The Jewish people were very much affected by the other two. The Syrian or eastern section under Seleucus lay directly north of Palestine. The southern or Egyptian section under Ptolemy was southwest of the Jewish homeland. In reality the Jews were sandwiched between these two powers and were passionately coveted by both the Seleucids and the Ptolemies.

*13. The Jews Under the Ptolemies.*

Shortly after the division of Alexander's kingdom Palestine fell to the Ptolemies in Egypt. Ptolemy Soter was the ruler and at first was very severe in his treatment of the Jews. Later, however, he came to appreciate their good qualities and treated them with consideration. Numbers of Jews were given places of authority and prominence. Soter was succeeded by Philadelphus, who likewise gave fair treatment to them. He was a very able ruler and was responsible for many achievements. He built the famous lighthouse, called Pharos, at the mouth of the Nile. Even more significant was his erection of the great library in Alexandria which was the important center of culture and learning in the Mediterranean world for several centuries. It was burned by the Mohammedans in the seventh century after Christ.

*14. The Septuagint.*

During the reign of Ptolemy Philadelphus, the famous Septuagint was produced in Alexandria. This was the translation of the Old

Testament from Hebrew to the Greek language. Hellenism had come to dominate the Mediterranean world to the extent that the Jews themselves were ceasing to speak the Hebrew tongue, and instead were using the Greek language. Devout Jews saw that if their children were to continue to study their scriptures these must be put in the Greek language. This was a most significant event, since with this translation available every person who spoke Greek could read the scriptures. It made the Old Testament with all its predictions of a Messiah available to hundreds of thousands of people who otherwise might never have had the opportunity of reading the Jewish scriptures.

*15. Significance of Hellenism.*

In order to appreciate the real problem which the Jews faced in this era the student should understand something of the meaning of Hellenism (the philosophy of the Greeks) which was now confronting them at every turn. Hellenism was a way of life which was radically different from that of the Jews or any Oriental people.

The civilization of Greece was essentially a city product. It developed in cities and must be propagated by city communities. In the Orient cities were collections of houses and peoples without much plan and were ruled by a tyrant, since the people were little more than slaves. On the other hand cities among the Greeks were well planned and artistically built. The people elected their officers, discussed public affairs and participated in their government.

To the Greek, life was good and should be enjoyed. Health was at the foundation. The gymnasium was a popular institution where the young men met for physical exercises and social activities. Activities of all kinds — games, contests, sports, dancing, music, poetry — were emphasized. Greek communities had a stadium for athletic contests, a hippodrome for chariot racing, a theater for dramatic presentations.

Literature and art occupied a prominent place in their lives. Being intellectually alert, they had their schools, their philosophical discussions, their training centers for students of art and sculpture. Every building must be adorned with sculpture. These adornments were statues of the gods, of prominent citizens, of philosophers and athletes. To the Greeks a city without art was unthinkable. They developed the most remarkable language of any people in history. It was an instrument of such beauty, precision and refinement that any other language seemed barbarous in comparison with it. No wonder that the Greek language conquered the world in a short time after the conquest of Alexander.

Manners and customs of living also were vastly different from those of Orientals. Their dress was gay, even gaudy, with mantles and broad brimmed hats. Their emphasis on proper styles and the attention they gave to proper personal appearance would impress the Jews as frivolous, and even wicked.

Pleasure of all kinds was not only legitimate but desirable. Life should be enjoyed today — tomorrow we may not have. No wonder Epicureanism became the accepted standard of thought and behavior for most of the Greek people. Religion, particularly as it related to future life, had but little place in their thoughts.

The problem facing the Jews under Greek control was: Could they accept Helenism and remain loyal to the faith of their fathers? Some felt that they could and hence a few openly accepted it. The big majority however, felt that they could not become Hellenists without betraying their faith. This heathenism must be resisted even unto death.

### 16. The Jews Under the Seleucids.

While the Ptolemies succeeded in getting control of Palestine in 323 B.C. this control was never securely established. The Seleucids and the Ptolemies were frequently at war with each other and the outcome of these struggles was almost always in doubt. Within twenty-five years after Alexander's death Jerusalem changed hands seven times. During the one hundred twenty-five years (323-198 B.C.) that the Ptolemies had nominal control of Palestine there were so many wars that an exact count cannot be made. Finally in 198 B.C. at the battle of Banias the Ptolemies were defeated and the Seleucids assumed control of the little country which had been between the upper and nether millstones for so long. The Jews thus came under the control of another race of conquerors.

Antiochus III, called "The Great," (223-187 B.C.) was the ruler of the Seleucid Kingdom when Palestine was taken from the Ptolemies in 198 B.C. He endeavored to conquer Egypt itself from the Ptolemies but was unsuccessful. We know but little of his treatment of the Jews, though it probably was not too harsh. Seleucus IV came to the throne in 187 B.C. and ruled until 176 B.C. There were no outstanding events in his reign. The hard years for the Jews came with Antiochus Epiphanes who succeeded Seleucus IV.

*17. Antiochus Epiphanes.*

Antiochus IV, the grandson of Antiochus the Great, had two nicknames. By some he was known as "Epiphanes" (the brilliant one); by others as "Epimanes" (the dullard). There were reasons for both, since, in some ways he was a very brilliant ruler, and yet in other respects he was unbelievably stupid. He was a passionate devotee of Hellenism and his ruling ambition was to force this philosophy on all his subjects. The Jews thus had to face one of the most critical situations in all their history.

Shortly after he became king Antiochus Epiphanes got into difficulties with the people of Jerusalem by the appointment of a high priest which the Jews would not accept. The same experience was repeated a short time later with the result that very unhappy relations developed between the king and his subjects. In 169 B.C. Antiochus was on a campaign in Egypt when the report came to Jerusalem that he had been killed. The Jews proceeded at once to celebrate, only to learn later that the report was false. When Antiochus returned to Jerusalem he wreaked his vengeance on the city and plundered the temple. Disorder and bitterness increased. Antiochus now devoted himself with fanatical zeal to bringing the Jews under absolute control. Some Jews in Jerusalem had accepted Hellenism and were persuaded by the king to join in his efforts to make all Jews conform. Many orthodox Jews were imprisoned, forty thousand were slaughtered and an equal number were sold as slaves. Still later he sent emissaries to all the synagogues where the people were assembled on the Sabbath and massacred thousands of men, women and children.

He was determined to destroy the worship of Jehovah. The temple was plundered and all feasts annulled. The Jews were forbidden to read their Scriptures, to observe the Sabbath or to perform the rite of circumcision. Two Jewish women defied his edict and had their boys circumcised. When apprehended, they were led through the streets with their children fastened to their necks, and were thrown headlong over the steepest part of the walls. To show his contempt for the faith of the Jews, he sacrificed a sow on the altar of burnt offering, cooked the meat, and then poured the broth over all the building. He caused an altar to the Greek god Zeus, to be erected on the temple area. These desecrations were the chief cause of the revolt of the Jews. At first Jewish resistance was passive, but later, in desperation, this resistance became a burning flame. The illustrious Antiochus underestimated the devotion of the Jews to their faith. Under the circumstances it appeared that their cause was hopeless, but such was not the case. Though they could not forsee it, they were on the threshold of one of the most glorious epochs in their history as a nation.

### 18. Maccabean Dynasty.

One of the most remarkable ruling families in the long history of the Jewish race was the Maccabean with which we are now concerned. The father of this family was an aged priest, named Mattathias, who lived in the little town of Modein, west of Jerusalem near the Philistine border. He had five sons, John, Simon, Judas, Eleazer, and Jonathan. He led the revolt which put his family to the forefront as rulers of the Hebrew people. The family is sometimes called Asmonaeans, a title derived from Asmoneus, one of their ancestors. They are more frequently called Maccabeans. There are various explanations given as to the origin of this name, though it probably was a sort of nickname meaning "hammerer." For several generations this dynasty was to exert a tremendous influence on the life of the Jewish nation.

### 19. Mattathias at Modein.

During the darkest days of the Antiochan persecution (167 B.C.) an event took place at Modein which started the revolution. An emissary of Antiochus appeared in the village to test the loyalty of the people to the king. He built an altar to Zeus and commanded Mattathias and his sons, as the leading citizens, to offer sacrifices to the pagan god with the promise of a large reward and the favor of the king. The aged priest refused to obey. When a younger man stepped up to obey the order, Mattathias, unable to control his anger, rushed forward and slew the young man, then turned and killed the emissary of the king. Realizing that the die had been cast the priest made an appeal to all loyal Jews to join him. He and his five sons together with a number of other zealots, then fled to the hills to declare open war against Antiochus.

When this bold stand had been taken larger groups of Jews took courage and joined the forces until a formidable army was recruited. This task of leadership in this uprising was too strenuous for Mattathias, who was already an old man. From his five strong sons he selected Judas to take the leadership of the new movement. The new leader was admirably suited for this difficult undertaking. He was intrepid and bold, a skilled strategist who appeared and disappeared swiftly. He was thoroughly familiar with the contour of the country;

he knew the ravines, mountains and caves. In his bold undertakings he had the loyalty and absolute co-operation of his patriots. A man of lesser stature could never have won independence from the merciless Seleucids.

### 20. Achievements of Judas.

To give the details of his wars with the Seleucids is obviously impossible in the limits of this chapter. We shall tell briefly of four of his victories. The Seleucid General Appolonius was sent first to crush these rebels led by Judas. Somewhere near Samaria Judas met the Syrian general and his army and completely routed them, gaining a store of supplies and much needed equipment. Next a large Syrian army was led by Seron, who planned to get to Jerusalem through the valley of Beth-horon. Judas trapped the army and almost annihilated it in the valley. Again he gained much booty. The third attempt to crush Judas was led by three generals whose combined forces numbered fifty thousand. They attempted to go through the passageway south of Mizpah. With only six thousand men Judas attacked them at dawn and took them by surprise. They fled in utter defeat. The fourth army to come up against Judas was led by Lysias, the commander-in-chief. His forces numbered sixty thousand. Just north of Hebron Judas attacked them with only ten thousand men and utterly defeated them. The Syrians withdrew, not to return until after the death of Antiochus Epiphanes two or three years later.

### 21. Worship Restored.

Taking advantage of the absence of the Syrians, Judas and his forces entered Jerusalem and cleaned up the temple court. They wept as they saw the desecration and wreckage before them. They destroyed all pagan altars and gods, then set up an altar to Jehovah, repaired the temple and put the city in order. On December 25, 165 b.c. the temple was rededicated to the worship of God. This occasion was memorialized by the "feast of the dedication." (John 10:22.)

Judas next proceeded to make war on several neighboring peoples who were sympathetic with the Syrians. He defeated the Idumeans in the south, later capturing Hebron, and then crushed the Philistines. He crossed the Jordan to administer defeat to the Ammonites as far north as Damascus. With the close of these campaigns he had gained possession of much of Palestine.

## 22. Jewish Independence.

Antiochus Epiphanes died of a loathsome disease while breathing out threats and slaughter against his enemies. Lysias now came against the Jews with a still larger force — one hundred thousand infantry, twenty thousand cavalry and thirty-two war elephants. Realizing that he was completely outnumbered Judas elected not to fight. He withdrew to Jerusalem to defend himself. Lysias besieged the city in his determination to crush Judas. A report of serious trouble back at Antioch caused Lysias to withdraw. However, before leaving, he came to terms with Judas and guaranteed to all Jews the privilege of religious freedom. Judas had won what Mattathias had prayed for. The Jews could now worship their God without molestation. However, they were not yet politically free.

The Hellenists did not keep their agreement and new conflicts arose. The brave Judas was forced again to fight the Syrians, and died on the battlefield in 161 B.C. Against overwhelming odds he had saved his people and their religion in their greatest peril. His name, even though the same as that of the most ignominious character in Jewish history, continues to shine with undying glory.

## 23. Successors to Judas.

At the death of Judas his brother Jonathan was the leader for a while. He was murdered by a Syrian general who hoped to gain the throne. However, Simon, another brother of Judas, moved swiftly and took charge. Demetrius II, king of Syria, needed the support of Simon and in order to get it bargained with this son of Mattathias. By the agreement reached Simon was recognized as Jewish high priest, and the payment of all tribute of the Jews to Syria was stopped forever. This pact made in 143 B.C. began a new era in Jewish history. At long last they had gained political independence. The subsequent reign of Simon was one of great prosperity. "They tilled their land in peace, and the land gave her increase, and the trees of the plain their fruit . . . Simon provided food for the cities and furnished them with the means of fortification . . . and he strengthened all the distressed of his people, he was full of zeal for the law, and every lawless and wicked person he banished. He made the sanctuary glorious, and multiplied the vessels of the temple." (I Mac. 14:8-15.)

Simon was assassinated in 135 B.C. along with a group of his friends, by Ptolemy, his son-in-law, who planned to seize the throne. However, John Hyrcanus, Simon's son, out-maneuvered Ptolemy and became the ruler. Under John Hyrcanus (135-105 B.C.) there was a period of rapid expansion. He annexed Idumea, Samaria and Perea to Judea. He beautified Jerusalem. He was the first Jewish ruler to issue coins. As high priest he offended the strict Pharisaic party and later identified himself with the Sadducees, the rival religious party of Jews.

### 24. Pharisees and Sadducees.

During this period which we are now considering the Pharisees and the Sadducees emerged as the two strong religious parties of the Jews. They were opposed to each other at almost every point and the rivalry between them was keen and often very bitter.

The patriots who stood by Judas Maccabeus desired religious freedom and were willing to die for it. They were known at first as Hasidim. As soon as religious freedom was won they stopped fighting since they had no political ambitions. Out of this group came the Pharisees.

There were some Jews who saw the good in Hellenism and who believed that they could accept it and still be loyal to their own faith. These were largely of the aristocratic class and, while not nearly so numerous as the Pharisees, they were very influential in national affairs.

The antagonism between these two strong parties became so severe that it ultimately wrecked the Maccabean kingdom and forfeited the political freedom of the Jews. John Hyrcanus died in 105 B.C. and was succeeded by Aristobulus I who ruled for only a year. He was succeeded by Alexander Janneus, who lived until 78 B.C. Both these were Sadducees. Janneus was vicious in his actions and was very severe in his treatment of the Pharisees. Janneus was succeeded by his wife, Alexandra, who was strongly pro-Pharisee. Under her rule the Pharisees were merciless in their treatment of the Sadducees.

When Alexandra died in 69 B.C. an era of civil war broke out between her two sons, Hyrcanus II and Aristobulus II. This bitter struggle for supremacy dragged on for six years, neither one being able to gain a decisive victory. In 63 B.C. Pompey the Roman general came upon the scene, and with his advent the period of Hebrew independence came to an end.

### 25. The Roman Empire.

The important place which the Roman people occupied in the history of the world is known, to some degree at least, by every student. The little city which sprang up on the banks of the Tiber river in Italy some seven centuries before the birth of Christ expanded until it became a kingdom which covered the entire basin of the Mediterranean and spread northward into Europe and eastward far into the Orient. For centuries it dominated the civilized world. Its contribution to civilization and its influence on the thought and lives of men have been surpassed by few other races.

It was in the Roman world that Jesus Christ lived and did his work. "In the fulness of times" — when conditions were just right — the Jewish Messiah made his advent. Palestine, the home of the Jews, was a part of the Roman empire. The Jews were subjects of Rome and, like all their neighbors, were governed by Roman officials. They resented this domination, chafed under its restrictions and frequently rebelled against it, but to no avail. Their rebellion against Roman authority finally brought their national destruction.

## 26. Pompey Conquers Palestine.

The triumphant Roman army under Pompey moved eastward into Syria in 63 B.C. With the conquest of Syria Pompey paused to await developments in Palestine. We have seen that at this time the Jews in Palestine were deadlocked in a bitter civil war between Hyrcanus II and Aristobulus II. Each of these claimants, feeling that he could not succeed without outside assistance and realizing that Pompey was now ready to move into Palestine, resolved to appeal to this Roman general. Each laid his case before Pompey, offered his resources and pled for his support. In his favored position the Roman general could take his time. Finally he announced his preference for Hyrcanus. Aristobulus hastily prepared to defend Jerusalem against the advances of Pompey. After a siege of three months Pompey captured Jerusalem and seized Aristobulus whom he sent, along with some of his supporters, to Rome as a prisoner.

When the Roman general had seized Jerusalem he horrified the Jews by entering the Holy of Holies, as well as by other profane deeds. Having disposed of Aristobulus, he now set up Hyrcanus as ruler in Palestine, but without a crown. He also laid upon the Jews a heavy annual tribute to be paid to Rome. Jewish independence was at an end. The Roman ruled the Jews.

## 27. Struggles for Power.

The next fifty years were filled with intrigues, revolts, bloody battles and changing fortunes for the Jews. Pompey had sided with Hyrcanus

II, but Aristobulus II, whom he had sent to Rome, managed to escape and returned to Palestine. This was the beginning of renewed civil war among the Jews. Pompey had made Antipater of Idumea (ancient Edom) the advisor of Hyrcanus II. He proved to be a powerful influence and ultimately assumed authority for Rome in the troubled affairs of Palestine. He was a strong supporter of Pompey who had placed him in power.

In the meantime affairs in the Roman empire had resolved themselves into a life and death struggle between Pompey and Julius Caesar for the place of supremacy. The contest was finally settled in the battle of Pharsalus in 48 B.C. In this battle Pompey was killed. Julius Caesar was now the undisputed master in Rome.

Antipater, who had supported Pompey, was clever enough to convince Caesar of his loyalty to him. Caesar therefore placed him in the position of Procurator of Judea, a position above that occupied by Hyrcanus. In the meantime Caesar manifested a very lenient attitude toward the Jews, not only in Palestine, but elsewhere in the empire. He granted them special favors, among which was full religious liberty.

### 28. Antipater in Palestine.

With the full support of Caesar, Antipater became at once a powerful political figure in Palestine. He was thoroughly loyal to Rome and at the same time seemed to be genuinely interested in the Jews. The Jews hated him, however, since he was an Idumean, and thus a descendant of their bitter enemies in former years. Antipater had two sons — Phasael and Herod, who later became procurators of Judea and Galilee. Antipater was poisoned after only a year in his position. Three years later Caesar was assassinated in Rome.

### 29. Herod the Great.

Herod, the son of Antipater, was born in 74 B.C. and died in 4 B.C., a short while after the birth of Christ. In his career as a politician and ruler he more than any other man, represented the Roman government in dealing with the Jews.

After the death of Julius Caesar the Roman empire was divided among three triumvirs, Octavius, Antony and Lepidus. Syria and the East fell to Antony. On the whole, Antony was favorable to Herod and this friendship with Antony aided him greatly. Herod further strengthened himself by his marriage to Mariamne, granddaughter of Hyrcanus, and one of the most beautiful women of the time. This marriage identified him with the Maccabean line. About this time civil strife broke out anew among the Jews, and Herod hurried to Rome to confer with Antony. He persuaded Antony that he alone could preserve order in Palestine, so Antony appointed him ruler over Judea.

The story of the disgraceful flirtation of Antony with Cleopatra, queen of Egypt, is known to every reader of history. During this time war broke out between Antony and Octavius. In the decisive battle of Actium Antony was defeated. About a year later Antony and Cleopatra committed suicide in Egypt. Octavius now became Emperor of Rome under the title of Caesar Augustus.

In the meantime the crafty and unprincipled Herod was strengthening his position in Judea. This was done largely through intrigue and murder. To recount the record of murders committed by him during his reign would require an entire volume. Suffice it to say no one under suspicion escaped. Many members of his family fell at his order. Even Mariamne, whom he loved most devotedly, was killed upon his command. After her death his remorse was so great that he came near losing his mind. His was literally a reign of terror.

Despite all this Herod was an able ruler and did much for his country, though the Jews hated him with intense bitterness. In his saner moments he honestly sought to be helpful to the Jews and seems to have genuinely coveted their good will. His greatest service to them was the rebuilding of their temple. He hoped that this generous gesture would cause them to feel more friendly toward him, but apparently it failed in this object.

Historians tell us that his last days were indescribably horrible. Stricken by a foul disease of the flesh he lay on his death-bed a rotting mass. He suffered the most excruciating bodily pains, which were perhaps less torturing than the memory of crimes committed and the consciousness of the bitter hatred held by all who knew him. He died in 4 B.C. "dispensing death with one hand and crowns with another."

### 30. The Birth of Christ.

Shortly before the death of Herod momentous events, though unrecognized by many, had been taking place. Four hundred years of silence at last had been broken. God had spoken again to the faithful of his people. The angel Gabriel had announced to a maid in Nazareth the coming of the Messiah, the real King of the Jews. While Herod lay on his death-bed in his palace at Jerusalem, Mary brought forth her first-born son and laid him in a lowly manger at Bethlehem. This new-born babe was Jesus Christ, the King of the Jews.

[1]Carver, William Owen, *Why They Wrote the New Testament,* p. 13.

*Chapter III*

## LIFE IN THE FIRST CHRISTIAN CENTURY

Introduction. 1. Age and Extent. 2. Graeco-Roman World. 3. Contribution of Greece. 4. Language and Literature. 5. Philosophy. 6. Education. 7. Contribution of Rome. 8. Roman Government. 9. Roman Emperors. 10. Militarism. 11. Commercial Enterprises. 12. Large Cities. 13. Society. 14. Morals. 15. Religion. 16. Providential Preparation.

## CHAPTER III
# Life in the First Christian Century

*Introduction.*

One who would understand a great movement must have knowledge of the world situation in which that movement originated and operated. The first step in the study of Christianity must be the effort to become acquainted with the life of the people among whom it arose. Jesus, the Son of God, lived among the people; his teachings touched their lives at every point; what concerned them was of concern to him; his work was related to the institutions, customs and work of the people.

Jesus came to the world at exactly the right time. "In the fulness of time," when conditions were favorable and the situation was propitious after long centuries of preparation, the Son of God became flesh and dwelled among men. One who is acquainted with the political, social, educational, economic and religious life of this century is, therefore, able to appreciate the significance of his ministry.

*1. Age and Extent.*

Jesus lived in the Roman world of the first century. While his home was in Palestine this little country itself was a part of the great Roman empire, which was the dominant world power of the time.

It was built "on the ruins of the past." It is customary for students to think of the first Christian century as ancient times, but this was not the case since civilization was already old. In fact Biblical lands had been inhabited at least 4,000 years before this century. For many centuries nations had risen, flourished and passed into oblivion in the very arena then occupied by the Romans. The period from the earliest known civilization up to the birth of Christ is more than twice the length of time from Jesus' day to our own.

The Roman empire lay around all the shores of the Mediterranean Sea. The word Mediterranean means "in the midst of the land." Life in the first century centered around this strategic body of water, which so often since has been the center of historic events and movements. The eastern boundary of the empire was the Euphrates river in the Near East while westward it extended to the Atlantic ocean. It reached up to the Danube river in Europe and went southward to the Sahara desert. This vast territory dominated by Rome was the home of many different nations which had been subdued by Roman arms and was held in absolute control by these same armies. It is estimated that these subdued national groups made up a population of approximately 100,000,000 people who paid tribute to and took orders from government headquarters in the city on the Tiber river.

### 2. Graeco-Roman World.

The civilization of the first Christian century is called "Graeco-Roman" because it was made up largely by the Greek and Roman element. The thoughts and habits of life native to the various peoples under the domination of Rome had gradually faded out and were supplanted by a combination of those of Greece and Rome who had in turn subjugated them. Even the Jews in Palestine, despite their fierce tenacity to the teachings of their fathers, were almost overcome by these "pagan" philosophies and ways of life. "The Romans gave the first century its political principles and administration, but the Greeks were the molders of its intellectual life. Greek influence dominated the culture of the entire civilized world. That world was politically Roman, culturally Greek, socially pagan, religiously Graeco-Oriental."[1]

One may say that the Greek influence was even greater than the Roman, for after the conquest of the Hellenistic world Rome did not attempt to eradicate the influence of Greek life and thought. In fact Roman people even became imitators of Greek literature and philosophy. It was not uncommon for the Roman lord to be taught by his Greek slave. "Greece captive led enthralled her captor," and there were good reasons for this.

Unquestionably Greek culture was the most powerful intellectual influence in all history. Hellenism, the Greek way of life, from the time of Aristotle and Alexander was to the Greeks a sacred trust to be given to the world. They were passionately devoted to its propagation. The fact that the domination of Hellenism in the first century was so nearly complete furnishes eloquent testimony to the fervor and devotion of its advocates.

It is easy to see that this was a part of the preparation of the world for the advent of Jesus. Without this as a vehicle it is doubtful that Christianity could ever have reached the peoples of the Mediterranean countries and eventually won its victory over the other religious systems in that century. "To one who contemplates in broad perspective the historical situation at the beginning of the Christian Era, it appears that

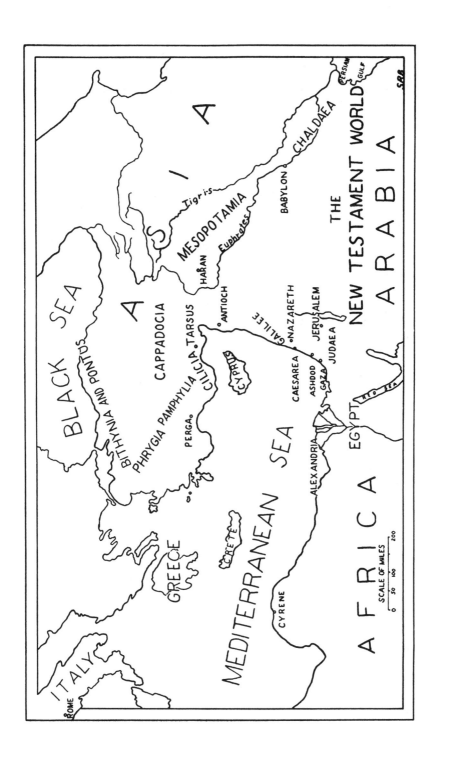

THE NEW TESTAMENT WORLD

Greek culture was just waiting to become the willing servant of the new religion."[2]

4. *Language and Literature.*

The Greek language is generally conceded to be the most effective vehicle ever developed for expressing thought. It had its origin as far back as a thousand years before the Christian era. It developed both in its character and in its scope or use until it reached its climax before the time of Aristotle and Alexander. Classical Greek literature is the type most familiar to students of literature, though in reality these "classics" were but one dialect of this marvelous language. As time passed the language underwent changes. In the first Christian century the dominant type was the Koiné, the language of the common man of the time. As a result of the conquests of Alexander this Greek Koiné became the spoken and written language of the Mediterranean world and remained such until 330 A.D. Thus at the opening of the Christian era most of the peoples of the known world were using a common language, and that language was the one best suited to the high mission of expressing the truths of the gospel to men. "Its possibilities of subtle distinction in the expression of thought are vast, and the writers of the New Testament were remarkably adept at using the finer capacities of the language. It is certainly no exaggeration to insist that the Greek New Testament is the most richly expressive text in all literature, and this fact is in no small measure due to the character of the language in which it was written."[3]

5. *Philosophy.*

In no realm did the Greek reach greater heights of attainment than in philosophy. One can not think of philosophy at all without paying tribute to the Greeks who contributed so much to its development. Heraclitus, Anaxagoras, Pythagoras, Plato, Socrates, Aristotle, Zeno, Epicurus and others are familiar to every well-informed person.

Through centuries of development it reached its heights with Socrates, Plato and Aristotle. Philosophy is related to life and has a more important place in the life of people than they realize. Essentially Christianity is a philosophy, a system of thought, and as such touches life. This being true it was inevitable that it should come in contact with, and even in conflict with philosophical systems in the Christian era. Slowly but surely these ancient philosophies were forced to give ground as Christianity won its way into the thinking of the first century. At no other point is the relation of Christianity to its environment of greater significance than its contact with the philosophic systems of the Greeks.

At the time of Jesus the four schools of philosophy contending for the mastery were Platonism, Aristotelianism, Epicureanism and Stoicism. These four systems had arisen from Socrates' great key word "know thyself." Prior to Socrates philosophy dealt with the external, but as a result of his teachings the emphasis came to be placed on the introspective. Aristotle dealt mainly with physics and metaphysics. Plato was chiefly concerned with ethics and aesthetics. Epicurus and Zeno gave consideration to the problem of how one should best act in the world. Epicurus said one should have a good time and not worry about the consequences. Zeno held that one should be brave, proud, and uncomplaining and keep himself above the level of a beast. The net result of these teachings was a wide-spread skepticism which left unanswered the deep questions of the human soul. It was left to Christianity to supply the answer to these questions.

## 6. Education

Few centuries before the time of the Renaissance had a higher state of intellectual activity and enlightenment than prevailed in the Graeco-Roman world of the first century. There were great universities and libraries at such cities as Tarsus, Alexandria, Pergamum, and Athens. Distinguished scholars lectured at these centers and some lecturers traveled from city to city. The Roman writers, Caesar, Cicero, Virgil, Lucretius and Horace had just passed off the scene, but their works were still read and studied. Livy and Ovid did their work at this time and Juvenal and Tacitus were to come a little later. It was by no means an illiterate age. The chief criticism or shortcoming of such activity was that it was limited largely to the upper and middle classes. There was no program for all the people and no doubt, most of the people of the lower and even middle classes were illiterate. However we may assume that these were not unlearned since the Christian people were largely from the middle and lower class and yet were expected to read and understand the Epistles of Paul.

We have abundant evidence of the progress made in scholarly pursuits by educators of this century. The mathematicians of Alexandria made remarkable discoveries in astronomy. Teachers of medicine and surgery were far advanced and the science of pharmacy was already in use. Architecture, sculpture, painting, music, law and oratory were widely taught and praticed. Professional writers or scribes reproduced manuscripts which book dealers retailed to the public.

### 7. The Contribution of Rome.

The renowned city of Rome which sprang up in Italy some seven centuries before the birth of Christ had passed through successive periods of conquest and expansion until it's sway extended over the Mediterranean world. This Roman Empire reached its highest perfection and power under Augustus Caesar, often called Octavian. (31 B.C.-A.D. 14.) Under this ruler one of the world's most efficient organizations was perfected with a resulting era of peace, security and progress that has seldom been equalled. Unconsciously Rome was preparing the way for the gospel of Christ. It would be difficult to overestimate this contribution. "Rome saved the decaying Hellenism, and Hellenism reciprocated by turning upon Rome the enchanting powers of her superior cultural and religious influence. The Roman had soon adopted the education, philosophy and religion of Greece. By spreading the stabilizing, organizing effects of her imperial administration over the Hellenistic world, the Empire rescued the waning results of Greek civilization and opened the way for its renewed advancement."[4] We may specify several aspects of this contribution.

The triumph of Roman armies had established "the Roman peace." Everywhere people lived in peace, life and property were secure, commerce flourished and peaceful pursuits were enjoyed.

The famous Roman roads which spanned the empire made travel easy and served to unite the various nations under Roman authority. One great route ran from Ephesus in Asia Minor to the Euphrates. The famous Egnation road stretched from the Adriatic Sea far to the East. Many smaller roads in other parts of the empire made travel, trade and communication relatively easy.

The Mediterranean Sea, so long plagued and plundered by pirates, was cleared of this menace by government ships. Over this body of water, except in the cold of winter, ships sailed back and forth and served to keep the various peoples of the empire in constant touch with each other.

Over these roadways and sea lanes Paul and other apostles traveled to various parts of the Mediterranean world carrying the gospel to the Gentiles.

## 8. Roman Government.

Unquestionably the greatest contribution which the Romans made to the world was in the field of government and law. The pattern of their government has been imitated by scores of nations since that time. Theirs was the most famous system of law ever devised, one to which all subsequent lawmakers are immeasurably indebted.

Naturally the government was centered in Rome. The two principal authorities were the Emperor and the Senate. The Senate was made up of several hundred prominent leaders who had gained prestige, usually by their wealth. The Senate was supposed to serve as a check to the power of the Emperor. But the Emperor had authority not only to veto the action of the Senate, but also to remove a Senator from office. Thus the Emperor had almost absolute authority.

Usually each conquered nation became a province of Rome. Such a state was allowed to retain its own laws and customs so long as these did not challenge the Roman. In some instances they retained their own rulers. In every case, however, these countries were the subjects of Rome, were under its control and paid taxes to Rome.

## 9. Roman Emperors.

Because of the historical importance of the emperors of Rome during this time we are giving brief consideration to several of these.

Augustus Caesar (31 B.C.-A.D. 14) was ruler at the time of Jesus' birth. (Luke 2:1.) It was he who really placed the empire on a foundation and gave it security. He established an era of peace, the famous *Pax Romana,* which contributed greatly to the spread of Christianity. He was not only the ablest of the emperors but is ranked as one of the greatest statesman in history.

Tiberius (A.D. 14-37) turned out to be a despot who was inefficient and unscrupulous. He had but little contact with Christianity.

Caligula (A.D. 37-41) was one of the most disgraceful and despotic of all. He encouraged the idea of emperor worship and in other ways exhibited his vain and fanatical notions.

Claudius (A.D. 41-54) had a reign of peace and prosperity despite the fact that he was a weakling. It was during his rule that much of Paul's missionary work was done, though the emperor deserves but little credit for this.

Nero (A.D. 54-68) unquestionably was the most vile and vicious of Roman rulers. His unjustifiable cruelty to thousands is well known. The "Neronian" persecutions of Christians constitute one of the most shameful chapters in even this brutal regime. He had the city of Rome burned in A.D. 64 and then placed the blame on the Christians. It was during his reign that Paul and Peter, as well as thousands of others, were martyred. His unpopularity grew to such proportions that he took his own life.

Vespasian (A.D. 69-79) won the title of emperor through his army. During his reign Titus, his son, destroyed Jerusalem in A.D. 70.

Titus became emperor at the death of Vespasian and ruled from 79 to 81.

Domitian (A.D. 81-96) was an able administrator but was guilty of great cruelty. It was during his reign that the fierce Domitian persecutions of Christians occurred.

*10. Militarism.*

Equally as famous as its governmental system was the Roman army which under the absolute direction of the emperor, conquered the Mediterranean world. It overshadowed every other institution. The Roman soldier was everywhere. Stationed at strategic posts the army kept down insurrections and guaranteed obedience to the government. Military men occupied the most influential places and were not only numerous but exacted recognition and obedience from all the citizens. The prominence of military men in Palestine in New Testament times is verified by the large number of references to them both in the Gospels and in Acts. The student will be impressed by the large part which these military men had in the experiences of Paul. Even Jesus himself did not escape the authority of the Roman soldier.

*11. Commercial Enterprises.*

Economic conditions in this first century were far from ideal. Slave labor was abundant while there was but little employment for public laborers. There was much idleness and unrest. Indeed, honest labor was frowned upon as unbecoming to respectable people. Wealth was centered in the hands of a few while the great majority of citizens were exceedingly poor.

Despite this there was much commercial activity. Roman roads and the Mediterranean Sea carried heavy traffic in merchandise. Remarkably "modern" methods of accounting were used. Banking and lending of money was carried on by wealthy men who charged high rates of interest. There were factories, wholesale houses, traveling salesmen, and countless retail establishments. It was a period of big business.

*12. Large Cities.*

One is impressed with the number of great cities in the Roman empire. Naturally Rome was the leading city. From a small village on the Tiber in seven centuries it had reached a place of greatest power and fame through the conquest of rival nations. Being the capital it held the place of supremacy among all the cities. Athens, the city of culture, and Corinth the commercial center, were both in Greece. Thessalonica and Philippi were likewise great centers of life and activity. In Asia, Ephesus the capital city, was world-famous chiefly as the home of the worship of Diana. It also was a great commercial city. Tarsus, the early home of Paul, was "no mean city." In Egypt ancient Memphis and Thebes were still alive and the important coastal city of Alexandria, which served as the home of a great library, was also a big center of trade and a cosmopolitan city.

*13. Society.*

In the first Christian century there were abundant evidences of decline in family and social life. The substantial virtues of earlier centuries, which had contributed to the greatness of Rome, were disappearing.

Two extremes in social life prevailed. The political and military leaders, as a result of conquest, were extremely rich. Though few in number they held most of the wealth of the empire. On the other hand there were millions of extremely poor people who had little if any property, whose employment was uncertain and whose existence was extremely hard. The middle class, without which no social order can exist very long, was practically non-existent.

Slavery was an entrenched institution which few questioned and apparently none was willing to challenge. The extent of it was amazing. To occupy a place of respectability a family must have a minimum of ten slaves. Prominent families considered two hundred slaves an adequate supply, though some lords owned thousands of them. Slave markets were common sights on the streets of Rome.

The lot of slaves in the empire was extremely hard. In legal language they were called, not *personae* (human beings), but *res* (things). They were bought and sold for profit. They were mated like cattle and their offspring were sold as "the increase of the herd." Treatment of them usually was extremely cruel. Runaway slaves were branded with the letter F (fugitive) on the forehead.

Some of this brutal treatment may be accounted for by the fact that the number of these slaves, usually enslaved after capture in war, was so great as to constitute a threat to the security of the government. Tacitus states that under the rule of Augustus and Tiberius almost half the population of the empire was made up of slaves.

We may be relieved to know that not always was such brutality and cruelty practiced upon slaves. There are records of a number of instances of humane and brotherly treatment, and even of intimate friendly relationships between owner and slaves. But such cases were perhaps exceptional.

There was a large freedman class who had purchased their freedom. Also there were the plebeians who were born free and considered themselves above both freedmen and slaves. But the vast majority of the poor were exploited by the rich who became more extravagant and unreasonable with their increase in wealth. In no sense could this social order be considered a democracy. It could not be expected to endure permanently.

### 14. Morals.

It is customary to think of the moral life of this first century as unspeakably bad. This is not altogether true since we have evidence to show that there were many good people, that family life in many instances was wholesome, and that virtue had not entirely perished. But as a whole morals were very low; in fact almost every sin one could mention was in evidence.

Immorality was openly displayed. Divorce multiplied so rapidly that eventually family life decayed. Suicide and infanticide became so common as to cause no comment. One writer says that baby skeletons by the cartload could be taken from the bottom of the Tiber river. Seneca, the Roman writer, declared: "Vice no longer hides itself; it stalks forth before all eyes. Innocence is no longer rare; it has ceased to exist." Paul was not being rhetorical when he gave his "ghastly picture of cruelty and terror and despair" in the first chapter of Romans.

### 15. Religion in the Empire.

All the nations comprising the Roman empire had religious systems. In fact, the empire was filled with the institutions of religion. Naturally the dominant ones were Greek and Roman, though practically every known god had some worshippers in the empire. By the first century, while the forms of religion persisted, the implicit faith which an earlier period had witnessed had passed away. Much of the worship was pure humbuggery! This was accompanied by a tide of skepticism which nearly engulfed the people of the period. Some doubters gave up the quest of truth in despair. Many became pessimists yielding to "dismal fatalism." Multitudes without much hope groped in darkness. But there was a deep and genuine longing for religious satisfaction. Men were burdened with the sense of human sin and the need for fellowship with the true and holy God. They yearned for a God who knew their need, loved them and wanted to redeem them. The reality of this deep longing for a knowledge of the true God is one of the best established facts in the history of this period. Little did the multitudes who hungered for fellowship with God know that this God for whom they longed was to reveal himself through his Son, Jesus Christ.

### 16. Providential Preparation.

It will be fitting to close this chapter by reviewing briefly the ways by which the world was providentially prepared for the coming of Christ. Dr. David Smith has eloquently stated these under four headings: The Jewish Dispersion, A Universal Language, The Roman Empire, The Decay of Pagan Religions.

The Jewish Dispersion was a process which covered several centuries. Starting with the deportation of the Israelites to Assyria in 722 B.C. it continued up to the time of Jesus. At this time Jews were everywhere in the empire, but particularly numerous in commercial centers. Multitudes of them were in ancient Mesopotamia. Damascus had such a large Jewish colony that in the time of Nero ten thousand were massacred. Those in Egypt numbered more than one million. As far west as Italy great colonies of them were to be found. On one occasion a Jewish embassy to Rome was welcomed by eight thousand of his fellow countrymen.

The Jews were true to their faith even in a foreign land, though always they were loyal to their adopted country. They established synagogues, maintained their faith, and indeed, won some pagan people to faith in Jehovah, their God. It is to be noted that the apostles who went to the cities of the empire to preach the gospel always went first to the synagogue where Jews assembled for worship. This institution thus proved to be a tremendous asset to missionary endeavors among the Gentiles.

A universal language was already in use in every part of the empire. The advantage which this offered is obvious. Wherever the heralds of the gospel went they found people using the Greek language. There was no necessity of mastering and using a strange language.

The Roman empire was responsible for creating certain situations that greatly favored the work of the church. The Roman genius for statesmanship had perfected an organization that established Roman peace, guaranteed stability and encouraged progress. Commerce flourished because of the famous Roman roads. Roman citizens were protected while law and order prevailed.

The pagan religions of the empire were impotent if not already dead. To be sure the forms continued to exist but their power was gone. There is abundant evidence of the deep hunger of heart which people of that century in the empire had for spiritual truth. In reality the world was crying for God. "They were seeking rest for their souls, and they found it after a sort in Judaism. But Judaism was insufficient. It was only a temporary resting place, a foretaste of a nobler satisfaction. And this is the deepest of all the providential preparations for the Gospel. The world was, if the phrase be pardonable, prospecting for a faith, and its unconscious prayer was answered by the advent of Christianity."[5]

[1]Dana, *The New Testament World*, pp. 22-23.
[2]Glover, *The World of the New Testament*, p. 29.
[3]Dana, *The New Testament World*, p. 180.
[4]Ibid., p. 163.
[5]Smith, *The Life and Letters of St. Paul*, p. 13.

*Chapter IV*

JEWISH LIFE IN PALESTINE

Introduction. 1. Home Land of the Jews. 2. Natural Divisions. 3. Political Divisions. 4. Chief Cities. 5. Ancient Roads. 6. Economic Life. 7. Home Life. 8. Rome in Palestine. 9. Antipater. 10. Herod the Great. 11. Herod's Successors. 12. Pontius Pilate. 13. The Jewish Temple. 14. Annual Feasts. 15. Synagogues. 16. Scribes. 17. The Pharisees. 18. The Sadducees. 19. Other Religious Sects. 20. The Sanhedrin. 21. State of Jewish Religion. 22. Messianic Expectations.

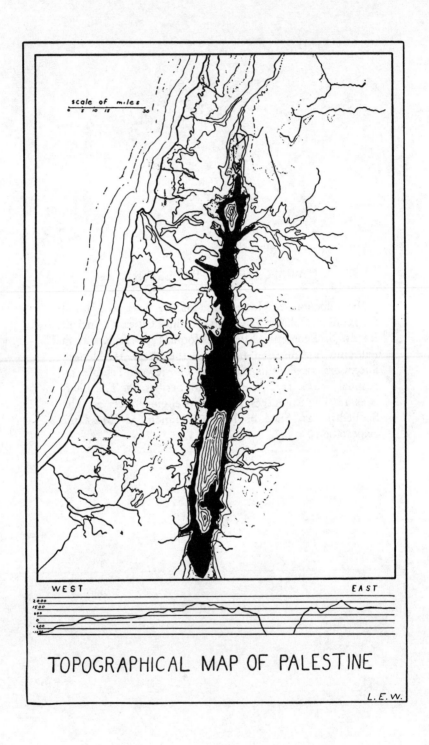

scale of miles
0  5  10  15          30

WEST                                          EAST

2000
1500
600
0
-400
-1292

TOPOGRAPHICAL MAP OF PALESTINE

L.E.W.

# CHAPTER IV
# Jewish Life in Palestine

*Introduction.*

As we have already seen, Jewish people were living in every part of the Roman empire during the first century. By the end of this century, through the labors of Paul and other apostles, the message of Christianity was taken to practically every region embraced by Rome at this time. It is well, however, to remember that Jesus was born in Palestine, that he spent all his earthly life within the confines of this little land, and that it was here that Christianity made its start. Palestine was the real home of the Jews and here, as nowhere else, we can see the real life of the Jewish people. It will be advantageous to the New Testament student therefore, to be familiar with the conditions of living among the Jews in Palestine at the time of Christ. "We can neither understand Him nor the fortunes which he encountered in seeking to incorporate with history the gifts He brought, without a clear view of the conditions of the sphere within which His life was to be passed."[1]

## *1. The Home Land of the Jews.*

Palestine, often called the Holy Land, was a tiny country of unbelievably small dimensions. Its area was only about 10,000 square miles. The entire country could be placed three times in South Carolina, seven times in Missouri and twenty-six times in Texas. Its importance in world history is out of all proportion to its size. It was bounded on the west by the Mediterranean Sea, on the north by the territory of ancient Syria, on the east by the Arabian Desert, and on the south by the semi-desert country occupied through the centuries by many transient peoples. It has a unique climate, the average yearly temperature ranging about like that of Georgia and other states in that latitude. The remarkable aspect of its climate is the two unvarying periods, the "rainy season" and the "dry season." Light rains begin falling in the early autumn. These become heavier until mid-winter and then taper off until rain completely ceases in early spring. The dry season lasts for approximately six months (April-September) during which time absolutely no rain falls in the country.

## *2. Natural Divisions.*

Nature has divided Palestine into four distinct sections which run throughout the length of the land from north to south. Beginning at the western boundary, the Mediterranean Sea, and going eastward, these divisions are: (1) The Maritime Plains, a series of low, sandy and fertile plains extending along the shores of the Mediterranean. (2) The Western Highlands, a great backbone of mountains forming the chief part of Western Palestine. (3) The Jordan River Valley, the deep depression running through the heart of the land. (4) The Eastern Highlands, the hills and plains of Palestine east of the Jordan.

(1) *Maritime Plains* — The Maritime or Coastal Plains lie between the Mediterranean Sea on the west and the mountains of Galilee, Samaria and Judea on the east. At the northern end this territory is very narrow, in some places scarcely a mile wide. It widens out as one goes south until at the lower end it attains the width of some twenty-five or thirty miles.

(2) *Western Highlands* — The second natural division of Palestine is the main plateau known as the Western Highlands. This long, high ridge, varying in height from 1,000 feet to 2,500 feet, begins in the Lebanon mountains in the north and runs southward to the desert of Arabia. It is customary to divide this highland into three sections: a. Galilee, b. Samaria, c. Judah or Judea. Between Galilee on the north and Samaria on the south is the famous plain of Esdraelon, the only break in the long western plateau, which has already been mentioned.

a. Galilee is a mountainous country, beautiful but not very productive. Its boundaries varied through the centuries, but its area may be given as approximately 1,600 square miles. Galilee is best known as the region where Jesus grew up and spent the major part of his life.

b. Samaria lies just south of Esdraelon and north of Judah. On the east is the Jordan River and on the west the plain of Sharon. Its area is approximately 1,600 square miles. It, too, is mountainous, but has some good agricultural and pastoral lands. It has had a very important place in the history of the Hebrews. Abraham and other patriarchs lived in it. It was conquered by Joshua and occupied by the Israelites for centuries. It was the home of the ten northern tribes (Kingdom of Israel).

After the conquest of the city of Samaria by Assyria in 722 B.C. this territory became the home of a mixed race of people, called the Samaritans. They have maintained their existence here until the present time. Only a few remain but they still worship God according to the ancient customs of their forefathers.

c. Judea makes up the lower part of the Western Highlands. In area it, too, is approximately 1,600 square miles. The country has three rather distinct sections; (1) the Eastern hills or "wilderness," (2) the Western hills sloping down toward Philistia, called the Shephelah, and (3) Southern Judea. Judea is more rocky and barren than any other part of the highlands, though it has been cultivated and used as a makeshift for pasturage through many centuries. While not as fertile as the other parts of Western Palestine, it is historically most important. Jerusalem was, and is now, the center of life for this region as well as all Palestine.

(3) *Jordan River Valley* — The most interesting and unique geographical feature of all the Holy Land is the Jordan River valley. There is nothing else just like it in the world. This great ravine starts at the top of the Taurus mountains in the north and runs far into the desert south of Palestine, a distance of 550 miles. In the mountains it is as high as 3,000 feet above sea level while at the deepest part of the Dead Sea it is nearly 2,600 feet below sea level. This gorge or rift varies in width from one to fourteen miles.

In Palestine proper there are three sections of this valley. We consider these in their order from north to south.

a. The Lake of Galilee, called also the Sea of Gennesaret, Sea of Tiberias, and Sea of Chinnereth, is one of the most beautiful little bodies of water to be found anywhere. The mountains on the east and west tower high above its clear waters. The surface of the lake is 682 feet below the level of the sea and at one point it is about 600 feet deep. It is shaped like a pear or a harp. In general its width is about seven miles and its length nearly twelve miles. It is fed by several streams from the mountains of Galilee and the hills to the east, but its chief supply comes from the upper Jordan in the north. It is a beautiful and refreshing body of water. The ancient rabbis said: "Jehovah hath created seven seas, but the sea of Gennesaret is his delight."

During the three years of his ministry, Jesus spent much of his time on or around this lake. Several of his disciples made their living by fishing in its waters. In this beautiful region he performed many miracles and delivered some of his most profound teachings.

b. The Jordan valley from the lower part of the Lake of Galilee to the upper end of the Dead Sea is a deep depression. Through the heart of this valley the Jordan river flows. It runs a very crooked course and because of its numerous windings measures about 110 miles in length though a straight line from the Lake of Galilee to the Dead Sea is only sixty-five miles long. In this distance the river falls about six hundred and ten feet. This rapid descent gives it the name of Jordan or "Descender." The river is not very wide, varying from one hundred to two hundred feet, except during the rainy season when it overflows its banks. These annual floods have strewn the valley with driftwood and covered it with mud. In ancient times there were no bridges across the Jordan, but ordinarily it was only from three to ten feet deep and could easily be forded. When General Allenby gained possession of Palestine in 1917 he had a bridge erected across the river opposite Jericho. This bridge bears his name and is in use today. The river can not be used for commercial purposes and the heat there in the summer (as high as 118 degrees) is so intense that but few people can live in the valley.

c. The large body of water into which the Jordan empties is called the Dead Sea. It occupies the deepest part of the great rift. The surface of its waters is 1,292 feet below sea level and at one point the sea is about 1,300 feet deep, thus the great gorge is about one-half mile below sea level. The sea is about fifty miles long and averages about ten miles in width. The remarkable thing about it is that it has no outlet. The only way for its waters to escape is by evaporation, and this extracted moisture forms an almost impenetrable haze which hangs over the sea constantly. But in the process of evaporation the chemical substances which abound in its waters are left behind. These waters are 25% solid matter and hence are so bouyant that one can scarcely sink in them. But they are poisonous to all life. In fact not a single living thing, plant or animal, is to be found here, hence its name, Dead Sea.

(4) *Eastern Highlands* — The fourth and last natural division of Palestine is the Eastern Highlands. Geographically it is so much like the Western ridge that a discussion of this is not necessary here. Just before the time of Christ several large and prosperous cities of Greek and Roman people were situated here. This region was called the Decapolis. Extensive and elaborate ruins of these can still be seen in the region southeast of the Lake of Galilee.

*3. Political Divisions.*

During the time of Jesus Palestine was divided into six distinct political regions which figured prominently in his life.

(1) *Judea,* the Judah of the Old Testament, was the most important since it was always regarded as the heart of the Hebrew nation. Within its borders was Jerusalem, the Holy City, always the center of national life. In the days of Jesus it was the headquarters of the Jewish faith.

Here was the temple, and here were centered all the religious traditions and practices of Judaism. Judea was the southern section of the territory west of the Jordan and was about 1,600 square miles in area.

(2) *Samaria* — Just north of Judea was Samaria, approximately the same size, in the center of the western highlands. At this time it was the home of the Samaritans, the people whose origin went back to the fall of Israel in 722 B.C. This sect was a distinct religious group with a system of worship somewhat like that of Old Testament people. There was very bitter feeling between the Jews and the Samaritans since every Jew regarded a Samaritan as a "half breed." This racial animosity was of long standing and was very pronounced in the days of Jesus.

(3) *Galilee* — This section of some 1,600 square miles was the northern part of the western highlands and was a mountainous country. The Galileans were separated from other members of their race and came to have distinct characteristics. They were mountain people, simple in habits, hospitable and teachable. It should be noted that Jesus spent his boyhood and young manhood in this region and that fully half the months of his public ministry were given to the Galilean people. This fact made it difficult for the "orthodox" Jews of Judea to accept him as teacher and Messiah.

(4) *Perea* — The region of Perea lay east of the Jordan opposite the territory of the Samaritans. While separated from western Palestine by only a little stream, in reality it was quite a different country since it was affected by Gentile influences much more than the western half of Palestine. Its length was approximately forty miles while in width it varied from twenty to thirty miles. It was inhabited largely by Jews who were not hostile to the devout Jews from the other side of the river who passed frequently through this territory in their travels between Galilee and Judea rather than traverse the territory of the hated Samaritans.

(5) *Decapolis* — The region immediately north of Perea and east of the Lake of Galilee, though it extended across the Jordan into Samaria and Galilee, was known as the Decapolis (ten cities). It was a sort of confederation of ten Greek cities banded together for mutual protection. The inhabitants were Gentiles and maintained their pagan character and customs, hence were usually scorned by Jews. At times there were more than ten of these cities and the names of the original ten are not certainly known. The gospel writers tell of a number of visits made by Jesus to this region.

(6) *Northeast Palestine* — The region northeast of the Lake of Galilee went by different names at different times. Several small districts (Gaulonitis, Auranitis, Trachonitis, Iturea and Batanea) were included in this region. Some Jews lived here near the Lake of Galilee though the other inhabitants seem to have been wild, restless and rebellious people who gave frequent trouble to their rulers. Jesus retired to this region on at least one occasion for special training of his disciples.

*4. Chief Cities.*

Since many of the big events in New Testament history took place in the cities of Palestine every student of the New Testament should know something of these cities.

(1) *Jerusalem* was the most important of all these. It is situated in north central Judea on a ridge of hills some 2,400 feet above sea level. It was wisely located on a promontory with the east, south and west sides marked by deep ravines or valleys. It could be easily fortified and defended, though it has been besieged more than seventy times during its history. It was captured by David's forces and became his capital about 1,000 B.C. Since then it has been one of the famous cities of the world. Here the temple was built and the religious and political life of the nation was centered. In New Testament times it was still pre-eminent in Jewish religious life.

(2) *Bethlehem,* the birthplace of Jesus is just six miles south of Jerusalem. In New Testament times it was but a village and had but little part in national affairs.

(3) *Bethany* was around the southern part of the Mount of Olives east of Jerusalem. Mary, Martha and Lazarus lived here and Jesus visited here on more than one occasion.

(4) *Jericho* was some fifteen miles northeast of Jerusalem in the edge of the Jordan Valley.

(5) *Nazareth,* the most important city in Galilee in relation to Jesus, was located in the southern part of the province overlooking the famous plain of Esdraelon. It was on two of the great roadways and was the boyhood home of Jesus.

(6) *Capernaum* was a busy city on the northwest shore of the Lake of Galilee. It was large and had considerable commercial activity. It served as headquarters for Jesus during his ministry in Galilee.

(7) *Tiberias* on the western shore of the Lake, was built on the pattern of a Greek city and was not prominent in Jewish affairs.

(8) *Caesarea* was on the Mediterranean coast about sixty miles northwest of Jerusalem. It too, was a Hellenistic city where Roman and Greek people lived, hence was not popular with the Jews.

(9) *Joppa* was also on the coast and was some fifteen miles south of Caesarea. It was strongly Jewish in character. Several important events in New Testament history took place there.

## 5. Ancient Roads.

From time immemorial certain well-traveled roadways have passed through Palestine. In the time of Jesus there were at least four principal ones. Two of these originated at Gaza in the extreme southwest. (1) Starting at Gaza one led northeast to Hebron, Bethlehem, Jerusalem, Jericho and up to Damascus. (2) The other one ran from Gaza along the coast northward to Joppa, Caesarea, and Ptolemais to Tyre. (3) Beginning at Jerusalem a very important road went northward through Judea, Samaria and Galilee to Capernaum on the northwestern shore of the Lake of Galilee. (4) The greatest of these highways called *Via Maris* (the way of the sea), came from Damascus southward and crossed the Jordan River north of the Lake of Galilee. It passed through Capernaum, then Nazareth and led down through the plain of Esdraelon to Ptolemais. These arteries of travel figured prominently in the life of the Jews in Palestine. Jesus himself used these frequently in his travels through the land.

## 6. Economic Life.

In the time of Christ the chief occupations of the Jews in Palestine were farming, grape producing, sheep-raising and fishing. Most of the populace secured a living from the cultivation of small plots of land, the members of the family doing the labor. Commercial activity on a large scale has never prevailed in Palestine because of circumstances, though there was limited trade in the necessary articles of living. Professional life was so limited as to be negligible.

## 7. Home Life.

While wealthy men owned large stone houses, elaborately furnished and ornately decorated, the common people were poor and lived humbly. Their houses were simple structures, often with only one large room where all the family ate, slept, and lived. These houses were built with flat roofs which served like our porches, as a place for visiting and sleeping. Their furniture consisted mainly of a few cooking utensils and dishes, small beds (mats), perhaps a few chairs, and occasionally a table. Their food consisted of the products of the flock — milk, cheese, and sometimes meat — vegetables, bread, and fruits.

As a rule families were large since children were expected and were welcomed. Boys were favored above girls, but there is no reason to suppose that girls were treated unkindly. The oldest son held the position of honor. Upon the death of the father he assumed responsibility for the family. If Joseph died shortly after Jesus was twelve years of age, as is usually assumed, Jesus became the responsible head of the family which consisted of his mother, three or four brothers, and at least one sister. The father was "head of the house," but the position of the wife and mother was honored and respected. Each child was expected to do some work in the home, but children, then as now, had their games and played at home and in the public places. There were certain occasions such as weddings, dinners, and family gatherings, where social life was enjoyed by all. The family was a unit and usually was characterized by great loyalty.

### 8. Rome in Palestine.

With the conquest of Palestine by Pompey in 63 B.C. some changes took place in the life of the Jews. They were treated generously as long as they were submissive to Roman laws. They were allowed to keep their religion and to worship, provided they did not violate the law. They had a legal tribunal, the Sanhedrin, which had jurisdiction chiefly in religious matters. They paid tribute to Rome which was humiliating to them. Their hatred of the Roman however, was very bitter since the zealots among them exaggerated their shame in subjection to an alien power. On the whole the Jews were not ill-treated nor abused as is commonly thought.

### 9. Antipater.

In the political changes resulting from the Roman conquest of Palestine Antipater of Idumea (Edom) had a prominent part. He was governor of Idumea which had been annexed to Judea. He was shrewd and unscrupulous, always courting the favor of the Roman whom he foresaw as the ultimate ruler of Palestine. He was poisoned by a Jew, but not before he had prepared the way for his son Herod.

### 10. Herod the Great.

Herod was born in 74 B.C. and died in 4 B.C. He was made governor of Galilee by his father when he was only twenty-five years old. He played the fool while serving as governor and incurred the opposition of the Jews. Yet few politicians of any time have been more astute and cunning than he. Through a long succession of schemes he was finally appointed king of Judea by the Roman senate. He played a conspicuous part in the life of the Jews up to the birth of Jesus.

## 11. Herod's Successors.

Upon the death of Herod, his son Archelaus was supposed to become king of Judea, but this never took place since he was a weakling who served as ethnarch until he was banished ten years later (A.D. 6). From A.D. 6 until 42 Judea was ruled by procurators. There were several of these, but the most important one was Pontius Pilate who ruled from A.D. 26-36.

Herod Antipas was made Tetrarch of Galilee and Perea and served from 4 B.C. to A.D. 39. Most of the life of Jesus was spent in the territory of Herod Antipas who, while an able ruler, was without morals or mercy. He was responsible for the death of John the Baptist.

## 12. Pontius Pilate.

Since Pilate is so prominently identified with the life of Jesus it will be well to speak briefly of him in this connection. He was a weakling without much character or conviction. His dealings were those of an opportunist. He was in almost constant conflict with the Jews who not only distrusted him but actually hated him. He misappropriated funds, disregarded Jewish religious customs and defied their leaders. His misdeeds served to make him a coward and to bring him into contempt. His weakness and utter lack of character is exhibited in his handling of the trial of Jesus.

## 13. The Temple.

From the time of Solomon (1000 B.C.) the temple in Jerusalem was the glory of the nation. This was true in Jesus' time. The Jews had had three temples. The first one, erected by Solomon, was destroyed by the Babylonians in 587 B.C. Zerubbabel rebuilt the temple which was dedicated in 516 B.C. Herod the Great, hoping to win the favor of the Jews, erected the third temple, which was not finally completed until A.D. 65. Only five years later Titus destroyed this one. All three temples occupied the same site on Mt. Moriah in the city, and were substantially of the same pattern. Each of these buildings faced the east. On the lower floor was the court of the Gentiles where the public could assemble and where animals for sacrifice were sometimes sold. Above this level was the real center of Jewish worship. It consisted of the Holy Place and the Holy of Holies.

The annual feasts brought great crowds of people to the city at stated intervals. The priests served in turns. The hours of prayer were nine, twelve and three. Indeed, this glorious temple was the heart and center of Jewish religious and national life.

### 14. Annual Feasts.

In the time of Jesus there were six great feasts observed annually by the Jews. Following our calendar these were Purim, Passover, Pentecost, Day of Atonement, Tabernacles and Dedication.

*Purim* was observed about the first of March. This observance originated with the deliverance of the Jews from the designs of Haman as told in the book of Esther. Usually it was a gay occasion observed in holiday spirit. The book of Esther was always read during the observance.

The *Passover,* the oldest of the feasts, occurred near the first of April. It commemorated the deliverance of the Hebrew people from Egyptian bondage and was most impressive and important. Usually very large crowds came to this celebration.

*Pentecost,* the feast of first fruits, came fifty days after the Passover, about the latter part of May. This was the time of grain harvest and one ceremony connected with its observance was the presentation of the two "wave-loaves" made from new wheat flour. This feast also commemorated the giving of the Law of Moses. It was at the feast of Pentecost that the Holy Spirit came upon the Christians in Jerusalem after the ascension of Jesus.

The *Day of Atonement,* which was really a fast, took place in late September. It was a solemn occasion on which the High Priest entered the Holy of Holies to make atonement for the sins of the people.

The feast of *Tabernacles* came five days after the Day of Atonement. It was a sort of Thanksgiving for the blessings of the year with especial reference to the blessings of God upon their fathers in the wilderness wanderings enroute to Canaan.

The feast of *Dedication* came in December and was held in commemoration of the dedicating of the temple after the victories of Judas Maccabeus in December, 165 B.C.

### 15. Synagogues.

The synagogue had a very prominent place in the religious life of the Jews at the time of Jesus. The details of its origin are not known, though it came into existence after the Exile. The word means *coming together* or assembly. Usually the word refers to a small building used by the Jews for teaching the law, for worship and even for social gatherings. Since these buildings met a real need they soon multiplied in number. There is no way of knowing how many of these were in Palestine at the time of Jesus, but the number was very large. Since the Jews built these wherever they resided, we may be sure that there were many of them in the Roman empire. Paul habitually went first to the synagogue when he reached a city to begin his missionary work. Usually these were simple structures, rectangular in shape. They were placed near a stream of water because of the ceremonial ablutions. In some cases they were outside the city limits.

The services of worship and the program of teaching were under the direction of the general officer known as the "ruler." Services were held regularly on the Sabbath day (our Saturday), and occasionally additional services were held on week days. The Old Testament was read and explained to both young and old. After the reading of the scriptures any qualified worshiper might make an exposition of the scripture lesson as Jesus did on at least one occasion in the synagogue at Nazareth. Paul and other missionaries also did this. Thus we can see the far-reaching influence of the synagogue in the life of the Jewish people.

*16. Scribes.*

After the Exile the office of Scribe came into existence. These officials exercised a tremendous influence in the time of Jesus. Originally, as the name indicates, they were the copyists of the sacred writings. Gradually their function changed and they were regarded as the authoritative interpreters of the scriptures. They claimed to have great reverence for the Old Testament writings, even counting every word in them. They gradually became a "dry ecclesiastical and scholastic class" who were concerned chiefly with the letter of the law. They even became greedy for power and determined upon selfish aggrandizement. "Whatever was most spiritual, living, human and grand in the scriptures they passed by. Generation after generation the commentaries of their famous men multiplied, and the pupils studied the commentaries instead of the text. Moreover, it was a rule with them that the correct interpretation of a passage was as authoritative as the text itself; and, the interpretations of the famous masters being as a matter of course believed to be correct, the mass of opinions which were held to be as precious as the Bible itself grew to enormous proportions. These were 'the traditions of the elders.' By degrees an arbitrary system of exegesis came into vogue, by which almost any opinion whatever could be thus connected with some text and stamped with divine authority. Every new invention of Pharisaic singularity was sanctioned in this way. Peculiarities were multiplied until they regulated every detail of life, personal, domestic, social and public. They became so numerous that it required a lifetime to learn them all; and the learning of a scribe consisted in acquaintance with them, and with the dicta of the great rabbis and the forms of exegesis by which they were sanctioned. This was the chaff with which they fed the people in the synagogues. The conscience was burdened with innumerable details, every one of which was represented to be as divinely sanctioned as any of the Ten Commandments. This was the intolerable burden which Peter said neither he nor his fathers had been able to bear. This was the horrible nightmare which sat so long on Paul's conscience. But worse consequences flowed from it. It is a well-known principle in history, that, whenever the ceremonial is elevated to the same rank with the moral, the later will soon be lost sight of. The Scribes and Pharisees had learned how by arbitrary exegesis and casuistical discussion to explain away the weightiest moral obligations, and make up for the neglect of them by multiplying ritual observances. Thus men were able to flaunt in the pride of sanctity while indulging their selfishness and vile passions. Society was rotten with vice within, and veneered over with a self-deceptive religiosity without."[3]

### 17. The Pharisees.

There were two very influential religious parties among the Jews, the Pharisees and the Sadducees. As a matter of fact, however, these parties were political as well as religious. The Pharisees were more numerous and powerful since they had in their party the representative religious leaders. In a sense they can be thought of as a fraternal order.

They were the chief exponents of the traditions of Judaism, the "guardians of orthodoxy." Their very name, "separatists," indicates the nature of their emphasis. They were patriotic, fervent in their faith, and wholly unsympathetic toward any who held different views. To them there was no good outside Pharisaism.

They had very definite doctrines which they enthusiastically proclaimed. They stressed special divine providence, though they did not deny free will. They believed in the future life, the resurrection of the elect of Israel, and the existence of angels. They were simple, even ascetic in living habits. They stressed external observances such as fasts, tithes, prayers, ablutions and sacrifices, to the exclusion of love to God and to men. It was natural that they should fail to accept the new teachings of Jesus. It was inevitable that Jesus should challenge them and then denounce them for their failure to see this truth.

### 18. The Sadducees.

The Sadducees, while much fewer in number, were of the aristo-cratic class and were very influential. They differed from the Pharisees at almost every point. They protested the emphasis placed on tradition by the Pharisees and demanded a return to the Bible. They were in reality skeptical and cold-hearted, wanted to live a life of self-indulgence and luxury, and did not concern themselves with annoying details of religious duties.

Insofar as they had religious views they were liberals. They denied the concern of God for human affairs. They denied the doctrine of immortality, the resurrection and the existence of angels. To them the written Old Testament only was authoritative. They accepted Graeco-Roman culture and considered themselves a sort of religious aristocracy.

### 19. Other Religious Sects.

In addition to these two leading parties there were several other religious sects among the Jews. The *Essenes,* not mentioned in the New Testament, were ascetics who lived largely in the wilderness of Judea. They were a mystical group interested in Persian and Greek philosophy. How vitally they affected the life of their times is debatable.

The *Zealots* were a party chiefly concerned with political matters. They desired above everything else the independence of the Jewish people as a nation. Their immediate aim was to throw off the yoke of Rome and set up a free nation again. In their devotion to this ideal they were frequently guilty of fanaticism.

The *Herodians* likewise were almost wholly politically minded. They favored the dynasty of Herod after Archelaus was deposed. They were of but little consequence in the religious life of the nation.

### 20. The Sanhedrin.

After their conquest, the Romans allowed the Jews to preserve some of their institutions so long as they did not challenge Roman authority. Thus the Jews had their Sanhedrin or supreme court. Its jurisdiction, however, was limited mainly to matters of religion. Civil cases of a more serious nature were handled by the Roman courts. For this reason the Sanhedrin could try Jesus on religious charges but his civil trial and the pronouncement of the death penalty must be by Roman officials. The Sanhedrin was composed of seventy-one members made up of both Pharisees and Sadducees. The members were chief priests and scribes, and were called elders. The high priest who served as president was frequently only the puppet of Rome appointed and deposed at the pleasure of the Roman ruler.

### 21. The State of Jewish Religion.

From this brief survey of the aspects of Jewish religion, it will be seen that the Jews had not lost interest in religion. Indeed, the casual student may assume that their religion was sufficient. But this would be a superficial and unwarranted conclusion. They did have a religion, but one which was a hollow mockery characterized by external appearances. "The nation was far more orthodox than it had been at many earlier periods of its history. Once its chief danger had been idolatry; but the chastisement of the Exile had corrected that tendency forever, and thenceforward the Jews, wherever they might be living, were uncompromising monotheists. The priestly orders and offices had been thoroughly reorganized after the return from Babylon, and the temple services and annual feasts continued to be observed at Jerusalem with strict regularity. Schools of theology, similar to our divinity halls, had sprung up, in which the rabbis were trained and the sacred books interpreted.

"But, in spite of all this religiosity, religion had sadly declined. The externals had been multiplied, but the inner spirit had disappeared. However rude and sinful the old nation had sometimes been, it was capable in its worst periods of producing majestic religious figures, who kept high the ideal of life and preserved the connection of the nation with Heaven; and the inspired voices of the prophets kept the stream of truth running fresh and clean. But during four hundred years no prophet's voice had been heard. The records of the old prophetic utterances were still preserved with almost idolatrous reverence, but there were not men with even the necessary amount of the Spirit's inspiration to understand what He had formerly written."[4]

### 22. Messianic Expectations.

In spite of the superficiality and poverty of formal religion among the Jews, there were some sincere, devout, and spiritually-minded people who still trusted in God and believed in the high spiritual mission of their race. Among all these religious leaders there was the hope of a coming Messiah. This hope varied among different groups and there were many different beliefs as to the nature and work of this Messiah. He might be a prophet, a priest, a king or even an angel. In the hearts of many there was a deep longing for something more satisfying than that which their official religion offered them.

[1]Stalker, *Life of Christ,* p. 25.
[2]Ibid., pp. 29-30.
[3]Ibid., pp. 29-30.
[4]Ibid., pp. 27-28.

*Chapter V*

## THE NEW TESTAMENT RECORDS

Introduction. 1. Variety of Contents. 2. Chronological Arrangement. 3. How and Why the New Testament Was Written. 4. New Testament Manuscripts. 5. Texts and Versions. 6. The Canon of The New Testament. 7. The Gospels. 8. Acts. 9. Letters of Paul. 10. General Letters. 11. The Apocalypse.

CHAPTER V

# The New Testament Records

*Introduction.*

Unquestionably the New Testament is the most important book, or collection of books, in all literature. These writings, all of which may be included in a book of some five hundred pages of average size, have been read and studied by more people than any other writings ever produced. They have a value and a significance which no other literature can ever approach. "The New Testament is a treasure. Generations of scholars have set eyes and hearts and hands to compass it, and to preserve it. A goodly army of martyrs have died for it. A multitude of saintly men have beset it about with commentary from their own lives and thoughts . . . The New Testament has given rise to tens of thousands of books; to ten hundred or more great songs, and paintings, and carvings in wood and stone and metal; and to thousands of hospitals and houses of mercy, schools and cathedrals and chapels. This single book has begotten a great and living tradition — in the light of which other treasures and other traditions come to judgment and valuation."[1] The chief reason for the unusual value and significance of the New Testament is the fact that it is the sole record of the origin and early development of Christianity. The writings of secular historians in the Roman empire contain practically nothing about the life of Christ or the early church. Two notable exceptions are the statements of Tacitus and Pliny, eminent Roman writers.

Somewhere about A.D. 115 Tacitus in his Annals (XV:44) says: "These people take their name from one Christus, who was put to death in the reign of Tiberius by the Procurator Pontius Pilatus; and the pestilent superstition was checked for a time. Afterward it began to break out afresh, not only in Judea, where the mischief first arose, but also at Rome, to which all criminal and shameful things flow in from every quarter, and find a welcome."

About the same time Pliny the Younger, while governor of Bithynia, spoke of the Christians: "They assemble on a fixed day before day-break, and sing responsively a hymn to Christ, as a god, at which time they bind themselves by means of an oath not to enter into any wickedness, or to commit thefts, robberies, or adulteries, or to falsify their work, or to repudiate trusts committed to them. When these things are ended, it is their custom to depart, and on coming together again, to take food, men and women together, yet innocently."

Josephus the eminent Jewish historian, about the end of the first century made one brief reference to Christ in his *Antiquities.* Speaking of the death of James he refers to him as the "brother of Jesus, the so-called Christ."

Whatever may have been the reasons for failure of secular historians to mention Jesus, the fact remains that were it not for the New Testament itself we would know very little of the life and teachings of Jesus and his Apostles. These New Testament writings are thus the only source book of Christianity.

*1. Variety of Contents.*

It is always well for the student to get a sort of preview of the material to be studied in a given course. His study can be much more meaningful if he knows beforehand something of the nature and extent of such a course. Since our New Testament is a compilation of writings of different kinds the student will need to get a glimpse of their nature, purpose and content.

It is customary to classify the books of the New Testament as biography (gospels), history (Acts), epistles, and the apocalypse. Such a classification is helpful but it is not always complete, and may be misleading. No book is wholly historical or purely biographical. In considering the gospels we should remember that they have other distinct values in addition to their importance as biographies of Jesus. Many of the New Testament books contain history, doctrine, some poetry and prophecy. Having said this however, it is still useful to follow the general classification.

The first four books are called *gospels,* which carries the idea of "good news." We sometimes speak of Matthew, Mark and Luke as the Synoptic (seeing with same eye) gospels because of the striking similarity of arrangement and content, and John as the "Fourth gospel." The traditional view is that each book bears the name of its author. In the main they deal with the earthly life of Jesus Christ. Not any one of them claims to give a fully-detailed account of all the experiences of Jesus in the "days of his flesh." They give a record of only a small part of what Jesus said and did. There is no complete detailed life of Christ. So far as we know no one ever attempted such a gigantic undertaking. John closes his gospel with the statement: "And there are also many other things which Jesus did, the which if they should be written every one, I suppose that even the world itself would not contain the books that should be written." (21:25.)

In general the gospels close with rather lengthy accounts of the trials, death, burial, resurrection and ascension of Jesus. But that which Jesus "began both to do and to teach" did not cease. A new movement had been launched, a new era had opened. The book of Acts is devoted to the recording of the progress of this new movement for a generation after the death of Jesus. Naturally this book also does not claim to record all details. It traces the main course of history and gives representative incidents up to the time Paul was in prison in Rome for the first time (A.D. 60-62). As a source book its value is inestimable. This book is sometimes called the Acts of the Holy Spirit and the Magna Charta of Christian evangelism.

The epistles or letters of Paul, usually listed as thirteen in number, were written out of the experiences of Paul and were sent to various churches and individuals to instruct and nurture new Christians. These letters are vital, dynamic documents dealing with the problems and difficulties in a certain situation. Usually they were intended for some critical situation, though their value was not exhausted in this particular use. They interpret the teachings of Jesus and are thus theological in general character.

In addition to the Pauline letters there are eight others which are often called General or Catholic epistles. Some of these are early (c A.D. 50) but most of them belong to the latter part of the first Christian century. These epistles give us a glimpse into the life of people where Christianity had become reasonably well established.

The last book of the Bible, Revelation, is apocalyptic in nature. In the visions of this book the Christian hope amid persecution and death is radiantly set forth.

While there is diversity in the contents of these writings there is a significant absence of inconsistencies and contradictions. Indeed a marvelous unity runs through all of these. "There is a unity of spirit in these writings, sometimes vast and deep, that points to a common revelation of divinity shared together. It suggests the music of the spheres or the communion of the saints."[2]

2. *Chronological Arrangement.*

The books in the New Testament are not arranged in the order in which they were written. There is some difference of opinion among scholars as to the dates of these books, and while their value usually is not greatly affected by the date it may be useful to the student to have a list of these books in the order of their writing as generally accepted by conservative scholars. Dr. A. T. Robertson in his book, *The Chronological New Testament,* arranges these in the following order:

| | | | |
|---|---|---|---|
| James | 50 A.D. | Ephesians | 62 A.D. |
| Mark | 50 A.D. | I Peter | 65 A.D. |
| I Thessalonians | 52 A.D. | II Peter | 67 A.D. |
| II Thessalonians | 52 A.D. | Jude | 67 A.D. |
| I Corinthians | 57 A.D. | Titus | 67 A.D. |
| II Corinthians | 57 A.D. | I Timothy | 67 A.D. |
| Galatians | 58 A.D. | II Timothy | 68 A.D. |
| Romans | 58 A.D. | Hebrews | 69 A.D. |
| Matthew | 58 A.D. | John (Gospel) | 85 A.D. |
| Luke | 58 A.D. | I John | 85 A.D. |
| Acts | 62 A.D. | II John | 85 A.D. |
| Philippians | 62 A.D. | III John | 85 A.D. |
| Philemon | 62 A.D. | Revelation | 95 A.D. |
| Colossians | 62 A.D. | | |

### 3. How and Why the New Testament Was Written.

Many volumes have been written on this subject. While we can not attempt any detailed discussion here, it may be helpful to call attention to some general principles involved.

These twenty-seven books were produced by no less than eight different men. The time of writing was from forty-five to fifty years (A.D. 50-100). Naturally the purpose in writing differed in each instance.

These books were produced by people who had had a vital experience with Jesus. Their writings grew out of this experience which was satisfying, compelling and urgent. These writings deal with life, and in no sense can be thought of as cold, mechanical, theoretical treatises unrelated to living.

It is but natural that they should be written. These writers accepted fully the Old Testament scriptures. They certainly were cognizant of the fact that while the Old Testament was divinely inspired it in itself was incomplete.Their life-changing experiences with Jesus and their part in the historic enterprise inaugurated by him laid upon them the compulsion of recording and amplifying their experiences and the truth which they enjoyed. They "accepted the call to complete" the Old Testament.

We shall do well to keep constantly in mind the fact that these writings were the product of men whose lives had been transformed by their experience with Jesus Christ in obedience to his great commission.

"Every one of its twenty-seven books was produced in connection with the work of the disciples in carrying out the commission of their Lord to give his gospel to all the peoples of the world; to seek always the kingdom of God and his righteousness; to cause all men to see what is the stewardship of the divine intention which for ages had been hid in God who created all things, with the purpose of making known to all the universe, through his church, his manifold wisdom, to the universal praise of the glory of his grace (Matt. 6:33; 28:16-20; Eph. 3:9-12).

"They were wrought out of the experiences of the witnesses; out of the moral and ethical struggles of the believers and the churches in a pagan environment; out of the antagonisms of the opponents and the persecutions of enemies of the cross of Christ; out of triumphs of faith and love in a wicked world; out of the necessity for the Christians to try to explain to themselves and to others the marvel of themselves and of their growing meaning in the world's life.

"So far from being any less the Word of God for being produced out of their experiences while carrying the gospel to men, the New Testament writings are all the more real as the Word of God to all generations of them that seek his face and find his glory shining in the face of Jesus Christ. It is not some ancient word spoken in remote days and encased in antique pages. No, it is 'alive, and active, and sharper than any two-edged sword, and piercing even right through soul and spirit, joints and marrow, and acting as judge of impulses and thoughts of the heart' (Heb. 4:12). It is exactly in harmony with the purpose and plan of Jesus for his Testament to come out of the growth of his gospel."[3]

The books were not written for "literary" purposes. There was no thought on the part of any of these writers that he was producing a piece of literature that would become immortal and make the author famous. At the same time it is good literature. To be sure it is not classical in style like that of Homer, for example, but it is the work of men of genius. "Genius shows itself everywhere, in both phrase and thought." While Paul and other writers were scholars they were not attempting to exhibit their scholarship nor make any bid for literary fame.

We are all deeply indebted to these men who were led of the Holy Spirit to write these books which have been miraculously preserved and are available for our use today.

### 4. New Testament Manuscripts.

The books of the New Testament were written originally on papyrus. Only the inner surface of these sheets of durable paper was used. At first these sheets were pasted end to end until the required amount of paper was secured, then the whole was rolled around a small rod to form what was called a scroll. A cord or ribbon was tied around the scroll which was kept in a safe place. In this way the original manuscripts of the New Testament were preserved and from them copies were carefully made.

Usually it is a shock to the student to discover that we do not have a single original manuscript of any book in the New Testament. These originals have disappeared and in all probability will never be recovered. All we have are copies of these first manuscripts. However, we need not be too disturbed about this since copies were made with the greatest of care and the authenticity of these books is not affected. It is generally held by scholars that our copies are faithful reproductions which are substantially identical with the originals.

By the fourth century these scrolls were being replaced by the *codex* in which the sheets were placed one upon another and bound in what we call book form. By this time papyrus was being replaced by parchment or finely prepared skins of certain animals. By the use of parchment in book form these "books" could be skillfully done and elaborately ornamented.

While we do not have the original manuscripts of the New Testament, we do have a great many of the old manuscripts of the New Testament which were copied by scribes. In fact there are in existence more than 2,500 of such manuscripts. A number of these which go back to the fourth century are exceedingly valuable. Naturally the older manuscripts are more valuable since they are nearer to the original and thus have less possibility of error in being copied. These manuscripts are in book form (codex) and are classified by scholars into two groups. The first are called *Uncials* because they are written in Greek capital letters. These are dated from the fourth to the ninth centuries. The second are known as *Cursives* because they were written in running hand. These date from the ninth to the fifteenth centuries, that is up to the time of the invention of printing.

The Uncials are by far the most important to New Testament scholars. While there are a large number of these Uncial manuscripts, only four or five of the most valuable ones can be mentioned in this study.

(1) *Codex Vaticanus* — This is the oldest and the most important of these manuscripts, dating around A.D. 350. It has about 800 pages 10 x 10½ inches and contains almost all of the Old and the New Testaments. It was brought to Rome as early as 1448 and is in the Vatican Library in Rome.

(2) *Codex Sinaiticus* — The discovery of this famous manuscript is a thrilling story. The Greek scholar, Count L. F. K. Tischendorf, first got a glimpse of this in the library of the monastery of St. Catherine on historic Mt. Sinai in 1844. It was not until 1859 that he was able to get it to Cairo and finally have it presented to the Czar of Russia. In 1862 it was photographically reproduced and published in an elegant edition and thus became available to New Testament scholars. The original was kept for a while in Petrograd, but is now in the British Museum. It is the only complete Uncial manuscript of the New Testament. It is usually dated around A.D. 375.

(3) *Codex Alexandrinus* — This famous codex also is in the British Museum. It dates around A.D. 425, consists of about 775 pages including most of the Old and New Testaments.

(4) *Codex Ephraim* — This one is in the National Library in Paris. It dates from the fourth or fifth Christian century. It is called a palimpsest or rescript because it is a manuscript from which the Biblical text has been partially erased and upon which some sermons of Ephraem were written. By the use of chemicals the original writing, i.e., New Testament books, was restored after the sermons had been erased.

(5) *Codex Bezae* — This Codex which was written in the sixth century, is in the University Library of Cambridge. It was presented to this Library in 1581 by Theodore Beza. It is a Graeco-Latin manuscript, the Greek of the left hand page and the Latin version on the right. Scholars tell us that the Latin does not always correspond exactly to the Greek text.

We must of necessity omit the discussion of these other interesting New Testament manuscripts. The remarkable, even miraculous, preservation of the text of the New Testament has left to us a rich heritage for study.

### 5. Texts and Versions.

The significance of these five famous codices is seen when we realize that they were used in making only the more recent translations of the New Testament. In view of the fact that we have so many manuscripts of the New Testament it is natural to raise the question as to what is the authoritative text. This has been the problem of scholars for several centuries. Erasmus, the eminent Dutch scholar, prepared what he considered a standard text as far back as 1516. Since then other scholars have devoted much time to this undertaking. Through the labors of such men as Bentley, Tischendorf, Westcott and Hort, Souter, Weiss and others, general unanimity of opinion has been reached on this important question.

The limits of this chapter will not permit us to discuss the various translations of the New Testament. As early as the second century these books were being translated into the languages of other people. An early Latin version appeared about A.D. 150, but the most famous Latin version was that of Jerome known as the Vulgate, A.D. 380, which included the entire Bible. Through the centuries translations have appeared in increasing numbers. In 1962 the New Testament had been translated into more than eleven hundred different languages and dialects.

### 6. The Canon of the New Testament.

The term "canon" as applied to accepted authoritative Christian writings was first used in Alexandria, Egypt, about A.D. 200. In modern usage the word *canon* means the list of books which are recognized as inspired and authoritative. The process by which the various books of the New Testament came to be agreed upon as authoritative was a long one. In fact, our information on this process is not as definite and detailed as we might wish.

To begin with we do well to remember that perhaps none of the writers of New Testament books felt that he was producing a book which might later become a part of a body of sacred writings to be used by posterity. They wrote out of the experiences under the conviction that they were witnesses of and participants in events which were the fulfillment of the Old Testament which they regarded as the word of God. The primary purpose of their writings was to meet an immediate need.

The bringing together of these various writings was really a matter of growth. The gospels and some of the epistles were circulated among

Christians within one generation after the death of Jesus and thus their value came to be recognized. As time passed others likewise were used by various groups. The general order of our present New Testament was recognized as early as Eusebius (A.D. 260-340). By A.D. 397 this was established and thereafter no serious question was raised about these books. "All were accepted as the revealed and inspired Word of God, whose unity of authorship is found in the Holy Spirit, whose unity of subject is found in Jesus Christ, and whose unity of fundamental beliefs and practices is expressed everywhere. It was recognized that this unity is not superficial but is rather inherent in and essential to the records themselves. That conviction remains until today."[4]

The matter of determining finally which books should be included in the canon of New Testament writings could have been done in two ways: (1) By the official decree of some council or group of leaders who would render a decision which would be accepted as final. (2) By the general test of usage by individuals and churches in meeting their problems in doctrine, polity and practice. It is true that some of these councils did make pronouncements regarding the books in the New Testament but so far as we know the church represented by these councils did not decide the matter. The people, represented by the churches, out of their experience in discovering what was genuine gradually decided it. By approximately A.D. 400 there was general unanimity among these groups of Christians in all parts of the Graeco-Roman world as to what books were authoritative and consequently entitled to be included in the canon. This was far better than the arbitrary decision of any small group of churchmen.

## 7. The Gospels.

We shall devote the remainder of this chapter to a brief consideration of the character and content of these New Testament books which are to be the object of our study.

For obvious reasons we begin with the gospels. These books are concerned with the life of Jesus, and while they have many striking similarities, they differ in many respects, and each book has individuality of its own.

Matthew, Mark and Luke are called the "synoptic" gospels because they are so much alike in arrangement, content, and even in phraseology. They appear to "see with the same eyes." Years ago careful students, noting the similarities in these gospels conceived the idea of arranging the contents of each gospel in chronological order and placing these accounts alongside each other in parallel columns. This arrangement is called a "harmony" of the gospels and is a very valuable device for careful students. For example, it is a great convenience to have each writer's record of the crucifixion, or any other event, on one page where the process of comparison is made simple.

(1) *Mark* — We begin with Mark because his book was the first to be written. It is generally agreed that the author was John Mark, a young man who later became a distinguished helper of Paul and an able missionary. We know a number of things about him. He was the son of Mary, a woman of Jerusalem whose home was a meeting place of the disciples. He was probably converted by Peter since this apostle refers to him as his "son." He accompanied Paul and Barnabas on their first missionary campaign as far as Perga where he forsook them and returned to Jerusalem. He pled with Paul and Barnabas to take him on the second campaign but Paul refused him and for this reason Paul and Barnabas separated. Paul took Silas with him while Barnabas and Mark went back to Cyprus to work. Ten years later he had regained the confidence of Paul and seems to have been with him in Rome.

It is possible that he wrote his gospel in Rome. The date may have been as early as A.D. 50. Some scholars hold that it is primarily Peter's gospel and that John Mark was only the amanuensis or scribe. All are agreed that it reflects strongly the influence and ideas of Peter.

It is the briefest of all the gospels. It is largely narrative, the style is direct and simple, and it moves rapidly. For this reason it is sometimes called the "motion picture" gospel. It gives numerous details and is characterized by vividness. It omits all the facts connected with the birth, boyhood and preparation of Jesus and begins with his ministry.

It is marked by energy and activity. He stresses the works of Jesus more than his words. He records but few of the sayings of Jesus, gives only four parables, but records eighteen miracles. The rapid succession of events is quite noticeable. He uses the word "straightway" forty-one times.

Mark emphasizes the awe and the wonder which the work of Jesus created. "The wonder-working Son of God sweeps over His Kingdom swiftly and meteor-like."

It was written to make an appeal to the Roman people, who were men of power and achievement. Everywhere he shows the power of

Jesus. He is presented as one who had power over demons, power to heal diseases and power over the forces of nature.

(2) *Matthew* — This writer was one of the twelve disciples of Jesus, though we do not have many details about him. He was the son of Alphaeus, and was known as Levi until Jesus called him. He was a "publican," one who officiated as tax-collector for the Romans, a position of the lowest rank in the eyes of the Jews. He is listed as among those present at the day of Pentecost. The manner of his death is not known though tradition says that he was a martyr.

Being accustomed to bookkeeping it may be that he kept careful notes on the work and the discourses of Jesus. At any rate he gives much attention to the teachings of Jesus. He gives by far the most detailed account of the Sermon on the Mount.

The date of the writing of his book is not certainly known. We do know that it was after Mark. It seems reasonable to date the book A.D. 58-60.

This book too, is marked by certain distinguishing characteristics. One will note that it is topical in emphasis and that these topics are arranged purposely in a certain order. For example nearly all of chapters eight and nine are devoted to miracles, while chapter thirteen is concerned with parables.

Matthew stresses the kingly nature of Jesus. The book opens with the royal descent of Jesus. Again and again he speaks of the kingdom. The book closes with a picture of all the nations gathering before the king as he sits on his throne.

The distinguishing characteristic is its purpose to appeal to the Jews. Jewish terms and expressions abound, and are never explained, as in the other gospels. There are sixty-five direct quotations from the Jewish scriptures. Frequently he uses the expression "that the scripture might be fulfilled." The numbers, so characteristic of the Jews, are frequently used. For example, the number seven occurs repeatedly. There are two chapters containing seven parables each, seven woes in chapter 23, seven petitions in the Lord's prayer, etc. Undoubtedly his chief purpose in writing his gospel was to convince the Jewish people that Jesus was the Messiah predicted in their scriptures.

(3) *Luke* — Competent scholars are practically unanimous in the opinion that Luke is the author of the third gospel. He is the only Gentile writer in the New Testament. His writings exhibit rare literary beauty. It is probable that he belonged to the Greek race, was once a

slave and later became a freedman. Some scholars believe that he once belonged to Theophilus who gave him his freedom and that he dedicated his gospel to Theophilus as a token of appreciation. The "we" sections in Acts show that he was a companion of Paul on his missionary campaigns. He was with Paul on the second campaign, joined him at Philippi on his return from the third campaign, went with him to Caesarea, stayed with him to Rome. Paul calls him the "beloved physician" and his "fellow laborer." The fact that he was a doctor or a scientist gives great significance to his gospel. He gives the fullest account of the birth of Jesus. He gives great emphasis to the healing ministry of Jesus. He was the first genuine scientist to face the problem of Christ and of Christianity. This he did with an open mind and yet in a reverent spirit.

The gospel of Luke gives evidence of familiarity with methods of research. In the opening statement he declares that he "has traced the course of all (these) things accurately from the first." His book impresses the reader as the work of an accurate scientist who is also an able historian. It is probable that he wrote the gospel about A.D. 58-60 from Caesarea.

This book naturally has certain very distinct characteristics. One notes the element of song and praise throughout. He gives the "songs" of Mary, Zachariah, the angels, and Simeon. It has a note of music and gladness, which is not found in the others.

In Luke's gospel we find unusual prominence given to womanhood and childhood. Elisabeth, Mary the mother of Jesus, Anna, the widow of Nain, Mary Magdala, Mary and Martha, and others are brought into his story.

Luke tells of a number of the poor and neglected people of Jesus' day who were brought under his beneficent influence. He mentions the publicans a number of times, the harlots, the prodigal son, Lazarus the beggar, Zacchaeus, the dying robber, and many others. He alone gives the familiar statement of Jesus, "I came to seek and save that which was lost."

The note of universality in Luke is distinctly characteristic. The angel's announcement of great joy which shall be "to all people," sending the seventy to all the cities which Jesus should later visit, the story of the Good Samaritan, the Perean ministry and many other references show this universal note. Indeed, it may be called the Gentile Gospel.

(4) *John* — Probably the most debatable problem in New Testament criticism is that of the authorship of the fourth gospel. Volumes have been written on this question and it is still unsettled. It is not essential to our purposes to attempt to state the arguments for and against the Johannine authorship. As I see it, those who insist that John, the beloved disciple and follower of Jesus, was the author still have the better part of the argument.

John was one of the twelve and was an eye-witness to much of what he relates as is indicated by the precise details which he gives. He became a disciple and was very active in the events connected with the earthly life of Jesus, and later as an apostle. His prominence is shown by the fact that he is so frequently mentioned and was one of the three so closely associated with Jesus. His later years were spent in active work in Asia where he was the recognized leader of Christianity and was known as the "disciple of love." He outlived all the other disciples, his death occurring in the late nineties of the first century. There is a tradition that he was submerged in a caldron of burning oil.

His gospel was written much later than the other three and for a different purpose. Assuming that its date was around A.D. 85, Christianity was no longer a Jewish sect confined to Palestine, but was known all over the Roman empire. Clement of Alexandria makes this positive assertion: "Last of all, John, perceiving that the external facts had been made plain in the gospel, being urged on by his friends, and inspired by the spirit, composed a spiritual gospel."[5] Despite persecution Christianity was triumphing and had attained a place in the thought and life of people which commanded attention and respect. Many of its teachings were accepted but at this time one central truth of Christianity was bitterly attacked. The deity of Jesus was the crucial issue. The Gnostics who did not accept the deity of Jesus, were both vocal and aggressive. John writes his gospel for all nationalities to emphasize that Jesus was the Eternal, Incarnate Word of God. He states this purpose in these words: "Many other signs therefore did Jesus in the presence of the disciples, which are not written in this book; but these are written, that ye may believe that Jesus is the Christ, the Son of God, and that believing ye may have eternal life." (John 20:30-31.)

This gospel is the greatest of all; in fact it is ranked by some scholars as the greatest book ever written. "The test of time has given the palm to the Fourth Gospel over all the books of the world. If Luke's Gospel is the most beautiful, John's Gospel is supreme in its height and depth and reach of thought. The picture of Christ here given is one that has captured the mind and heart of mankind. . . . The language of the Fourth Gospel has the clarity of a spring, but we are not able to sound the bottom of the depths. Lucidity and profundity challenge and charm us as we linger over it."[6]

In order to prove that Jesus is the Christ John makes much use of testimony. Seven distinct lines of testimony are presented (John the Baptist, the Scriptures, Jesus Himself, God the Father, The Holy Spirit, etc.).

It places great emphasis on the spiritual nature of Jesus and his work, yet without minimizing his humanity. Its chief characteristic, however, is its assertion of the Incarnation of Jesus. The Word "became flesh" and dwelled among men.

## 8. Acts.

This book of history, written by Luke as a continuation of the story contained in his gospel, is one of utmost importance from the standpoint of history. Without it we would have almost no record of the events connected with the expansion of Christianity after the resurrection and ascension of Jesus. Its chief purpose seems to be to give an account of the labors of the apostles in establishing Christianity among the Gentiles. It makes no claim to give all the experiences of all or even of any one of the apostles, but gives representative cases to show how Christianity was received and established.

This book, together with the letters of Paul, are our sources of study of Apostolic Christianity, and as such will be considered more in detail when we reach that point in our narrative.

## 9. The Letters of Paul.

The New Testament contains thirteen letters usually accepted as the works of Paul. These grew out of Paul's experiences as a missionary, teacher, preacher and statesman. They were written usually to some church to assist in an emergency which had arisen. Since we are to deal with these later it will be sufficient for our purposes here simply to name these letters in the order in which they probably were written. There are four groups of these. (1) I and II Thessalonians, written about A.D. 52-53, dealing with the second coming of Christ. (2) I and II Corinthians, Romans and Galatians, written AD. 55-58 to expound the doctrine of Justification of Faith. (3) Philippians, Philemon, Ephesians, and Colossians, written in Roman imprisonment about A.D. 60-62 dealing with the deity and humanity of Jesus. (4) I and II

Timothy, and Titus, A.D. 65-67, written to these young ministers to furnish counsel on pastoral problems.

### 10. General Letters.

There are eight other letters in the New Testament, sometimes called General Epistles, because of the more general groups to which they are addressed. These were written by several different men to different people and vary in date from about A.D. 50-90. These have distinct value as we shall see when we reach that point in our studies.

### 11. The Apocalypse.

This last book in the New Testament is better known as the Revelation. To many it is a book of mystery. It has been more generally misinterpreted and abused than any other book in the Bible. Obviously this will be considered in the closing chapter in the study of the New Testament which we are now ready to begin.

---

[1]Battenhouse, *New Testament History and Literature*, p. 2.
[2]Ibid., p. 4.
[3]Carver, W. O., *Why They Wrote the New Testament*, pp. 139-140.
[4]Adams, J. McKee, *Our Bible*, p. 62.
[5]Eusebius, *Church History*, pp. 6, 14, 7.
[6]Robertson, A. T., *Word Pictures in the New Testament*, Vol. V, p. IX.

# PART TWO

*The Life of Jesus Christ*

*Chapter I*

## THE BIRTH AND BOYHOOD OF JESUS

1. The Supernatural. 2. The Pre-existence of Christ. 3. Chronology of His Life. 4. The Annunciations. 5. Mary and Joseph. 6. The Virgin Birth. 7. The Roman Census. 8. The Birth of Jesus. 9. The Time of His Birth. 10. Recognition of the King. 11. Escape Into Egypt. 12. At Home in Nazareth. 13. Joseph's Family. 14. Visit to Jerusalem. 15. The Eighteen Years in Nazareth.

CHAPTER I

# The Birth and Boyhood of Jesus

## *1. The Supernatural.*

The student will be impressed with the frequent mention of miraculous happenings in the gospels. The New Testament opens with supernatural events and the gospels close with the record of the resurrection and ascension of Jesus. Again and again the writers of New Testament books relate these occurrences with a naturalness that makes them an integral part of the narrative. At the outset one must face the question, can we accept these as authentic? Did these miracles occur? Naturally people differ in their answers. Some say frankly that miracles never took place. According to this view these supernatural events would be a violation of the laws of nature, hence are not to be accepted. This school insists that all these are to be discarded, because we can not understand them nor accept them on the basis of reason. There are others who, realizing the difficulty involved, evade the issue by asserting that after all it does not matter greatly. Why should one be too much concerned about these questions when no final solution may be found? At least this is the easy position to take. There are still others who believe in these supernatural occurences, even though they are not able to explain them on a basis of pure reason. They hold that these are not to be discarded simply because we may not be able fully to understand them. The fact that we can not explain them does not mean that they are not true. In faith they accept the supernatural as the acts of God who has infinite wisdom and limitless power: "With God all things are possible."

Without attempting even a brief discussion of this problem two or three general remarks may be made. (1) These accounts of supernatural happenings are a natural and integral part of the gospel record. Some who do not accept miracles have attempted to delete them from the narrative so as to have an account which can be accepted on a rational basis. But this deletion leaves an insipid and pathetic record without meaning or force. (2) What is really involved in the whole question is our conception of God and of Christ. "We have to consider whether Jesus is a mere product of evolution or is the entrance of God into man. The distinction is important from every point of view. If Jesus is only a man who gives us his opinion about God, he is interesting and helpful so far as he sets us a good example, but not an object of worship and a Saviour from sin. If, as we believe and know, he is the Son of God who died on the cross for the sins of the world, there is no ground for doubt about the presence of God in unusual ways in the life, death and resurrection of Jesus."[1] (3) It should be some comfort to the student to know that millions of other Christian people, among them some of our greatest thinkers and scholars, have faced the difficulty, and have exercised faith by accepting the supernatural, even though they were not able to give a scientific explanation of such occurrences. Everyone who holds this view is in respectable company.

## 2. *The Pre-existence of Christ* (John 1:1-18).

It is common for immature students to think of Jesus Christ as having had his beginning with his birth in Bethlehem. It is true, of course, that his birth was the beginning of his life as a man. However, his existence as the Son of God goes back to the beginning of time. This truth is stated in the familiar words of John's gospel: "In the beginning was the Word, and the Word was with God, and the Word was God. The same was in the beginning with God. All things were made by him; and without him was not anything made that hath been made. In him was life; and the life was the light of men." (John 1:1-4.) According to John the roots of the life of Jesus reach back into eternity. He is declared to be the Son of God, on an equality with God, with power to create. He was with God. In the "fulness of time" he became flesh and dwelt among men. The fact of his incarnation (becoming flesh) is stated by Paul: "Have this mind in you, which was also in Christ Jesus; who, existing in the form of God, counted not the being on an equality with God a thing to be grasped, but emptied himself, taking the form of a servant, being made in the likeness of men; and being found in fashion as a man, he humbled himself, becoming obedient unto death, yea, the death of the cross." (Philippians 2:5-8.)

The great miracle in the birth of Jesus is the incarnation, God becoming human flesh and dwelling among men. We may not be able to comprehend this but we may believe it. "He came unto his own (world) but they that were his own (family) received him not." The eternal Christ was born as a baby in Bethlehem. For thirty-three years he lived (tabernacled) among men. This little arc in the circle of his eternity is often called the "days of his flesh." In these days he revealed God; he made God comprehensible to men.

### 3. *Chonology of His Life.*

Oriental people were not time-conscious like modern Western people. In writing the life of a great person we are careful to arrange all details in proper chronological order. The writers of the gospels did not do this in their accounts of the life of Jesus. To be sure the general order is chronological, beginning with his birth and closing with his death and resurrection, but these writers made no effort to arrange the details in the exact order in which they occurred. They were more concerned with the topics or general subject matter. It is not possible, therefore, for the student to find any complete chronological arrangement of these events. But this does not lessen the value of the accounts. For example, the fact that scholars do not agree on the time and place for the Sermon on the Mount does not affect the value of this great deliverance. There is not much difficulty in agreeing on the order of events in the life of Jesus up to the opening of his public ministry. We shall speak of the question of the length of his ministry and the general order of events when we reach that point in our studies.

### 4. *The Annunciations* (Luke 1:5-72; Matthew 1:18-25).

All the facts about the birth of Jesus are given by Matthew and Luke. Mark and John do not tell of his birth, but begin their records with the opening of his public ministry. The story of the advent of Jesus begins with the annunciations. The angel Gabriel made three announcements: one to Zacharias the priest, one to Mary in Nazareth, and one to Joseph. These announcements are significant in that they break the long silence of four hundred years and herald the beginning of momentous events.

It was probably in the year 6 B.C. that Zacharias, during the performance of his regular duties as priest in the temple, received his visitation from Gabriel. This aged priest was startled by the angel's announcement that he and his wife, though both were well past the age, were to become parents of a boy. The character and work of this forthcoming son were denoted. This announcement was so unexpected and startling that even a pious and devout man like Zacharias would hesitate to believe it. Because of his doubt this priest should become dumb and remain so until after the birth of the boy. Naturally this visitation delayed the ministry of Zacharias in the temple and the delay aroused the curiosity of the people who waited.

Six months later Gabriel appeared to Mary, a young woman of Nazareth in Galilee, and announced to her that she was to become the

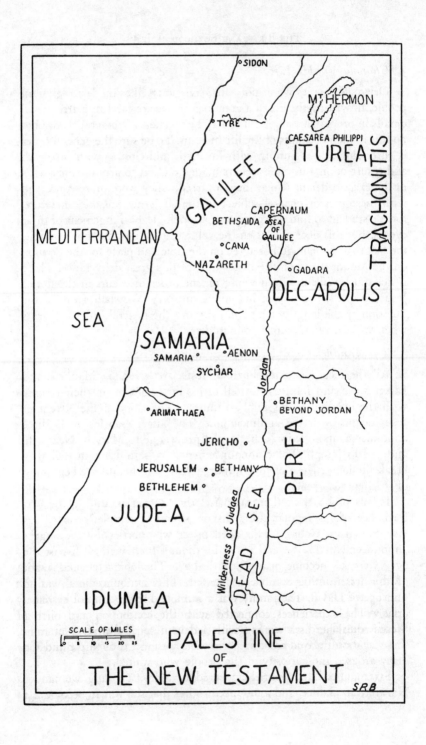

SIDON

MT HERMON

TYRE

CAESAREA PHILIPPI

ITUREA

GALILEE

TRACHONITIS

CAPERNAUM
BETHSAIDA
SEA
OF
GALILEE
CANA
NAZARETH
GADARA

MEDITERRANEAN

DECAPOLIS

SEA

SAMARIA
SAMARIA
AENON
SYCHAR

Jordan

BETHANY
BEYOND JORDAN

ARIMATHAEA

JERICHO

PEREA

JERUSALEM   BETHANY
BETHLEHEM

DEAD SEA

JUDEA

Wilderness of Judaea

IDUMEA

SCALE OF MILES
0   5   10   15   20   25

PALESTINE
OF
THE NEW TESTAMENT

SRB

mother of the Messiah. With great delicacy and beauty Luke gives the details. (1:26-38.) No wonder these amazing words should trouble Mary. No wonder that she asked for further light on this remarkable event. Mary rejoiced as the angel gave in bold outline the nature of the Messiah's work. Knowing full well the problems this would create for her and her family and Joseph, to whom she was betrothed, she nevertheless acquiesced gladly. The "Magnificat," Mary's song of praise on this occasion, gives us an insight into the depth and beauty of her character. She needed some one in whom to confide so she probably told her parents, and perhaps Joseph also. She knew of the secret of her cousin Elisabeth, so she hastened to the home of Zacharias and Elisabeth in the hill country of Judea for a visit. These two devout women with a common secret would find mutual help and encouragement.

Regardless of whether or not Mary went to Joseph with her problem certainly he would learn sooner or later what had taken place. This created a problem for him. Betrothal with the Jews was much more sacred and serious than "engagement" in modern life. Mary belonged to Joseph though not yet legally married to him. In view of this unusual occurrence it would inevitably raise the question as to the character of Mary. Was this a miraculous occurence or was Mary untrue to him? In order to insure the cooperation of Joseph in this matter the angel appeared to him with the statement: "Fear not to take unto thee Mary thy wife: for that which is conceived in her is of the Holy Spirit." (Matthew 1:20.) "And Joseph arose from his sleep, and did as the angel of the Lord commanded him and took unto him his wife; and knew her not till she had brought forth a son; and he called his name Jesus." (Matthew 1:24-25.)

### 5. Mary and Joseph.

We know nothing of the family of Mary, and not a great deal about Mary herself. It is probable that she was of the tribe of Judah and the lineage of David. The family was a humble one though not extremely poor. The experiences connected with the conception and birth of Jesus reveal her as a woman with a devout spirit and reverent mind. She was well acquainted with the Old Testament as is indicated by her song.

We may be safe in assuming that she was a young woman in good health, attractive in appearance and pure in heart. Surely God would have chosen only a woman of the finest character and nobility of soul to be the mother of his Son.

Likewise our information about Joseph is meager. He lived in Nazareth, though his family home had been in Bethlehem. He was a carpenter, called by Matthew *the* carpenter of Nazareth, which would indicate that he was well known and had good standing in the city. The work of a carpenter was not simply that of a repairman, but implied new construction. The behavior of Joseph in his willingness to take suspicion upon himself by marrying Mary is commendable. In every experience Joseph shows up well. He was a man of genuine piety, of simple faith, of real industry, with sympathetic understanding and deep devotion to Mary.

### 6. The Virgin Birth.

In at least two respects the birth of Jesus was unique. It was the incarnation, the miracle of one who was God from the beginning emptying himself and becoming a human being. Jesus stands alone in this respect in human history. His birth is unique also in that he was conceived by the Holy Spirit and was born of a virgin. He was not the son of Joseph or any other man, but the son of God. The "virgin birth" of Jesus therefore, is not only unique but tremendously important. From the first century to the present time this question has been debated; perhaps no other question has been discussed more often or more voluminously. The great majority of Christian people subscribe to the doctrine, though there are some who reject it, claiming that this matter does not affect their faith in Christ. It is worthy of note, however, that every great creed of both evangelical and Catholic Christianity affirms the doctrine.

It is obvious that the limits of this study make it impossible to treat the matter fully. We can summarize very briefly the arguments for it held by thoughtful Christian people. The situation itself is unique — unlike any other in history. If Jesus was the Son of God miraculous circumstances must have attended his coming. He existed from the beginning and "emptied himself" to become a man. We may also ask: "If Jesus was born of human parents, who then was his father?" Not Joseph, for this is disclaimed. The only alternative is that of scandal. The character of Mary and of Jesus would be besmirched. One should recall also the fact that Jesus never called Joseph or any other man his father. He refers always to God as his father.

The unanswerable argument for the virgin birth is the documentary evidence. The four gospels give us the facts in the earthly life of Jesus. Two of these emphatically state the fact of his virgin birth. Matthew tells it from the viewpoint of Joseph. Luke, the physician and historian who gives the fullest account, writes from the standpoint of Mary from whom he probably got all the facts in his research before writing. It is true that neither Mark nor John give the story of his virgin birth. But Mark begins his account with the public ministry of Jesus and gives no facts about his boyhood or training. John affirms that Jesus was with God before the creation of the world and refers to him as the "only-begotten" of the father. To hold that Mark and John did not believe in the virgin birth because they did not record it is utterly unreasonable. One might as well assert that they did not believe in his boyhood.

To refuse to accept the evidence given by the gospels is to discredit them as historical documents, and this is not easily done.

There are some who claim that Paul did not accept the virgin birth because he does not specifically state it in his writings. Again this is argument from silence. The fact that Paul did not mention the Sermon on the Mount does not mean that he questioned it. Every picture which Paul gives of Jesus is in keeping with the representation of him in the gospels. It is possible, indeed probable, that Paul felt no need to defend this, since it was so generally accepted. He defended other truths but not this one.

We may say finally that nowhere in the New Testament does any writer challenge the fact of the virgin birth. The evidence presented above should seem conclusive. "The direct testimony of two Evangelists, and the logical implications of the other two; the necessities of the case and the consciousness of eternal sonship of Jesus; the assumption by Paul and the profound passages in which he discusses deity becoming human; the absence of any challenge of the virgin birth by a New Testament writer and the anathemas against those who deny that Jesus has come in the flesh; the warnings against speculation and the exhortation to hold fast the faith; these, taken altogether, should assure us that the doctrine standeth sure, and hearten us to preach it with confidence and courage."[2]

7. *Roman Census* (Luke 2:1-3).

Luke tells us of this census. "Now it came to pass in those days, there went out a decree from Caesar Augustus, that all the world should be enrolled. This was the first enrollment made when Quirinius was governor of Syria." Up until recent years practically every New Testament scholar was puzzled by these statements of Luke. Some declared that Luke was in error in his account. However, archaeological discoveries have shown that Luke was right. In fact there are reliable references to the very census of which Luke speaks. It came in 6 or 5 b.c. in Palestine. Under this decree every male citizen must go back to the ancestral home to enroll himself for taxation. Joseph lived in Nazareth at the time, but since citizens must enroll themselves at the original home of their tribe, and since Joseph belonged to the tribe of Judah, it became necessary for him to make the long journey from Nazareth, through the plain of Esdraelon and ancient Samaria, past Jerusalem down to Bethlehem.

8. *The Birth of Jesus* (Luke 2:3-20).

The order that forced Joseph to go to Bethlehem served unknowingly to fulfill the prediction of the ancient prophet: "But thou, Bethlehem Ephratah, though thou be little among the thousands of Judah, yet out of thee shall He come forth unto me that is to be ruler in Israel."

Legally it was not required that Mary should go with Joseph to Bethlehem. But since she was "great with child" and the big event might occur at any time she chose to go with her husband rather than remain at home without him. It is probable that she rode on a little donkey, the common beast of burden, led by Joseph. Surely it was a tedious and tiresome trip, but not a sad one. Traveling this ancient route they would see many historic places. They would by-pass the great city of Jerusalem in their haste to dispatch their official business. Upon arriving in Bethlehem they found to their dismay that "there was no room for them in the inn." They were not too poor to pay for such accomodations — no room was available! I have often wondered why some understanding person in the hotel that night did not offer his room to these weary travelers. We should not be too censorious of the inn-keeper; he didn't know the story as we do, and it was probably his kindness that found a place for them at all. This place may have been a grotto or cave, a simple shelter where the cattle were fed, or even an open spot out behind the caravansary.

Thus it happened that in the best quarters available, a stable near the inn, the baby Jesus was born. Were there any kindly friends there to assist? We do not have the details. After the custom the baby was wrapped in swaddling clothes (long bands of white cloth wound around the little body) and laid in the manger.

It is not possible to determine the exact spot where Jesus was born, nor is it necessary. Helena, the mother of Emperor Constantine, the first Roman emperor to embrace Christianity, had a church building erected over the spot then identified as Jesus' birthplace. Today the Church of the Nativity occupies the place, and travelers go down a stairway to a little room directly underneath the altar to see the spot marked by a great star in the stone floor. This may or may not be authentic; the important thing is that Jesus the Son of God was born.

## 9. The Time of His Birth.

There is considerable confusion as to the time of the birth of Jesus. He was not born December 25 in the year A.D. 1. It was some six centuries after the birth of Jesus before any attempt was made to reckon history from this event. Dionysius Exiguus with what data he had, worked backward and fixed what he thought was the correct date. On the basis of his calculations the Christian calendar, still in use, was established. The difficulty is in the fact that his date was later proved incorrect. He should have gone back four or five years further. The year in which Jesus was born was 5 B.C. or 4 B.C. Scholars base their belief in this date on several different lines of evidence, such as the time of the death of Herod, the beginning of the ministry of John the Baptist, the building of the temple, etc. Without attempting to present the arguments we may say that scholars are practically unanimous in this judgment.

There is no way of determining exactly what time of the year this event occurred. It could hardly have been in midwinter since shepherds did not keep their flocks on the hills at night during cold weather. Late in the summer or early in the fall would seem to be the proper time.

## 10. Recognition of the King (Luke 2:21-38; Matthew 2:1-12).

Even though his birth was unheralded the gospels tell of several groups who shortly came to pay tribute to the newborn king. An angel of the Lord appeared to a company of shepherds in the fields nearby who kept watch over their flocks by night, and announced the glad tidings of the birth of a Saviour. The angel told them where and how to find the child, and suddenly the angelic choir burst into song. These shepherds hastened to the village and found Mary and Joseph and the babe lying in the manger. Their story of the visit of the angels with the announcement about Jesus caused all that heard it to wonder. Having paid tribute to the baby the shepherds, who represented the "common people," returned to their flocks in the field. "Mary kept all these sayings, pondering them in her heart."

On the eighth day after his birth the child was circumcised and later was presented in the temple at Jerusalem according to the law of the Jews. Here Mary and Joseph were met by the aged Simeon, who was a God-fearing and devout man to whom the assurance had already been given that he should not see death till he should see "the Christ of the Lord." (Luke 2:22-28.) Simeon took the child in his arms and blessed God for the realization of his promise. He was now ready to depart in peace. He spoke of the work to be done by Mary's child. He should be set for the rising and falling of many. He will be "the touch stone of human hearts and of human history." Then Simeon added a warning to Mary, "Yea, and a sword shall pierce through thine own soul." Did she recall these words of prophecy as she stood thirty-three years later and watched him die on the cross?

From Jerusalem they returned to Bethlehem where they continued to live. Matthew relates the story of the Magi who came from the East to worship the boy Jesus. Following a star they reached Jerusalem and called upon Herod the king, thinking that he would know about the new-born king. Herod was embarrassed but after assembling all the chief priests and scribes to learn from them the prophecy of the birth of the king in Bethlehem, he sent these wise men on to Bethlehem with the request that they return to tell him about this king so that he too, might go to worship him. The wise men left Jerusalem, went to Bethlehem, found and worshiped the babe, but being warned in a dream, they did not return to report to Herod, but followed another route homeward.

There are many questions about these wise men which can not be answered. We do not even know the number, their names, nor their country. Was the star which they followed a comet or a regular star? These men did worship the child, making gifts of gold, frankincense and myrrh. Wise men have their place in the worship of Christ even as the shepherds have.

*11. Escape Into Egypt* (Matthew 2:13-23).

The next incident in the life of Joseph, Mary and the boy Jesus exhibits the worst qualities in the charcter of Herod, the king of Judea. Already he had killed a considerable number whom he felt might some day take his throne. In his last days, tormented by disease and physical pain, he was unspeakably mean and vicious. He suspected every one, including even his own family. When the Magi came with the announcement of a new-born king of the Jews naturally he would be inflamed. Unable to learn the truth, and being outwitted by the Wise Men who did not return to report to him, his anger knew no bounds. Herod was troubled, "and all Jerusalem with him." Determined that this new-born king should be killed, he issued his order for the murder of all male babies in Bethlehem under two years of age. His special officers who carried out such orders would see that this child should never live to become king of the Jews. How many baby boys perished in this "Slaughter of the Innocents" we shall never know. The hand of God rescued Jesus from the death-trap of Herod.

Again an angel appeared to make known to Joseph and Mary what they should do. They were to flee to Egypt out of the jurisdiction of Herod and remain there until they should be told to return. Thus into the ancient land where their ancestors served as slaves the family came to live. They probably remained here for at least a year.

*12. At Home in Nazareth* (Luke 2:39-40).

In 4 B.C. to the relief of every one, Herod died. "In perverted ingenuity he devised a scheme to compel a national mourning when he died. He summoned the chief men of all the nation to Jerusalem, and shut them up in the Hippodrome. He then charged Salome and her husband that the moment the breath left his body the soldiers should be let loose among them and all should be slaughtered. Surely if evil was embodied in any one man, when incarnate love came into that world, it was the corrupt mass that lay upon the royal bed, and still plotted death."[3]

Again the angel appeared to Joseph with the word to return to the land of Israel for, "they are dead that sought the young child's life." Accordingly Joseph began the journey back home and upon learning that Archelaus, Herod's son whose reputation was as bad as that of his father, was reigning in Judea, he was instructed to proceed to Nazareth where greater safety was promised. Thus it happened that Jesus was to grow up in Nazareth of Galilee. And we can believe that this was providential. For various reasons Nazareth was fitted to be the place of his boyhood. The village lay on the southern ranges of lower Galilee in the midst of the most beautiful part of Palestine. The boy would be surrounded by the beauties of nature. From the hill of Nazareth one

can see the historic plain of Esdraelon with its "twenty battle fields" —
the spot where so many great events of Hebrew history had occurred.
Nazareth was at the cross-roads of the ancient highways traversing
Galilee. The road from Jerusalem to Capernaum was within sight. The
famous Via Maris came through Nazareth from Damascus to the
coast. The east and west route over which Roman armies marched,
passed through the village. Any boy would be intrigued by the cosmopolitan company of travelers that passed through the town every day.
No doubt Jesus as a boy had seen many a young man begin a journey
"into a far country." There was much wickedness in this little city as
attested by the common proverb, "can any good thing come out of
Nazareth?" Here he could see life at its worst and could gain some
understanding of man's need for redemption. "Here, then, He grew up
and suffered temptation, who was tempted in all points like as we
are, yet without sin. The perfection of His purity and patience was
achieved not easily as behind a wide fence which shut the world out,
but amid rumor and scandal with every provocation to unlawful
curiosity and premature ambition."[4]

### 13. Joseph's Family. (Mark 6:3).

Joseph and Mary had their home and reared their family in Nazareth. Since Joseph was established in business the home would not be
too humble, nor yet too imposing. It was probably a modest house with
simple furnishings like others of the middle class. Joseph earned a
livelihood by his work as a carpenter. After they had settled in
Nazareth other children came into the home. Jesus had four half
brothers — James, Joses, Judas, Simon — and at least two sisters.
With a mother like Mary it would be a busy but a happy home. She
and Joseph would teach them much of the Old Testament scriptures.
In the synagogue Jesus would receive the regular course of instruction
for children of the time. In this humble but happy home the boy
Jesus grew up. "The child grew and waxed strong, becoming full of
wisdom and the grace of God was upon him." (Luke 2:40.) His
childhood must have been like that of any normal boy except
without sin.

These years in Nazareth up to the time he began his public ministry
at thirty years of age, are often called the "silent years." Wisely
the gospel writers do not tell, except for one big event, any of his
experiences during these years. However, other writers have invented
many so-called events which are both ludicrous and blasphemous.

*14. Visit to Jerusalem* (Luke 2:41-50).

When a Jewish boy reached the age of twelve years custom demanded that he be presented to the Rabbi, take part in the temple worship and become a "Child of the Law." So when Jesus had attained this age he went with Joseph and Mary to Jerusalem to attend the great Passover feast, though he probably had gone with them on other occasions before this time. To make such a journey would be a memorable experience for any boy. Jerusalem was the holy city, enshrined in the heart of every Jew. To go with a large group of other pilgrims, to share in the excitement and adventure of such a journey, to visit kinspeople and family friends, to have some part in the impressive ceremonies — all this would stir the soul of Jesus.

When the week of the feast was over and the caravan had started back home Joseph and Mary had assumed that Jesus would find his place in the company and did not seek him until the group made camp for the night. It is not too much to assume that this boy had shown his reliance and dependability so often beforehand that his parents naturally were not anxious about him. However, one can easily imagine their distress and alarm when the most careful search for him through all the company ended in failure. After a restless and anxious night they journeyed all day back to Jerusalem. Then on the next morning, "after three days they found him in the temple, sitting in the midst of the doctors, both hearing them, and asking them questions: and all that heard him were amazed at his understanding and his answers."

The reaction of Mary as revealed in her first words to him upon finding him safe, is perfectly natural. How relieved she was, and yet a motherly reproach escaped her lips. In the reply which Jesus made to her we have his first recorded words. And these words reveal his own genuine surprise and constitute a rebuke. "Why is it that ye were seeking me? Did ye not know that I must be about my Father's business?" He could not understand why they had not come at once to the temple. They should have known of his ways, his habits and his interest. These first words reveal an amazing consciousness of his high mission in the world. At twelve years he sensed his unique relationship to his father, and felt the obligation of it.

Joseph and Mary did not understand "the saying which he spoke unto them." They returned home and "he was subject unto them."

*15. The Eighteen Years in Nazareth* (Luke 2:51-52).

Since Joseph is not mentioned after the passover when Jesus was twelve years of age, it is generally assumed that he died shortly afterward. This may be true but proof is lacking. As the oldest son in the family Jesus would take up the trade of Joseph. He himself became a workman at the carpenter's bench and apparently was known as "the carpenter." In becoming a laborer he has dignified the toil and labor of workmen everywhere. Surely he did the best of work and did his full share. We may think of him as the counselor and comrade of his mother in her responsibilities with the other children and the household.

Luke gives the only word about these eighteen years before Jesus began his public ministry. But these words are amazing and sufficient. "He cut his way ahead intellectually (in wisdom), physically (in stature), spiritually (in favor or grace), both in religious relation (with God) and in social coordination (with men). This sentence yields us a rich fund of information if we analyze it and then study the outcome in the mature Messiah envisaged in the gospel picture. We shall greatly err and miss much in our understanding of Jesus if we do not allow full force to Luke's statement that 'He forged his way ahead.' That means problems, hindrances, difficulties, opposition; and toil, labor, pains, persistence; and loyalty to an ideal ever more clearly defining itself. He was naturally extraordinary; He achieved distinction and uniqueness."[5]

[1]Robertson, A. T., *Studies in the New Testament,* pp. 63-64.
[2]McDaniel, Geo. W., *The Supernatural Jesus,* p. 122.
[3]Grant, G. M., *Between the Testaments,* pp. 106-107.
[4]Smith, Geo. A., *The Historical Geography of The Holy Land,* p. 434.
[5]Carver, W. O., *The Self Interpretation of Jesus,* pp. 27-28.

*Chapter II*

## JOHN THE BAPTIST

1. Plan of Study. 2. John, the Forerunner. 3. Birth and Boyhood. 4. Beginning His Ministry. 5. Denouncing Sin. 6. Portraying the Messiah. 7. Baptizing Jesus. 8. Explaining His Mission. 9. Greatness of Soul. 10. Denouncing Herod and Herodias. 11. In Prison at Machaerus. 12. Encouraged by Jesus. 13. The Death of John. 14. His Contribution.

## CHAPTER II

# John the Baptist

### 1. Plan of Study.

In the books dealing with the life of Christ the work of John the Baptist is usually discussed as a part of the ministry of Jesus since the experiences of John are woven into the narrative of Jesus' life. However, some writers have departed from the usual order by giving an entire chapter to the career of John the Baptist before taking up the ministry of Jesus. In this way the work which John did is given special emphasis, and the student is better prepared to appreciate the ministry of John. We are to follow this plan in our discussion of the work of John and of Jesus.

### 2. John, the Forerunner.

The chief purpose of John's ministry was to prepare the way for the Messiah. For four hundred years the voice of the prophets had not been heard. The expectation of a Messiah had faded from the minds of most of the Jews who were absorbed in formalism and secularism. A voice was needed to arouse the people, to call them to a new study of their scriptures, to rebuke them for their sins, and to present the demands of a just and righteous God. There was need to rekindle the flame of Messianic expectation which had burned so low. "If one is disposed to question the wisdom of the mission of John as a herald of the King, let him reflect on what would have been the reception accorded Jesus without the preparation made by the Baptist. 'He came unto his own and his own received him not.' They rejected him after all? Yes, but John prepared some soil for the Messiah's sowing. Those who first responded to Jesus came from the group of John's disciples. The people will go from John to Jesus . . . Brief as was the ministry of Jesus, it probably lasted as long as it did, humanly speaking, because of the ministry of John. . . . The Christian movement began with John. The ground was made ready by him. John came not merely to prepare men's minds for the Messiah, but their lives also. If the Messiah comes, who is worthy to go forth to greet him."[1]

### 3. Birth and Boyhood (Luke 1).

For good reasons Luke gives a rather remarkable account of the birth of this man who was to arouse the nation and present Jesus. Zacharias, the aged priest, while in the course of his duties in the temple, received the startling news that he and his wife Elisabeth should find the answer to their prayers and see the realization of their dreams in the birth of a boy. When Zacharias had finished his term of service in the temple he and Elizabeth returned to their home in the hills of Judea. In due time the dream came true. A boy was born, and in obedience to former instructions, was named, not Zacharias (or Junior), but John. The location of their home and many other details which we should like to have are not given. We do know that Zacharias and Elisabeth were already old, and that they were genuinely pious and in every way worthy to be the parents of a boy whose career was to be so remarkable. The "prophecy" or *Benedictus* uttered by Zacharias is modeled on Old Testament prophecies and closes with a marvelous picture of the work to be done by this son of Zacharias and Elisabeth.

"For thou shalt go before the face of the Lord to make ready his
        ways;
To give knowledge of salvation to his people
In the remission of their sins,
Because of the tender mercy of our God,
Whereby the dayspring from on high shall visit us,
To shine upon them that sit in darkness and the shadow of
        death;
To guide our feet in the way of peace."
                                            (Luke 1:76-79.)

What pride and joy must have been in the hearts of this aged couple and with what devotion they must have given themselves to the training of their son. We may imagine that he grew strong in body out in the hills, that he was instructed in the scriptures, that he was taught all the virtues of life and that he spent much time in meditation in the solitudes of the desert country. How long his parents lived we can not tell. Being already old at the time of his birth it is probable that they did not live to see him become a man. Luke tells us that "he was in the deserts until the day of his showing unto Israel." While in the desert he developed faculties of observation and learned of life there as is reflected in his preaching. At any rate, he was ready when the time came.

*4. Beginning His Ministry* (Mark 1:2-4; Matthew 3:1-4; Luke 3:1-2; John 1:23).

A new epoch opens with the work of John. He spoke with the authority of a prophet and his work evoked a response like that of the prophets of old. It probably was A.D. 25 to 26 when this new prophet, now thirty years old, broke the silence and began to stir the hearts of the people. He selected the valley of the Jordan river as the scene of his labors, and probably moved up and down this historic valley with his message. It seems that he spent much of his time in the wilderness of Judea which embraced about one-third of Judea, the region lying near the Dead Sea.

John himself was a striking figure. Mark tells us that he was clothed with camel's hair and had a leather girdle about his waist. This was probably a garment of sackcloth woven of camel's hair and may have been consciously copied from the dress of the great Elijah. Mark also tells of his diet — locusts and wild honey. Some scholars insist that the honey was tree-honey, and that locusts were the fruit of the locust tree or carob-bean. It seems much more reasonable, however, to take the language in its simple meaning. There was an abundance of wild honey in the wilderness, and from time immemorial people have eaten locusts (insects) as the Bedouin still do in that region. We who eat oysters and shrimp should not find this too offensive to the taste.

John however, was able to attract people and move the multitudes not because of his dress or his diet. His powerful personality and his message were the secrets of his reputation and power. He was impressive, regal and strong. Here was no trickster, no charlatan. His sudden appearance and the impression he made remind us of the great Elijah of old.

Essentially it was the message of John which drew the crowds and stirred the people. He preached on sin and judgment, repentance and forgiveness. His basic message was, "Repent ye, for the kingdom of God is at hand." The words rang out sharp and clear and echoed throughout Judea. The call to repent challenged attention at once. John had the moral earnestness to demand a new life on the part of his audience. They listened with respect. But it was the second part of his proclamation that sent a thrill through the great crowds — "For the kingdom of heaven is at hand. . . ."

"What startled the people was not so much that the day of doom hung in the background as that the Messianic era had arrived. The wild delight of Andrew as he ran to Simon and cried, 'We have found the Messiah,' helps us to understand the enthusiasm that was created by the wonderful words of John. Brother would tell brother what he had heard. They would gather in groups to talk it over. Each one felt that he must hear the prophet for himself. In each heart the 'kingdom of heaven' was interpreted to mean what he most wished. The rainbow of promise was stretched over each life."[2]

Immense crowds came to hear this strange preacher whose words stirred them to the depths. Mark says that all the country of Judea came. Matthew says that "all the region round about Jordan" came. Luke speaks of the multitude that kept going forth to hear him. During the course of his ministry many thousands from all Palestine must have gone down to hear the new prophet. It is worthy of note that the religious leaders from Jerusalem itself joined the throngs that came under the spell of this strange messenger.

5. *Denouncing Sin* (Mark 1:4-6; Matthew 3:5-10; Luke 3:3-14).

John could announce the approach of the Messiah but he must also assert that the people were not ready for his coming. The kingdom was to be charcterized by righteousness and holiness — and only those who possessed these qualities could have any part in it. All others were to be rejected as the farmer winnows away the chaff with his fan, and the owner of the vineyard cuts down every tree not bearing fruit. To proclaim such a message required courage. It meant the confession of sin, the prayer for forgiveness, willingness to be obedient. His keyword was *repent*. Again and again he denounced sin in every quarter and called men to repentance. "Like the prophets of old he lashed the people for their sins." They were to give evidence of their turning from sin by submitting to his baptism. This preacher of righteousness denounced all alike. The religious leaders themselves were not exempt; indeed, his denunciation of them is the severest of all. They thought to excuse themselves on the basis of their descent from Abraham. But this was not sufficient. These leaders, like all others, must bring forth fruit worthy of repentance. What must have been the reaction of the multitudes as they heard this fiery prophet cry out to the scribes and priests of Jerusalem, "You offspring of vipers, who warned you to flee from the wrath to come?" "It was plain to see that a man as well as a prophet had appeared in Israel, one who stood unabashed before those in high stations, who understood the weakness of the men of his day, and who had the courage to lay them bare. A new era had dawned, a time of pulsing reality instead of dry rabbinism or vague apocalypticism. John struck the moral nerve and it twitched."[3]

*6. Portraying the Messiah* (Mark 1:7-8; Matthew 3:11-12; Luke 3:15-18).

As the work of John progressed, multitudes heard him and repented. Devout souls searched the scriptures and inquired about the Messiah. Could this strange man whose work was causing such a remarkable response be the Messiah? Could it be that their Messiah was already among them, his work already being done? In response to these questions John was quick to assert that he was not the Messiah. "There cometh after me he that is mightier than I, the latchet of whose shoes I am not worthy to stoop down and unloose. He (the Messiah) shall baptize you with the Holy Spirit and with fire, whose fan is in his hand, thoroughly to cleanse his threshing floor, and to gather the wheat into his garner; but the chaff he will burn up with unquenchable fire." This vivid description served to quicken their anticipation of the Messiah and caused men to wonder where he was and when he would appear. John did not give these details since he himself did not know. He had never seen Jesus, but he knew that he must come soon. So he continued his work yet more earnestly looking for the anointed one. Then came Jesus to the Jordan unto John!

*7. Baptizing Jesus* (Mark 1:9-11; Matthew 3:13-17; Luke 3:21-22).

As the work of John continued the news spread over the land. Up in Nazareth of Galilee Jesus, now thirty years old, more anxious and eager than any other man, must have known that the time had come for him to begin his work. "Palestine is athrill with the sensation of the New Prophet of the Hills, the Evangelist of the Jordan. Not for four hundred years has one so spoken for the living God. Every community is stirred. It is all the talk. No hamlet is unmoved. From every section companies are forming for pilgrimage down to the great camp meetings in the Jericho valley. Some have returned to Nazareth and tell in excited tones to awed throngs of the wonderful preacher and his burning message: 'The day of the Lord is at hand.'

"I think Mary noticed a strange light in the eye of her First-born. There was a far-away air about Him, as if He felt in His soul the call to a new career. He was more than usually reticent. He spent more time out in the hills alone. Each morning He took with Him to the little shop a 'roll of the Book.' From it He would read a bit, then lay it upon a shelf while He worked and thought; then read again, and turn almost absentmindedly to work again. All this Mary's keen, discerning eye saw. There was nothing for her to say. Then there came an evening when she noted that He carefully put away His tools, swept the shop out all clean and shut the door with a care that spelled finality. He came into the house and laid up His scroll and went out into the solitude of the night.

"Mary could not think of sleep. She got together a 'change of raiment' and prepared a simple lunch, all of which she made into a neat packet. Then she got ready a simple breakfast. In the morning twilight she saw Him coming in from his night with that Father about whose affairs it is needful for him to be. Mary met Him, very quietly, and led Him to the waiting breakfast. As they sat and He ate she watched Him furtively, lovingly, longingly. They did not talk much. Rather they felt each other and mingled their souls in spiritual converse and questioning. As He finished Mary went and brought out the packet and handed it to Him. She helped Him adjust it, thus to touch Him with her hands in gentle caress. A moment they gazed into the deeps of each other's eyes. Very gently He placed His arm about her, drew her to Him as they stood together there in the doorway, planted a kiss on her upturned face. No word was spoken. He turned about, walked past the little shop, followed the path as it wound eastward and south and then, more than a quarter of a mile below, passed around the point out of sight into the highway leading down to Judea and the Jordan. Mary turned into her house with a great surge of mingled feeling and fell on her face on His bed. She knew that her wonderful Son had gone out into the world to do His work, to attend to the affairs of His Father."[4]

Thus Jesus joined the throngs of pilgrims going to the Jordan. Two or three days later he stood in the crowd to hear John speak, and then presented himself to be baptized by him. "At last John and Jesus are face to face. . . . Out of the ages the two men of destiny meet. John had spent his years in preparation for this moment. It is the culmination of his life-work. It is the beginning of the ministry of Jesus."[5]

Up to this time John had not seen Jesus. But when Jesus asked for baptism at his hands he knew that here at last was the Messiah. John hesitated, and even insisted that he was not worthy to baptize him. No doubt the very presence of this sinless man convicted John of his own sin and made him aware of his need of a redeemer. Jesus insisted that John must baptize him for "thus it becometh us to fulfill all righteousness." John obeyed his Master and baptized him in the waters of the Jordan. "And Jesus, when he was baptized, went up straightway from the water: and lo, the heavens were opened up unto him, and he saw the spirit of God descending as a dove, and coming upon him; and lo, a voice out of the heavens, saying, This is my beloved Son, in whom I am well pleased." (Matthew 3:16-17.)

At this point many interesting and intriguing questions arise which, however, can not be discussed within the scope of these studies. Suffice it to say that John had done his duty, that he rejoiced at the manifestation of the Messiah and that he could continue his work with even greater zeal and confidence. Jesus was now ready to begin his ministry.

## 8. Explaining His Mission (John 1:19-36).

After the baptism of Jesus John's work must go on. He would continue to denounce sin, to call men to repentance, to prepare the way for the kingdom, to present Jesus. John (1:19,24) tells us that a formal delegation, probably from the Sanhedrin in Jerusalem, came to learn from John more about the nature of his work and his claims for himself. John, with characteristic humility, disclaimed being the Messiah or even Elijah, asserting that he was but the voice of one crying in the wilderness.

More than this on two different occasions John postively identified Jesus as the Messiah. "On the morrow he seeth Jesus coming unto him, and saith, Behold, the Lamb of God, that taketh away the sin of the world! This is he of whom I said, After me cometh a man who is become before me: for he was before me." (John 1:29-30.) "Again on the morrow John was standing, and two of his disciples; and he looked upon Jesus as he walked and saith, Behold, the Lamb of God!" (John 1:35-36.) These words so vividly uttered would cause men to look at this man whom John was so unmistakably identifying as the expected Messiah. One wonders how any one could question John's confidence in the Messiahship of Jesus.

## 9. Greatness of Soul (John 3:22-36).

The true nobility of John is revealed in an experience which now took place. For months John had been the foremost figure in all the land. His fame had gone afar. Few men had enjoyed such great popularity and public acclaim. He was the hero of many. His own disciples were jealous of his fame. Jesus had begun his work and was drawing great crowds. Some who had been followers of John went with the crowds to Jesus. His disciples therefore became alarmed at the popularity of Jesus and the waning fame of their idol. In a spirit of jealousy, and with words carefully calculated to stir envy in the heart of John, they came with a report to him, "He that was with thee beyond the Jordan, to whom thou hast borne witness, behold the same baptizeth, and all men come to him." (John 3:26.) In this they misjudged John. He hastened to reply in words that would declare unmistakably his freedom from jealousy and his loyalty to the One he had baptized and pointed out as the Messiah. "John answered and said, A man can receive nothing, except it have been given him from heaven. Ye yourselves bear me witness, that I said, I am not the Christ, but that I am sent before him. He that hath the bride is the bridegroom; but the friend of the bridegroom, that standeth and heareth him, rejoiceth greatly because of the bridegroom's voice; this my joy therefore is made full. He must increase, but I must decrease." (John 3:27-30.) This was a severe test for John, as it would be for any man. "When for a lifetime a man has stood on the pinnacle of influence, but at last his day is over and another appears to take his place, it is a miracle of grace if he is able to look on his successor with friendliness and good-will."[6] But John measured up to the test. He recognized that he himself was not the true light; he had had the joy of bearing witness to that light. "He (John) has shone like a star in the early dawn. He has hailed with joy the coming of the full day. Now that day has come, he fades away . . . . The law and the prophets were until John. John is the link between the Old Covenant and the New. His work is finished, but it stands as its own monument. It can never be duplicated nor forgotten. He formed the bridge by which the first Jews passed over from Moses to Christ. We are on the other side of the Jordan now, but let us never forget the bridge by which we crossed over."[7]

*10. Denouncing Herod and Herodias* (Mark 6:18; Matthew 14:4; Luke 3:19-20).

The next account of John's work is the story, given briefly by Mark and partially by Matthew and Luke, of his condemnation of the adulterous union of Herod Antipas and Herodias, with its culmination in John's imprisonment and death.

Herod Antipas (4 B.C.-A.D. 37), the tetrarch of Galilee and Perea, was the son of Herod the Great. He was an able ruler, a builder of cities, a friend of the Romans, and yet cautious in his dealings with the Jews. He was first married to the daughter of Aretas, the king of Arabia. Later he became infatuated with his niece Herodias, who at the time was the wife of his half-brother, Herod Phillip of Rome. He divorced his wife, and married Herodias. This involved him in a war with Aretas who defeated him. This scandal in high places was, of course, the cause of much comment among the people. John denounced this unholy alliance and for his courageous stand was ultimately beheaded.

We do not know the details, or even the occasion that brought this forth. Some think that the Jews, being outraged about it, asked John publicly his opinion on it. Others think that one of the Pharisees tricked him into it, then reported to Herod. Mark simply states: "John said unto Herod, It is not lawful for thee to have thy brother's wife." (6:18.) Being a man of convictions and with courage to state them he could not have done otherwise though he knew full well the danger in which it placed him.

*11. In Prison at Machaerus* (Mark 6:17; Matthew 14:3; Luke 3:19-20).

Matthew, Mark and Luke all tell us that John was imprisoned because of his reproof of Herod and Herodias. It is clear that Herodias, and not Herod himself, was responsible for this. There are good reasons for believing that Herod had a certain admiration for John, that he heard him often and at times was inclined to be partial to him. There are some who believe that Herod invited him to his palace so as to hear him. The exact details are not given, but we may be sure that Herodias "set herself against John" and resolved that he should pay for his public denunciation of her. She would goad Herod until he had to take action against John. Mark says Herod "sent forth and laid hold upon John, and bound him in prison for the sake of Herodias." (6:17.)

John was incarcerated at the old fortress of Machaerus which was about seven miles east of the Dead Sea at the northern end. Archaeologists have discovered the old fortress so that we are able to reconstruct the details. This was fortified by the Maccabean princes about 100 b.c., was destroyed by the Romans and then rebuilt by Herod the Great. At this time it was in the hands of Herod Antipas. This citadel was on a conical hill, higher than Jerusalem across the Jordan. The palace was built over two dungeons which have been discovered, one of which certainly John occupied. In this cold, lonely dungeon John lived until the time of his execution about a year later. We know but little of his life here, except that it must have been uncomfortable, lonely and dreary. He was shown some leniency in that his friends could visit him occasionally. What a contrast to the glorious days down in the Jordan where the multitudes hung upon his words and sang his praises!

*12. Encouraged by Jesus* (Matthew 11:2-19; Luke 7:18-35).

John's disciples did not disband after his imprisonment, though their leader was gone. These disciples brought him news of the great crowds who followed Jesus. They reported on the works of Jesus and the miracles he was performing. This would cause John to think and perhaps to wonder. He was in "a prison mood." It was under these circumstances that John "sent by his disciples and said unto him, art thou he that cometh, or look we for another?" (Matthew 11:2-3.) This raises the very pertinent question of the doubt of John. Did John really doubt that Jesus was the Messiah? While we can not deal adequately with this matter here we may say that the circumstances naturally had much to do with his questioning. He was affected by his own depressing situation. It was but natural that he wanted some word of assurance from the one he had introduced as the Messiah. At any rate, he took his doubts to Jesus.

The response of Jesus to the inquiry of John has often been mis-understood. Jesus was not unsympathetic, and certainly not hostile to John. When the disciples of John found Jesus he was busily occupied, and continued his work until there was a convenient opportunity to speak with them. His simple word to them was to "go tell John what things ye have seen and heard. The blind receive their sight, the lame walk, the lepers are cleansed and the deaf hear, the dead are raised up, the poor have good tidings preached to them." (Luke 7:22.) This would be sufficient answer for John. It was indeed a compliment to him.

Upon the departure of these messengers Jesus paid eloquent tribute to the great preacher then in prison, "I say unto you, Among them that are born of women there is none greater than John: yet he that is but little in the Kingdom of God is greater than he." (Luke 7:28.) Did John ever hear these words of affection and encouragement? It is possible that some friends carried them to him. Somehow we hope they did.

*13. The Death of John* (Mark 6:14-29; Matthew 14:11-12; Luke 9:7-9).

Herodias was determined upon the death of John. "With the persistence and stealth of a tigress she watched for her opportunity."[8] The opportunity came with the birthday of Herod. The event was to be celebrated in the palace where were assembled "his lords and the high captains and the chief men of Galilee." (Mark 6:21.) This was an occasion of state, pomp and display. The chief function in the celebration was the dinner itself. The guests were gorged with fine food and rich wines. Herod was host and in generous mood. Herodias had planned well for the consummation of her purpose. Her scheme was as degrading as could ever be imagined. She was stooping to use the physical charms of her own daughter, Salome, by her former husband. Salome, as vile as her mother, was willing to aid in the scheme. Without regard to the disgrace which the occasion demanded she "came in and danced." An ancient Latin inscription reads: "It was disgraceful both to dance and for a virgin to come into the banqueting-hall to men who had drunk freely." Herodias was willing to prostitute her own daughter for her foul purpose. Herod may have been too drunk to realize the depths to which Herodias had stooped, or it may be that he didn't care. At any rate, this voluptuous exhibition pleased him greatly. No doubt she was greeted with loud applause by the grandees present, and Herod now excited called out to the dancer, "ask of me whatever thou will, and I will give it thee." Later he swore to her; "whatsoever thou shalt ask of me, I will give it thee, even to the half of my kingdom." (Mark 6:23.)

Salome and her mother Herodias had anticipated just this. Their scheme was working. She then went out for a conference with her mother and re-appeared 'with haste.' She now announced to Herod: "I will that thou forthwith give me in a charger the head of John the Baptist." The drunken king had promised too much and "was exceedingly sorry." It was too late now, however. He must keep his promise, because of his oath, because of his guests, and no less because he dared not refuse Herodias. The trap had sprung and John the Baptist was to die.

The evil deed must be done at once. "Straightway the king sent forth a soldier of his guard, and commanded to bring his head. And he went and beheaded him in the prison." (Mark 6:27.) The details of this dreadful deed are not given in the gospels. Was John given any warning? Was he beheaded in his sleep? Did he resist? We can not know. A lewd dancing girl had literally danced his head off, and a drunken king had weakly submitted.

Herodias got her wish. The soldier "brought his head in a charger, and gave it to the damsel; and the damsel gave it to her mother." (Mark 6:28.) Salome had done her part. "She took it daintily in her hands lest a drop of blood should stain her gala dress, and tripped away to her mother, as if bearing her some choice dish of food from the king's table."[9] There is a tradition that Herodias now took her bodkin and pierced the tongue that at last was silenced. She had triumphed over the mighty preacher. John had met his fate. Jesus will meet his later.

No doubt the news of this disgraceful deed spread quickly. Evidently some of the disciples of John were nearby and heard it, for Mark tells us that "they came and took up his corpse and laid it in a tomb." (6:29.) The place of burial was probably one of rock-hewn tombs near Machaerus.

Matthew adds to his account of John's burial the words "and they went and told Jesus." We are not told what Jesus said or did. We may be sure, however, of his appreciation and love for John. He who wept at the tomb of Lazarus must have grieved at the tragedy which befell his forerunner and loyal friend.

## 14. His Contribution.

John had done faithfully what he came to do. He aroused the nation; he denounced the sins of the people, he called them to repentance; he announced the kingdom of God; he baptized and presented the Messiah. He was loyal to the last. He was faithful unto death.

"I can not write the last lines in this book about John without the humble tribute of my own heart's love. Few personalities in history hold my admiration and enthusiasm with a firmer grip than does the rugged and picturesque figure who still stands silhouetted on the horizon at Bethany beyond Jordan in Gilead, the land of Elijah of old. I see him standing 'and he looked upon Jesus as he walked.' His heart has gone with that look; he keeps on looking till he says 'Behold, the Lamb of God.' He can say no more. There is no need to say more, not for John. And he never saw him more on the earth."[10]

[1]Robertson, A. T., *John the Loyal*, pp. 50-52.
[2]Ibid., pp. 54-55.
[3]Robertson, *Studies in the New Testament*, pp. 53-54.
[4]Carver, W. O., *The Self Interpretation of Jesus*, pp. 32-34.
[5]Robertson, A. T., *John the Loyal*, p. 113.
[6]Stalker, *The Two St. Johns*, p. 233.
[7]Robertson, *John the Loyal*, pp. 175-176.
[8]Broadus, *Commentary on Matthew*.
[9]Ibid.
[10]Robertson, *John the Loyal*, p. 306.

*Chapter III*

## THE EARLY MINISTRY OF JESUS

1. Introduction to His Ministry. 2. The Length of His Ministry. 3. An Analysis of His Ministry. 4. Divisions of His Ministry. 5. His Baptism. 6. The Temptations. 7. His First Followers. 8. His First Miracle. 9. First Visit to Jerusalem. 10. Conference With Nicodemus. 11. Better Results in Judea. 12. Jesus in Samaria. 13. Going Into Galilee.

CHAPTER III

# The Early Ministry of Jesus

*1. Introduction to His Ministry.*

Jesus was born in Bethlehem, grew up in Nazareth, and was baptized in the Jordan river. His long years of preparation for his work were spent in Nazareth. When he reached the age of thirty years John the Baptist was stirring the nation with his preaching in the valley of the Jordan. The time for which Jesus had waited and prepared was now at hand. He must begin the ministry for which he came into the world.

The gospel writers devote almost all their attention not to his early years, but naturally to the events in his public ministry, with the greatest emphasis on the latter part of this ministry. The records of the first year of his public service are very scant. In fact were it not for John's gospel we would not know anything about the first year. The records in Matthew, Mark and Luke may be said to begin with his Galilean ministry.

*2. The Length of His Ministry.*

Since the gospel writers were not generally concerned with arranging their accounts of his work in chronological order, it is difficult to determine the number of years in this ministry. Taking all the facts into consideration we may be sure that the length was either two and a fraction years or a bit more than three years. A majority of scholars favor the longer period and hold that his public ministry extended over some forty months.

Dr. James Stalker in his *Life of Christ* has aptly characterized these years of his ministry as (1) the year of *obscurity*, (2) the year of *public favor*, (3) the year of *opposition*. While this characterization is general it is helpful. The first year was one of beginnings when he was getting acquainted, was finding his first disciples and was establishing himself. Apparently much of it was spent in Judea. The second year was marked by his exceeding great popularity. He performed miracles, taught the multitudes and attained nation-wide fame. This was almost altogether in Galilee. The third year was marked by waning popularity, and ever increasing opposition. It culminated in his rejection and crucifixion in Jerusalem at the great feast of the Passover (March-April). The first part of the year was spent in Galilee, the last half in other areas of the country.

*3. An Analysis of His Ministry.*

We need not be too much disturbed if we can not arrange the events of his public career in the exact order of their occurrence. While there are differences of opinion on numerous minor matters the general order is clear. Perhaps no chronological arrangement would be without objections, but it will be helpful to the student to get a glimpse of this brief ministry in its broad outlines. For this reason we are giving the analysis made by Dr. David Smith in his book, *Our Lord's Earthly Life.*

"Introduction

| | | |
|---|---|---|
| "5 B.C. | Birth of John the Baptist | March |
| | Birth of our Lord | August |
| | Flight to Egypt | October |
| 4 B.C. | Return to Nazareth | October |
| 7 A.D. | His first Passover | April 9 |
| 26 A.D. | His Baptism | January |
| | Wedding at Cana | early March |

I First Year of His Ministry

| | | |
|---|---|---|
| 26 A.D. | Passover | March 21 |
| | At Bethabara | April and early May |
| | Arrest of the Baptist | early in May |
| | At Sychar | close of May |
| | Settlement at Capernaum | beginning of June |
| | Inland mission | close of June till late summer |
| 27 A.D. | Passover | March or April |

II Second Year of His Ministry

| | | |
|---|---|---|
| | Passover | April 9 |
| | Ordination of the Twelve | May |
| | Mission in southern Galilee | May till early summer |
| | Visit to Nazareth, Commission of the Twelve, Deputation from the Baptist. | |
| 28 A.D. | The Baptist's execution | January |
| | Retreat to Bethsaida-Julias | February |

III Third Year of His Ministry

| | | |
|---|---|---|
| | (Passover | March 29) |
| | In Phoenicia | April-June |
| | In Decapolis | June |

Retreat to Caesarea Philippi ......... close of June to mid-August
Peter's confession,
First announcement of Passion,
The Transfiguration,
Healing the epileptic child,
Second announcement of Passion.
Back in Capernaum ........................................................ till August
Revisiting inland Galilee ................................... till mid-Sept.
Passage through Samaria ................................ September 23
At Jericho .................................................................... September 24
At Bethany ............................................................... September 25
Arrival at Jerusalem ........................................... September 26
Ministry at Jerusalem .............................. till close of December

29 A.D. At Bethabara ........................... probably till close of February
Raising of Lazarus ............................................ close of February
At Ephraim ....................................................................... till April 10
At Jericho ............................................ over Sabbath, April 11
Supper at Bethany ............................ Sunday evening, April 12

End The Passion-Week

Triumphal Entry ............................ Monday morning, April 13
Last Supper ........................... evening of Thursday, April 16
Crucifixion .................................................... Friday, April 17
Resurrection .............................. Sunday morning, April 19
Ascension .............................................. Thursday, May 29."[1]

Whether we accept this arrangement in detail or not, it is sugges-
tive and may serve to help the student keep his bearings and stay on the
main track. In the treatment of these experiences in the career of Jesus
in this text we are following the chronological order given in the
*Harmony of the Gospels* by A. T. Robertson. By this plan we can
follow the main current of the story and thus are able better to
understand and interpret these events. To give adequate treatment to
each event would carry us far beyond the limits of this text. When
one considers the countless number of books written to expound and
interpret the life of Jesus he will understand that in a brief treatment
of the life of Jesus many interesting and important happenings must
of necessity be omitted.

### 4. Divisions of His Ministry.

Before beginning our studies in the life of Jesus we should get a
glimpse of the main divisions of his public ministry. (1) His Early

Ministry, which began with the baptism early in the year 26 or 27 and lasted about one year, was spent largely in Judea. (2) The Great Galilean Ministry lasted approximately eighteen months and, as the name indicates, took place in the province of Galilee. (3) The Ministry in Withdrawals which extended over a period of some three months, was in the regions around Galilee. (4) The Later Judean Ministry covered approximately three months in Jerusalem and Judea. (5) The Perean Ministry came in the winter and early spring as he made his way to Jerusalem for his crucifixion. (6) The Last Week was spent in Jerusalem at the time of the great Passover Feast. (7) His Condemnation and Death came on Thursday and Friday of this last week. (8) His Resurrection took place early Sunday morning after his crucifixion on Friday. His Ascension occurred forty days after his resurrection.

5. *His Baptism* (Mark 1:9-11; Matthew 3:13-17; Luke 3:21-22).

The baptism of Jesus marks the beginning of his public ministry. This significant event took place in the Jordan river. Jesus went to John the Baptist for this purpose and insisted on being baptized, even though John demurred. All others were baptized as a public confession of sin; not so with Jesus. He was without sin and hence could not repent nor confess. His acceptance of baptism was his formal approval of the ministry of his forerunner. In this he "fulfilled all righteousness." His baptism was miraculously attested. There came to Jesus the visible manifestation of the presence of the Holy Spirit in the form of a dove resting upon him and the words of approval of the Father in him as his Beloved Son. John and Jesus rejoiced in this experience. The Son of God had now begun his work.

6. *The Temptations* (Mark 1:12-13; Matthew 4:1-11; Luke 4:1-13).

Immediately after his baptism Jesus faced a period of testing which is usually known as his Temptations. These experiences are extremely important. He was the Messiah come to claim his kingdom. But he was at once challenged by Satan. According to tradition the scene of this struggle was Mt. Quarantania in Judea, west of Jericho and some fifteen hundred feet above the Jordan valley. It is a wild, desolate region suited to this grim struggle. This period of testing lasted for forty days. It is customary to think of only three temptations during this time. We may gather from the gospels however, that there were more than three. Luke says "during forty days being tempted of the devil." Later he adds the statement, "and when the devil had completed every temptation, he departed from him for a season." (4:2, 13.)

Matthew's account asserts that Jesus was "led up of the spirit in the wilderness to be tempted of the devil." (4:1.) This testing was according to purpose. This was a "conscious grappling of the two leaders in the struggle for man. The devil had overcome Adam and Eve and was keenly aware of the importance of defeating the Second Adam. The hope of the race was at stake now. Satan knew who Jesus was and accepts him as the Son of God, but dares to tempt even him."[2]

The first temptation was in the realm of physical appetite. "And the tempter came and said unto him, If thou art the Son of God, command that these stones become bread." It was the temptation to use his supernatural powers to satisfy his own appetite. Jesus had not eaten for forty days and was hungry, but he would not use his power to satisfy his own needs. He replied in the words of the Old Testament. (Deut. 8:3.) "Man shall not live by bread alone, but by every word that proceedeth out of the mouth of God."

The second test was equally subtle and dangerous. Taking Jesus to the holy city and setting him on the pinnacle of the temple Satan said to him, "If thou art the son of God, cast thyself down." It is to be noted that Satan this time quoted, but misapplied a statement from the scriptures. (Ps. 91:11-12.) This was the temptation to yield to selfish vanity and gain the attention and the applause of the crowds. It was a cheap, easy, sensational way to get his work started. Again Jesus resisted the evil one and again quoted from the Old Testament, "Thou shalt not tempt the Lord, thy God." (Deut. 6:16.)

The third temptation offered Jesus a quick and easy way to become the king of the world. "Again the devil taketh him unto an exceeding high mountain, and showeth him all the kingdoms of the world and the glory of them; and he said unto him, All these things will I give thee if thou wilt fall down and worship me." Satan assumed that Jesus planned to be the king, and he offered him a short-cut to it. It will be so easy if he will but compromise and worship Satan who will give him these things. This way would by-pass all the sufferings and hardships, rejection and crucifixion. But Jesus again refused to yield and used the word of God (Deut. 6:13), "Thou shalt worship the Lord thy God, and him only shalt thou serve." He chose to win his kingship. He would take the long, hard way which involved torture and death. It would be a fight to the finish!

Jesus had won his first great battle, but there will be others. The devil left him "for a season" and angels came and ministered unto him. "Jesus emerged from the wilderness with the plan of His life, which, no doubt, had been formed long before, hardened in the fire of trial. Nothing is more conspicuous in His after-life than the resolution with which He carried it out. Other men, even those who have accomplished the greatest tasks, have sometimes had no definite plan, but only have seen by degrees in the evolution of circumstances the path to pursue; their purposes have been modified by events and the advice of others. But Jesus started with His plan perfected, and never deviated from it by a hair's breadth. He resented the interference of His mother or His chief disciple with it as steadfastly as He bore it through the fiery opposition of open enemies. And His plan was to establish the kingdom of God in the hearts of individuals, and rely not on the weapons of political and material strength, but only on the power of love and the force of truth."[3]

### 7. *His First Followers* (John 1:35-51).

Upon the completion of his temptations Jesus came down unto Bethany near the Jordan where John was still faithfully at work. How will he start his ministry? John was his friend, and naturally those who were followers of John would be most likely to become his friends. On two occasions here John saw Jesus and in rapture declared him to be the Messiah or the Lamb of God. (John 1:29, 35.) John gave his testimony and two of his disciples attached themselves to Jesus. "And the two disciples (Andrew and John the brother of James) heard him speak and they followed Jesus." These were the first disciples of Jesus. Perceiving that they were following him Jesus turned to them with the question, "What seek ye?" "Where do you live?" they inquired. Then Jesus gave them the invitation; "Come, and ye shall see." This is still the valid invitation to Christian faith. These two went with Jesus to his lodging place, a quiet spot nearby, where they spent an unforgettable day with this new teacher. It is worthy of note that John, one of these two, in writing his gospel more than sixty years later, remembered the exact hour, "and it was about the tenth hour." During this time these two disciples were so completely captivated by Jesus that they went out and found their brothers. Andrew brought Simon Peter, and John brought his brother James. Note the tone of joy and finality in the word of Andrew to Simon Peter, "We have found the Messiah!" This was the first meeting of Simon Peter and Jesus. On this occasion Jesus "looked upon him, and said, Thou art Simon, the son of John: thou shall be called Cephas (which is by interpretation, Peter)." Then Jesus found Phillip who shortly afterward found his brother Nathanael. These three pairs of brothers — Andrew and Simon, John and James,

Phillip and Nathanael — formed the nucleus of the followers of Jesus and became the first disciples or "learners." (John 2:11f.)

*8. His First Miracle* (John 2:1-12).

With these six disciples Jesus now went up into Galilee. He was ready to begin his work. The occasion of his visit was a wedding in Cana, a little village four miles northeast of Nazareth on the road to Capernaum. It was the home of Nathanael and it is probable that Jesus and the others were guests in his home for the time.

While a marriage feast was an occasion of great festivity and joy, it also was one of serious importance. The sacred vows of betrothal culminated in the marriage ceremony, usually at night. On this evening the bride was led from her paternal home, with music and parade to that of her bridegroom where the marriage formula was pronounced. After this ceremony the wedding supper was served.

On this occasion a large company of relatives and friends had assembled. Mary, the mother of Jesus, was already there, busy assisting the family in all the duties of serving the supper. An event now took place which had great significance in that it revealed the new relation which must exist between Jesus and his mother, and also in the fact that Jesus had power to perform miracles. The attendance had exceeded all expectations and the family was embarrassed to discover that the supply of wine (refreshments) was quickly exhausted. In this crisis Mary went to her Son with an appeal for help. The words of Jesus to Mary, sometimes interpreted as being inconsiderate and harsh, were not really so. Jesus was only making it clear to his mother that from now on he must do his work in his own way without interference, even from her.

In performing this first miracle Jesus relieved the embarrassment of his host and displayed his divine power so that all might know. We need not be too concerned just how he could do this. He was the Son of God and had supernatural power. "The conscious water saw its God and blushed." The simple vintage used on such occasions was three parts water and would correspond to our so called "soft-drinks" of today. It would be blasphemous to use this as an argument for Jesus' approval of the modern liquor traffic.

*9. First Visit to Jerusalem* (John 2:13-22).

From Cana Jesus went to Capernaum, the busy city on the northwest shore of the Lake of Galilee, for a brief visit. He was accompanied by his mother, his brothers and the disciples.

It was early spring and the great Passover feast was soon to take place in Jerusalem. Doubtless Jesus had attended these annual gatherings more or less regularly since he was twelve years old. Now that he had begun his ministry it was natural that he should go. The Messiah would present himself in the holy city and would assert his claims there.

Upon his arrival he went at once to the temple where the people were making their sacrifices and observing the ceremonies of the feast. Jesus was astounded at what he saw there. The court of the Gentiles, the lower level of the great temple, presented a scene of wild confusion, noise and bickering. Those who sold animals for sacrifices, and the money-changers, had moved in and had made a market-place of the holy temple. It was indeed, not only a profanation of the holy place but was the operation of a graft which brought in immense sums of money to unscrupulous manipulators. Filled with righteous indignation Jesus cleaned out the whole court. "He made a scourge of cords and cast all out of the temple, both the sheep and the oxen: and he poured out the changers' money and overthrew their tables: and to them that sold the doves he said, take these things hence; make not my Father's house a house of merchandise." (John 2:15-16.) These unscrupulous dealers fled before the Son of God, as he denounced them. "A certain fiery and starry light shone from his eyes and the majesty of the Godhead gleamed in his face." Why did these men flee without resistance? They recognized in Jesus a great personality whose very aspect in righteous indignation was unendurable. Then too, this act, which was altogether just and right, would receive the support of all the people who resented this nefarious practice. This exhibition of his power and assertion of his authority would startle the people. They recognized a new figure among them.

There were many other miracles which Jesus did during this first official visit to Jerusalem which are not given in the gospels. "During the feast many believed on his name, beholding the signs which he did." Among the religious leaders some did not believe, and already there were evidences of bitter hostility toward him. "But Jesus did not trust himself unto them, for that he knew all men." Jesus was not deceived by the enthusiasm of some because of his miracles.

*10. Conference with Nicodemus* (John 2:23-3:21).

Although many of those who followed Jesus in Jerusalem were not genuine, Jesus did make a deep impression on some of the people.

An example of this influence is given by John in his account of the long conversation of Jesus with Nicodemus. Some of the most effective work which Jesus did was in private conversation with individuals. More than half the wise sayings of Jesus in the gospels were spoken in private talks with individuals.

Nicodemus was an exceptional man. He was a "ruler" of the Jews, a man of culture and social position and a man of sincere religious spirit. He was a Pharisee and a member of the Sanhedrin. He recognized in Jesus something he had never yet encountered. He was so impressed that he sought a private interview with this new teacher, and arranged an appointment with Jesus "by night." The fact that Nicodemus came to Jesus by night certainly is no evidence of cowardice on his part. It was the natural thing to do.

The student should read carefully John's account of this remarkable conversation. (John 2:23-3:21.) Note the sincere and courteous approach of Nicodemus; the positive assertion of Jesus on the necessity of the "new birth"; Nicodemus' apparent bewilderment; the patient words of Jesus implying that Nicodemus as "the teacher of Israel" should know this truth; and Jesus' assertion that "we speak that we do know"; and Jesus pointing to the cross through the use of an incident in the wilderness experiences of Israel.

In this conversation we have the most familiar quotation in the New Testament: "For God so loved the world that he gave his only begotten Son, that whosoever believeth on him should not perish, but have eternal life." (3:16.) This great declaration, "Luther's Little Bible," summarizes better than any other single statement the glorious mission of Jesus.

Nicodemus did not understand all this at once. We shall find him coming into the picture later on. He did come to appreciate the message of Jesus and at the end he proved his loyalty to Jesus.

*11. Better Results in Judea* (John 3:22-36).

We do not know how long Jesus remained in Jerusalem, though it would appear that his stay there was not extended. He was aware of the hostilty of the rabbis and the superficial interest of the people. Leaving the city he and his disciples "came into the land of Judea, and there he tarried with them and baptized." Though we do not have the details of place and time it is quite evident that his ministry out in the province was encouragingly successful. The common people gave him a hearing and responded to his messages. His success aroused the jealousy and anger of the Pharisees in Jerusalem. The fight between Jesus and them was already shaping up.

It was at this time that the disciples of John the Baptist, who was then in prison, came to him with John's inquiry. Sometime after this John was beheaded. In view of the rising opposition of these Pharisees and the critical situation in official quarters, Jesus and his disciples left Judea to go back to Galilee where he had plans for a more extended ministry.

## 12. Jesus in Samaria (John 4:5-42).

Having decided to go from Judea to Galilee Jesus probably startled his disciples and others with the announcement of the route which he was to follow. "He must needs pass through Samaria." The Samaritan people and their territory were both avoided by all good Jews. In traveling between Judea and Galilee orthodox Jews went eastward through Jericho, crossed the Jordan and went north through Perea, and then recrossed the river to enter Galilee. In going through Samaria Jesus exhibited his interest in the hated Samaritans.

In his gospel John recounts one significant experience of Jesus in Samaria. This too, was a conversation which had far-reaching consequences. It took place at Jacob's well about a mile south of the village of Sychar. This well, originally one hundred and fifty feet deep, had furnished water for the people of the country since the days of Jacob (c 1700 B.C.). The well which has served as a sort of shrine for many centuries, is still a source of an abundant supply of water for people nearby.

Jesus and his disciples reached the well late in the afternoon. He sent his disciples to Sychar to buy food and he "being wearied with his journey" sat by the well to rest. Tired though he was, he spared not himself to deal with one who came to the well for water. This one with whom he was to deal was quite a different type of person from the scholarly Nicodemus. She was a woman, a Samaritan, and one whose whole life was blackened by sin.

In the study of this classic example of the methods of Jesus the student should note his courtesy, patience, tact, and persistence. See him as he established his point of contact and led her finally to see that he was the Messiah which her own forefathers, as well as the Jews, had been expecting. He did not hesitate to converse with a Samaritan, contrary to Jewish custom; he dealt with her though she was a woman whose rights were not then recognized; he defied custom in his effort to help one who was so obviously a "sinner." Then, as always, Jesus remembered that the Son of man was come "to seek and to save that which was lost."

The effects of this conversation were immediately apparent. The disciples upon their return from Sychar, were astonished to find their Master talking with a woman. While they did not question him about it they marveled at it. The effect on the woman was life-changing. She had seen the light, she had drunk of the water of life, she was a transformed person who hurried to tell what she had experienced. The entire experience was a moving one for Jesus. When the disciples offered him the food which they had procured at his suggestion he could not eat but replied to them, "I have meat to eat that ye know not of." He was profoundly stirred as he realized that even the basest of sinners could be redeemed. His redemptive message could save unto the uttermost. He could visualize the possibility of saving all mankind. As he contemplated these things he saw coming a great company of people who had heard the testimony of his new convert. "Behold," said he to the disciples, "Lift up your eyes, and look on the fields, that they are white already unto harvest." Small wonder that Jesus was moved as he contemplated the redemption of the world.

The effects of this on the community were nothing less than startling. "From that city many Samaritans believed on him." "And many more believed because of his word: and they said unto the woman, Now we believe . . . for we have heard for ourselves, and know that this is indeed the Saviour of the world."

## 13. Going Into Galilee (John 4:43-45).

After two busy and fruitful days in Samaria Jesus and his disciples continued their journey northward through the valley of Esdraelon up into the hills of southern Galilee. He has had a succesful ministry both in Judea (outside Jerusalem) and Samaria and now is ready to begin what proved to be a long and popular ministry in the land of his boyhood.

[1]Smith, David, *Our Lord's Earthly Life,* pp. xiii-xv.
[2]Robertson, *Studies in the New Testament,* p. 81.
[3]Stalker, James, *Life of Christ,* p. 45.

*Chapter IV*

## THE GREAT GALILEAN MINISTRY

1. Galilee of the Gentiles. 2. Nature of This Ministry. 3. Rejected at Nazareth. 4. Headquarters at Capernaum. 5. Calling Four Fishermen. 6. A Ministry of Healing. 7. The First Tour of Galilee. 8. Back in Capernaum. 9. Call of Matthew. 10. Sabbath Controversies. 11. Selecting the Twelve Apostles. 12. Sermon on the Mount. 13. Second Tour of Galilee. 14. A Busy Day. 15. Teaching by Parables. 16. Around the Lake. 17. Third Tour of Galilee.

CHAPTER IV

# The Great Galilean Ministry

*1. Galilee of the Gentiles.*

In every respect this land to which Jesus had now come was a fitting place for the scene of his labors. "It consisted for the most part of an elevated plateau, whose surface was varied by irregular mountain masses. Near its eastern boundary it suddenly dropped down into a great gulf, through which flowed the Jordan, and in the midst of which, at a depth of seven hundred feet below the Mediterranean, lay the lovely, harp-shaped Sea of Galilee. The whole province was very fertile, and its surface thickly covered with large villages and towns. But the center of activity was the basin of the lake, a sheet of water thirteen miles long by six broad. Above its eastern shore, round which ran a fringe of green a quarter of a mile broad, there towered high, bare hills, cloven with the channels of torrents. On the western side, the mountains were gently sloped and their sides richly cultivated, bearing splendid crops of every description; while at their feet the shore was verdant with luxuriant groves of olives, oranges, figs, and every product of an almost tropical climate. At the northern end of the lake the space between the water and the mountains was broadened by the delta of the river, and watered with many streams from the hills, so that it was a perfect paradise of fertility and beauty. It was called the Plain of Gennesaret, and even at this day, when the whole basin of the lake is little better than a torrid solitude, is still covered with magnificent corn-fields, wherever the hand of cultivation touches it; and, where idleness leaves it untended, is overspread with thick jungles of thorn and oleander. In our Lord's time, it contained the chief cities on the lake, such as Capernaum, Bethsaida and Chorazin. But the whole shore was studded with towns and villages, and formed a perfect beehive of swarming human life. The means of existence were abundant in the crops and fruits of every description which the fields yielded so richly; and the waters of the lake teemed with fish, affording employment to thousands of fishermen. Besides, the great highways from Egypt to Damascus, and from Phoenicia to the Euphrates, passed here, and made this a vast center of traffic. Thousands of boats for fishing, transport and pleasure moved to and fro on the surface of the lake, so that the whole region was a focus of energy and prosperity."[1]

The character of the population was such as to afford Jesus an opportunity for his work. Judea, especially Jerusalem, was the ancient headquarters of religion. Steeped in centuries of custom and tradition the people of Judea were not responsive to new truth. So devoted were they to their institutions that they closed their minds to anything which appeared to challenge their own customs and beliefs. Not so with the Galileans. Here was a sort of heterogeneous population made up of various types and nationalities. Their habits of life were simple; they displayed the hospitality typical of mountain people: they were not bound by custom and tradition. These "common people heard him gladly." To be sure moral standards were low, sin and wickedness were everywhere present and the people were in darkness. Here Jesus found an opportunity for his work of regeneration. They "that sat in darkness" would see a great light. "His great wisdom as a teacher flared up as a great light in the midst of their darkness." While it is true that the general acceptance of Jesus' ministry, after months of unprecedented popularity, was disappointing since many of the people were superficial followers and turned from him, nevertheless the results were not altogether disappointing. Many of the people were loyal to him. It is worthy of mention that in Galilee he found all of his twelve disciples except Judas Iscariot from Judea, who betrayed him.

## 2. Nature of This Ministry.

Jesus began his work in Galilee in the summer or early fall of the year 26 or 27. The length of this ministry was about eighteen months. In general he considered Capernaum on the Lake his headquarters though he made at least three separate tours of the province during these months. This ministry is known as the year of public favor. His popularity was tremendous. Great crowds attended him almost all the time. Several different times the gospel writers describe the number of people about him. He fed at one time five thousand men, besides the women and the children. They crowded him by day and even at night. He sought to escape the pressure of crowds by going away. Luke tells us of some audiences so large that "they trod one upon another." The whole province rang with his fame. His name was on the lips of every one. All sought to see him. The country was stirred and the people were fired with excitement about him.

What were the reasons for this great public favor? Two main factors contributed to it. He performed a great many miracles, some of which the gospels record, and of course there were many which the writers did not attempt to recount. These extraordinary works of healing would be the cause of the wildest publicity. All who were sick — and they were many — wanted to be brought to him. "The streets of the villages and towns were lined with the victims of disease as his benignant figure passed by." In addition to his works of healing he performed many other miracles, such as feeding the multitudes, walking on the waters of the Lake, and stilling the storm.

But there was another good reason why the multitudes followed him. His preaching and teaching were fresh, vital and challenging. "He spoke in the synagogues being glorified of all." "There is no power whose attraction is more unfailing than that of the eloquent word. Barbarians, listening to their bards and story-tellers, Greeks, listening to the restrained passion of their orators, and matter-of-fact nations like the Roman, have alike acknowledged its power to be irresistible. The Jews prized it above almost every other attraction, and among the figures of their mighty dead revered none more highly than the prophets — those eloquent utterers of the truth, whom Heaven had sent them from age to age. Though the Baptist did no miracles, multitudes flocked to him, because in his accents they recognized the thunder of this power, which for so many generations no Jewish ear had listened to. Jesus also was recognized as a prophet, and accordingly, His preaching created wide-spread excitement. . . . His words were heard with wonder and amazement. Sometimes the multitude on the beach of the lake so pressed upon Him to hear, that He had to enter into a ship and address them from the deck, as they spread themselves out in a semicircle on the ascending shore. His enemies themselves bore witness that 'never man spake like this man'; and meager as are the remains of His preaching which we possess, they are amply sufficient to make us echo the sentiment and understand the impression which He produced. All His words together which have been preserved to us would not occupy more space in print than half-a-dozen ordinary sermons; yet it is not too much to say, that they are the most precious literary heritage of the human race. His words, like His miracles, were expressions of Himself, and everyone of them has in it something of the grandeur of His character."[2]

His teaching and preaching were characterized by numerous sayings which are brief but packed with truth which would stick in the mind. He used many figures of speech identified with the familiar things of life. His use of parables was one of the most powerful aspects of his teaching. While he did not originate this method of teaching he did immortalize it. His parables are still the best known stories in literature.

The spoken words of Jesus, as Dr. Stalker reminds us, were so effective because of the bearing and charcter of Jesus himself. He spoke with *authority*. His statements were not the repetitious words of some scribe, rehashing what had been said by others; they were words that carried authority and moved the minds and hearts of men. "The people were astonished at his doctrine, for he taught them as one having authority, and not as the scribes." (Matthew 7:28-29.) His addresses were also characterized by *boldness*. He made no rash statements but everywhere he exhibited courage by his bold statements. "Lo, He speaketh boldly." A third quality characterizing his preaching was *power*. He was possessed by truth and the spirit which overflowed and seized the souls of his hearers. "His word was with power." Finally his preaching and teaching had the quality of *graciousness*. He respected and loved all men. His words were marked by courtesy, consideration, gentleness and love. "They wondered at the gracious words which proceeded out of his mouth."

A message given by a man of such character would attract and challenge people. A new voice was being heard. They could not analyze it and did not fully understand it but they responded to it.

*3. Rejected at Nazareth* (Luke 4:16-31).

Having examined the character of this period of his public ministry we shall now follow the general current of events during his stay in Galilee. We can not discuss every recorded incident but we may select for treatment the more significant ones in our effort to interpret his work in this part of his career.

Apparently one of his first stops was at Cana, where he had performed his first miracle. Here again he exhibited his supernatural powers, this time by healing the son of a nobleman who lived there.

He then went to Nazareth, his boyhood home. He went "as his custom was" to the synagogue on the Sabbath day. Here he accepted the invitation to speak. Having read a part of the prophecy of Isaiah which, partially at least, defined the functions of the Messiah, he boldly announced to them, "Today hath this scripture been fulfilled in your ears." As the people listened to "the words of grace which proceeded out of his mouth," they were startled. They then reasoned saying, "Is not this Joseph's son?" He grew up here; we know him. How could one we knew be the Messiah? The reaction against him set in and became so pronounced that they rejected him, led him out to the brow of the hill to cast him down. "But he passing through the midst of them went his way." He had offered himself to the people of his own city, but they rejected him! He must find another place to live and do his work.

### 4. Headquarters at Capernaum (Matthew 4:13-16).

Leaving Nazareth he went some twenty miles northeastward to the city of Capernaum at the upper end of the Lake. Here he found a busy and prosperous city in the heart of a populous district where there were ten other cities. It was situated in the richest spot in Palestine and thus was a great agricultural center. It was on the Via Maris, the old international highway that ran southward from Damascus to Egypt. It was, therefore, a busy trading center where he found an ideal situation in which to do the work which he was now ready to begin in Galilee.

### 5. Calling Four Fishermen (Mark 1:16-20; Matthew 4:18-22; Luke 5:1-11).

It seems that the six disciples who had been with him since he found them with John the Baptist had for some reason returned to their homes before he went up to Nazareth. From the first Jesus knew that he must build his kingdom around a small group of dependable men who would live with him, learn his plans, and develop into leaders who could carry on his work. He was now ready to find his men.

Passing along the shores of the Lake he found Simon, later to become Peter, and his brother Andrew. He challenged them to leave their work and follow him to become fishers of men. "And straightway they left the nets and followed him." A little further on he saw two others, James, the son of Zebedee, and John his brother. They likewise accepted his invitation to join him. Three of these (Andrew, Simon and John) were in the original company of six disciples.

Because of their former association with Jesus these men evidently did not hesitate to follow him. Their decision to give up a lucrative business was not hasty nor ill-considered. They knew what they were doing. Henceforth these men are to remain with him. He now had a start in his contemplated plans for his kingdom.

### 6. A Ministry of Healing (Mark 1:21-34; Luke 4:31-44).

Mark and Luke tell of two miracles performed by Jesus at this point, with the resulting fame which they brought to him. The first of these took place in a synagogue in Capernaum, the ruins of which may be seen today. The services began at nine o'clock in the morning of the Sabbath. Jesus was there and spoke words which because of their authority stirred the crowd. He then astonished them by healing a demoniac who was in the assembly. This miracle which proved his power over unclean spirits had an electrifying effect. "And they were all amazed insomuch that they questioned among themselves, saying, What is this? A new teaching!" (Mark 1:27.) Immediately after the services Jesus and his disciples went to the home of Simon, whose wife's mother lay seriously ill of a fever. Jesus "came and took her by the hand, and raised her up; and the fever left her, and she ministered unto them." (Mark 1:31.)

The report of these two mighty works would spread like wildfire. The entire area would be aroused. All who were sick wanted to be brought to this mighty man. All three synoptic gospels tell what occurred at the close of this day. As the sun was setting "they brought unto him all that were sick, and them that were possessed with devils. And all the city was gathered together at the door. And he healed many that were sick with divers diseases and cast out many devils." (Mark 1:32-34.)

7. *The First Tour of Galilee* (Mark 1:35-45; Matthew 4:23-25, 8:2-4; Luke 5:12-16).

After this busy day Jesus slipped away quietly and went to a desert place to pray. He needed a season of prayer and meditation since overnight he had become so popular that his situation was becoming complicated. Simon and others finally found him and told him of the crowds already assembled waiting for his ministry. Then it was that he announced his intention of departing from Capernaum for a season to let the excitement die down. They must remember also that he came to minister to other people and towns. "And Jesus went about in all Galilee, teaching in their synagogues, and preaching the gospel of the kingdom, and healing all manner of diseases and all manner of sickness among the people. And the report of him went forth into all Syria. . . . And there followed him great multitudes from Galilee and Decapolis and Jerusalem and Judea and from beyond Jordan." (Matthew 4:23-25.)

The details of this journey are not given. We do not know even to what places he went, nor how long the journey lasted. Only one incident, which may be considered representative, is given. It is the healing of a leper. This dread disease claimed many victims then, as it still does. It was a skin disease, always regarded as unclean, which worked slowly, becoming ever more painful until it terminated in death. The poor victim mentioned here had heard of Jesus and, defying the law, came and worshiped him and piteously begged to be made clean. In compassion Jesus stretched forth his hand and touched him and instantly cleansed him. Again the result was an immense throng of people pressing in upon him. Again Jesus "withdrew himself in the deserts, and prayed." (Luke 5:16.)

8. *Back in Capernaum* (Mark 2:1-12; Matthew 9:1-8; Luke 5:17-26).

Having returned to his home he found multitudes awaiting him. The story of his healing the palsied man who was let down through the roof of Peter's home is given by Mark, Matthew and Luke. Among the group inside who witnessed this miracle "were Pharisees and doctors of the law sitting by which were come out of every village of Galilee and Judea and Jerusalem." (Luke 5:17.) These had learned of his work and were moved by curiosity and by envy to investigate. They were critical of his work and could not disguise their ill-will as they saw him deal with this palsied man. Jesus, sensing their critical attitude and ill-concealed hostility, openly defied them. Already these religious officials were building up their scheme for curbing the activities of this wonder-working teacher whose works they could not understand but whose power they feared.

9. *Call of Matthew* (Mark 2:13-17; Matthew 9:9-13; Luke 5:27-32).

Jesus had four disciples already committed to him, but was seeking others to add to his group. Because of the prominent place which Matthew (Levi) later occupied the details of his call to discipleship are given by all three synoptic gospels. Again Jesus was on the shores of the Lake teaching the multitudes when he found his next full-time follower. Matthew was not a fisherman as were the first, but was a tax collector. The Roman government imposed heavy taxes upon the Jews the paying of which was exceedingly odious to them. Any collector of these would have been hated by them; for one of their own race to serve as collector was in their eyes an unpardonable offense. But it was a lucrative position because the collector with full military authority behind him could practice graft. Matthew, even though hated by his fellow men, was a man with many good qualities. He had promise and Jesus saw in him what he wanted and needed. His "place of toll" was on the busy shore of the Lake and no doubt Jesus had seen him many times. Matthew was not only familiar with the marvelous works of Jesus but probably was personally acquainted with him. This explains the statement that Matthew immediately rose up and followed him. It was not a sudden decision. He gladly accepted the call and in appreciation gave a reception in honor of Jesus. At this dinner he had many "publicans and sinners" as his guests along with Jesus. To the consternation of the scribes and Pharisees Jesus not only attended this reception in the home of a publican, but sat down and ate with all these sinners. To their cynical slurs Jesus replied in the familiar words: "They that are whole have no need of a physician, but they that are sick: I came not to call the righteous but sinners." (Mark 2:17.)

10. *Sabbath Controversies* (John 5:1-47; Mark 2:23-3:6; Matthew 12:1-14; Luke 6:1-11).

The scene of Jesus' experiences now shifts from Galilee to Jerusalem. The occasion was a Passover feast. The question of what year it was is a mooted one. If there were four Passover feasts in his ministry, as many hold, it means that his public ministry covered a little more than three years. Some scholars believe that this feast was at the end of the second years of his work; others hold that it was at the end of the first. We may never be able to decide this question, which after all is not important.

Already we have noted the spirit of criticism and hostility which the Jewish religious leaders had exhibited toward Jesus. This hostility was to become more and more pronounced until it finally culminated in his death. In this visit to Jerusalem their smoldering fear and hatred came out into the open. Jesus met it squarely and the clash was a fiery one. The issue was the observance of the Sabbath. The Jews venerated the Sabbath and observed it most scrupulously as their most sacred institution. It began at sunset (6:00 P.M.) Friday and lasted until the same hour Saturday. The observance of this day had developed into a very complicated and burdensome chore. The Mosaic restrictions had been elaborated and multiplied until they numbered into the hundreds. Many of these regulations were utterly ridiculous. For example, wearing false teeth on the Sabbath was considered carrying a burden, as was the plucking out of a grey hair, or picking a head of wheat, or even writing together two letters of the alphabet. These multiplied regulations had made the keeping of the Sabbath, even for the Rabbis, practically impossible. So these Rabbis and others resorted to casuistry and deception. The whole system had destroyed the very spirit of the Sabbath.

This was the setting for Jesus' experience in Jerusalem. The issue was raised when Jesus healed a lame man on the Sabbath. When attacked by these Jews for his work of mercy, Jesus defended his action, identified himself with the Father and on this basis insisted that the Sabbath had not been violated.

He openly claimed to be the Son of God and the appointed judge of mankind, but he did not here assert that he was the Messiah for this would have had political consequences. All his words made a profound impression on his hearers. These religious leaders would not forget.

As Jesus returned from Jerusalem to Galilee an incident occurred which raised again the question of observing the Sabbath. They passed by a wheat field which bordered the roadway and his disciples plucked some heads of wheat, rubbed them in their hands to remove the chaff and ate them. This was perfectly in accord with the Mosaic law (Deut. 23:25) but was a violation of the Pharisaic tradition. Certain Pharisees, probably planted spies, immediately challenged this and to their protest Jesus replied by quoting the experiences of David in eating the shewbread — which the Pharisees could not answer — and then asserted that "the Son of Man is the Lord of the Sabbath."

After they reached Galilee another incident arose on the same issue. In the synagogue on the Sabbath he healed a man with a withered hand. Again the Jews challenged him and again he justified his action on the basis of the real purpose of the Sabbath.

*11. Selecting the Twelve Disciples* (Mark 3:13-19; Luke 6:12-16).

Jesus had now reached a crisis in his ministry in Galilee. Already he had met increasing criticism of his work both in Jerusalem and in Galilee. A break with the whole system of Rabbinic traditions seemed imminent. He could not tolerate their system of unnumbered and ridiculous regulations. Real religion meant more than the observance of these regulations.

Upon going down to the Lake he found immense crowds of people waiting. He healed them and taught them, and his fame continued to spread. He was now ready to take another step. He was to call in final form twelve men for the special task of building his kingdom. The general ministry to multitudes here and there must be supplemented by an organization that would give strength to his movement and guarantee its existence. Before selecting his twelve men he spent a whole night in prayer since so much depended on his choice.

The time of this selection was certainly a short time after his return from Jerusalem. The place was probably his familiar haunt, the mount called the Horns of Hattin, some eight miles south of Capernaum and about four miles west of the Lake.

Before going up into the mountain he "calleth unto him whom he himself would, and they went unto him." From these selected ones he called out twelve men whom he called *apostles* since they were to be sent out. These were men who had been with him longest and who had been tested and proved. There are four lists of them (Mark, Matthew, Luke, Acts) given in a little different order. We may follow Matthew (10:2-4) in naming these, though of course the same men are in each list. These were Simon Peter, Andrew, James, John, Philip, Bartholomew (Nathanael), Thomas, Matthew, James (the Less) the son of Alphaeus, Judas (Thaddeus), Simon the Canaanean, and Judas Iscariot. We do not have space to comment on the character of each of these, though the student will find it a profitable study in personalities. These men were henceforth to be with Jesus, to receive special instruction and to serve as his immediate helpers.

## 12. *The Sermon on the Mount* (Matthew 5-7; Luke 6:17-49).

Immediately after the selection of these apostles Jesus delivered the famous Sermon on the Mount. The time and place were, of course, the same as for the choosing of the twelve apostles. The purpose was to declare publicly both to these apostles and the large group around him, the principles and ideals that must characterize the lives of those who are to be subjects in his kingdom. It is a sort of inaugural address — a declaration of principles and policies. It was an important occasion and Jesus had prepared himself to speak frankly, fully and authoritatively.

Only two of the gospels give the record of this address. Luke's report is very brief; Matthew devotes three full chapters to it. Even Matthew's account is not a verbatim report, but is a summary or resumé, though carefully and logically arranged. It must have been a long discourse, probably consuming several hours. No doubt his words provoked comment and questions from his hearers. This discourse is so significant that it should be thoughtfully studied by every reader. While we must resist the temptation to comment on this deliverance, every statement of which is so provoking, we must give a brief analysis of it. In this we are following the outline given by Dr. Robertson in his *Harmony of the Gospels*.

(1) The Introduction (Matthew 5:3-12, Luke 6:20-26). The Beatitudes and the Woes. The privileges of the Messiah's subjects.
(2) The Theme: Christ's Standard of Righteousness in contrast with that of the Scribes and Pharisees (Matthew 5:13-20).
(3) Christ's Ethical Teachings Superior to that of the Scribes in Six Items or Illustrations (Murder, Adultery, Divorce, Oaths, Retaliation, Love of Enemies) (Matthew 5:21-48).
(4) The Practice of Real Righteousness Unlike the Ostentatious Hypocrisy of the Pharisees, as in Almsgiving, Prayer and Fasting (Matthew 6:1-18).
(5) Single-hearted Devotion to God, as Opposed to Wordly Aims and Anxieties (Matthew 6:19-34).
(6) Captious Criticism, or Judging Others (Matthew 7:1-6, Luke 6:37-42).
(7) Prayer and the Golden Rule (Matthew 7:7-12).
(8) The Conclusion of the Sermon: The Lesson of Personal Righteousness Driven Home by Powerful Parables (Matthew 7:13-8:1).

We may call attention to several aspects of this famous sermon. Because of its significance various statements in it are more frequently quoted than almost any other words of Jesus. It is intensely practical; it deals almost altogether with human behavior. The theological teachings of Jesus will come later. The effect of the sermon was amazing. "When Jesus ended these words, the multitudes were astonished at his teaching: for he taught them as one having authority, and not as their scribes. And when he was come down from the mountain, great multitudes followed him."

*13. Second Tour of Galilee* (Luke 8:1-3).

Shortly after this great deliverance Jesus and his newly appointed disciples and a number of women who had been healed of infirmities, took a second tour of the province of Galilee. "He went about through cities and villages, preaching and bringing the good tidings of the kingdom of God." (Luke 8:1-3.) The time involved and the exact route followed are not given, but this does not matter. He was concerned with carrying his good news to as many as possible. This gave him an opportunity also for training his disciples. Without attempting to go into the details of this second tour we may note several incidents which occurred during this time. He performed still another miracle of healing in the curing of the slave boy who belonged to the centurion; he restored to life the son of a woman who lived at the village of Nain; he denounced the wickedness of the cities of Bethsaida, Chorazin and Capernaum, and then opened his heart to needy men everywhere in his immortal invitation, "Come unto me, all ye that labor and are heavy laden, and I will give you rest." One other event belonging in this time is the spontaneous expression of appreciation of Jesus by a poor woman who anointed his feet with oil while he was a guest in the home of Simon.

*14. A Busy Day* (Mark 3:19-35; Matthew 12:22-50).

Mark and Matthew relate a number of activities in the life of Jesus to show how full his days were. He healed a man "possessed with a devil, blind and dumb." This deed of mercy amazed the people and brought forth a bitter accusation of the Pharisees who asserted that Jesus was in league with Beelzebub, the prince of devils, and because of this was able to cast out demons. Jesus showed the absurdity of such an argument and then denounced these "hypocrites" for their wickedness and deceit. These Pharisees demanded a sign of Jesus to prove his claims. All Jesus' miraculous works, many of which the Pharisees had seen, should have been sign enough for any one. After refusing such an unnecessary request Jesus gave a positive prophecy of his resurrection from the dead, though they did not understand this at the time. This busy day also included another experience which has been widely misunderstood. He was interrupted in his labors by some who announced that his mothers and brothers were in the crowd and were eager to see him privately. It is generally assumed that his family had been deeply disturbed by the growing animosity of the religious leaders toward him and of his bitter clashes with them. No doubt the report was current that Jesus was "overwrought" and might be mentally ill. How far his family shared this feeling is not known. At any rate Mary, his mother, and his brothers might naturally feel that Jesus should relieve himself of the terrific pressure of duties and go back home for a rest. Jesus did not stop his work to talk privately with Mary but instead insisted that all human relationships must be subordinated to the higher spiritual relationships of the kingdom. He was not discourteous to his mother in thus continuing his work. Mary must understand that his work must come first, even ahead of her claims upon him. It is neither irreverent nor presumptuous to imagine that Jesus later sought out his mother and talked with her privately. At any rate, he loved his mother devotedly and she certainly followed him with her prayers and her admiring reverence even to the cross. This same busy day included a long period of teaching his disciples and the crowds by the use of parables.

*15. Teaching By Parables*  (Mark 4:1-34; Matthew 13:1-53; Luke 8:4-25).

During this busy day Jesus employed a significant method of teaching. He spoke in parables to the crowds by the sea, and to the disciples. There are three periods in the ministry of Jesus when he made profuse use of parables: in Galilee, in the Perean ministry, and during the last week of his life in Jerusalem. On this occasion he used nearly a dozen parables which are familiar to all students of the New Testament. These parables as given by Matthew were: The Sower, The Seed Growing of Itself, The Tares, The Mustard Seed, The Leaven, The Hidden Treasure, The Pearl of Great Price, The Net, and The Householder.

Since this method of teaching was so significant in the work of Jesus it will be well for the student to give some consideration to parabolic teachings. Other teachers have used parables, but those of Jesus are immortal. The word *parable* means to place along by the side of. In general his parables were of three kinds. (1) In the form of a proverb: "Physician heal thyself." (2) Paradox: "It is easier for a camel to go through the eye of a needle." (3) Narrative or story, which is by far the most common form. In this form a parable does not have to be actual fact, but it must be truth.

The parables of Jesus are unexcelled for literary beauty: "They are the finest literary art in the world, combining simplicity, profundity, elementary emotion and spiritual intensity." (Sanday.)

There were several reasons why Jesus used them. (1) To attract attention. Jesus knew, as does every speaker, the power of a good story. (2) To stimulate inquiry on the part of the disciples. He wanted to stir their minds and make them think. (3) In parables Jesus could state truth in crisp form so that it would be easily remembered, and later "digested" or understood. (4) With the increasing opposition of his enemies who sought occasion to misquote and misrepresent his sayings there were times when Jesus wanted to convey his meaning to his disciples without his opponents being able to comprehend it.

Because expositors often do injustice to parables in interpreting them it will be helpful to keep in mind two or three principles of interpretation. We should always seek to understand the language of the parables. Each parable should be studied and interpreted in its proper setting or context. As a general rule Jesus sought to make one main point by the use of a parable. We make a serious mistake in trying to apply every little detail in these parables. For example when Jesus compared his second coming to that of a thief entering a house he never meant to place himself in the category of a burglar. He meant only to show that his coming would be unannounced.

16. *Around the Lake* (Mark 4:35 to 6:6; Matthew 8:28 to 9:34; Luke 8:22-56).

This busy day in the life of Jesus was not yet finished. The crowds continued to press in on him. He was weary, but rest seemed out of the question. He therefore suggested to the disciples that they take him in one of the little boats to the other side where they might escape the crowds and rest for awhile. Pulling out from the shore Jesus relaxed and soon fell asleep. "Faintness, weariness and exhaustion dominated the physique of the human Jesus, and he lay immersed in profound slumber, fanned by the breeze of the lake and soothed by the gentle rythmic motion of the boat. Here is a picture unspeakably sublime of the human Saviour in repose, in the boat on the bosom of the beautiful sea of Galilee. Near him, his disciples converse in subdued tones about the happenings of the day, while others quietly manage the sails and guide the gliding craft over the placid waters. The last glimmerings of the day fade from the western horizon and the night spreads its mantle over this peaceful scene. The myriads of glittering stars dot the Syrian sky and furnish all the needed light for the sailing craft now midway the placid sea."[3]

But the scene was soon changed. A sudden storm, so common on this lake, now burst upon them and they were in grave danger. In their alarm they aroused Jesus who quietly stilled the storm. At his words, "Peace! Be Still!," the tempest ceased and the waters were calm. These seasoned sailors who knew the danger of such storms must have been deeply impressed by this miracle. "What manner of man is this, that even the winds and the sea obey him?"

Coming to the other side of the lake they found no opportunity for rest. Immediately they were met by a demoniac of Gerasa whose frightful malady moved Jesus with such compassion that he healed him. The results of this miracle were quite different from what might have been expected. "And they began to beseech him to depart from their borders." The only course left open to him was to return to Capernaum. The heart of Jesus must have been gladdened when upon preparing to leave the man who had been healed came with the plea that he might be allowed to go along with Jesus, just to be with him. This was not wise so Jesus told him, "Go to thy house, unto thy friends, and tell them how great things the Lord hath done for thee and how he had mercy on thee." Surely he went back and gave faithful witness among his own people. Back in Capernaum and its environs Jesus continued his mighty miracles of healing. The gospels give the story of four or five of these: The daughter of Jairus, the woman with an issue of blood (chronic hemorrhage), two blind men, and a dumb demoniac. The multitudes still thronged Jesus and he performed many other works of mercy which are not recorded. The Pharisees were still present to criticize and to pervert his words.

*17. Third Tour of Galilee* (Mark 6:1-13; Matthew 13:54-58, 9:35-11:1; Luke 9:1-6).

Before beginning his third and last tour of Galilee Jesus took his disciples and went again to Nazareth to offer the people of his home town a second chance to receive him. But again the result was disappointing. "They were offended in him." "And he could there do no mighty work." "And he marveled because of their unbelief." This was his last visit to Nazareth.

At this point we come to a new departure in the method of Jesus' work. Hitherto he had gone with his disciples; now he sent these twelve men out "by two and two; and he gave them authority over unclean spirits." After these months of training with him they were to go forth without him and try themselves out. How well had they learned, and how successful would they be?

Having given them detailed instructions Jesus resumed his own work. It is thought that he probably came into many of the cities where he had sent his disciples. At some later time he returned to Capernaum and in due time all twelve joined him there to tell him about their experiences and accomplishments.

His Galilean ministry was now about to come to a close. A situation had arisen which made it necessary for him to adopt a new course in his ministry.

¹Stalker, James, *Life of Christ*, pp. 56-57.
²Ibid., pp. 64-65.
³Shepard, J. W., *The Christ of the Gospels*, p. 232.

*Chapter V*

## SPECIAL TRAINING OF THE TWELVE DISCIPLES

1. The Year of Opposition. 2. The Ministry of Withdrawals. 3. The First Retirement. 4. Second Retirement. 5. Third Retirement. 6. Fourth Retirement. 7. Testing the Disciples. 8. The Transfiguration. 9. Closing Days in Galilee. 10. Ready for Jerusalem.

# Special Training of the Twelve Disciples

*1. The Year of Opposition.*

The end of the Galilean ministry in the spring brought Jesus to the last year of his life. One year remained, and this was to be the hardest. It is known as the year of *opposition*. We have noted frequently the rising tide of opposition on the part of the Jewish religious leaders. During the last year this became ever more pronounced and bitter until it finally culminated in his crucifixion. Because of its importance we should examine the causes of this opposition.

From the beginning the learned and influential Sadducees had assumed an attitude of indifference and opposition to this "peasant reformer." They were occupied with other affairs and gave but little attention to this one from Galilee who claimed to be the Messiah. It was only when the movement had gained such momentum as to threaten to become a political revolt which might upset their business and involve them with the Roman authorities that they became concerned about it.

However, with the Pharisees and the Scribes, the more numerous and popular party who were deeply interested in ecclesiastical affairs, it was different. The members of this party, which might be compared in modern life to our ministers, were deeply concerned about Jesus. From the first they had heard him and had detected signs of danger to their position. These "conservators of respectability and orthodoxy" knew almost at once that here was one so utterly different that his teachings could never be accepted — nor could he be silenced. They decided against him early in his public career and their adverse decision became more deeply fixed each passing month.

The fact that most of the official religious leaders of the Jews would not and could not recognize and accept the Son of God is both appalling and tragic. There were various reasons why they did not accept him. They were blinded by sin and could not discern the light. Centuries of distorted teaching had prejudiced their thinking that they could not recognize the true Messiah. The fact that Jesus was of seemingly humble origin also caused them to reject him. They had been taught to associate the Messiah with riches, power and worldly splendor. Moreover they did not like his choice of men to be his disciples. They were humble, working men — fishermen, farmers, and even a hated publican. Jesus had ignored the official religious group in calling his followers. Another very good reason for their opposition was that he himself did not practice, nor teach his followers to practice, many established observances so dear to the Pharisees — such as fasts, washing hands before meals, and so on. To the Pharisees no one could be genuinely religious or claim to represent God without the punctillious observance of these man-made institutions. Thus Jesus was not only un-godly, he was a deceiver. Perhaps the chief cause of their hostility was the teaching of Jesus concerning the Sabbath. To them the proper observance of this holy day necessitated literal obedience to the thousands of minute man-made regulations which they had set up. To Jesus "the Sabbath was made for man."

Having concluded that he was an imposter they would never go back to re-examine their first decision. They had crossed the line. Even the miracles of Jesus did not serve to convince them that he was the Son of God. From now on they would intensify their opposition and would enlist all possible allies in their fight on him. Thus it was that the very people who should have been the first to receive him were the ones who fought him and finally brought him to his death.

## 2. The Ministry of Withdrawals.

The fame of Jesus was greater than ever after his last tour of Galilee. Immense crowds were always about him. He had launched a movement that stirred all Galilee and the regions roundabout. The Pharisees now became more daring and unscrupulous in their opposition. John the Baptist had been beheaded by Herod Antipas and government officials were eyeing the work of Jesus. Trouble might arise from this area at any moment. So Jesus decided upon a new course. He would take his disciples away into quiet places for a while. These withdrawals or retirements were carefully planned.

It was now springtime, just a year until the end of his ministry. This period of retirements was to be spent in special work, which would last approximately six months, from spring to autumn — from April to September.

There were four of these retirements, each to some region near Galilee. It is perhaps significant that in every case he went outside the territory of Herod Antipas and in most instances was in the region ruled by Philip who was not openly hostile to Jesus. These withdrawals were: (1) Across the Lake of Galilee to the regions of Bethsaida-Julias in eastern Palestine, (2) To the territory of Tyre and Sidon in ancient

Phoenicia, northwest of Galilee, (3) To the Decapolis, southeast of the Lake, (4) To the region of Caesarea-Philippi some distance north of the Lake.

There were good reasons for these periodic withdrawals. (1) Jesus knew now that the Galileans were following him for superficial reasons and that their purpose was to make him an earthly king who could supply their material needs. (2) The opposition of Jewish leaders was becoming more offensive and intolerable. (3) Herod Antipas appeared to be ready to employ the forces of state against Jesus. (4) Both Jesus and his disciples were greatly in need of rest after the strenuous ministry in Galilee. These retreats into cool, quiet places would benefit them greatly. (5) He must give his disciples some intensive training which he could not do among the dense crowds of Galilee. It was only twelve months until the end. Could he get the disciples ready by that time?

3. *The First Retirement* (Mark 6:30 to 7:23; Matthew 14:13 to 15:20; Luke 9:10-17; John 6:1 to 7:1).

Having completed their third tour of Galilee his disciples met him again at Capernaum where they reported to him in detail their experiences on this tour. Seeing the crowds and knowing that he must get his disciples away he secured a boat so that they could cross to the eastern shore of the lake. Here they were met by an immense crowd of people who were hungry. In his compassion for them Jesus performed his great miracle of multiplying the five loaves and two fishes and fed 'five thousand men, beside the women and the children." After this he sent his disciples back to the western side of the lake, then he dismissed the multitude and went alone out in a desert place to pray. He saw a grave danger in what had just occurred. He "perceived that they were about to come and take him by force, to make him king." They were planning a political move to elect him king on the basis of an earthly ruler. This would be utterly ruinous to his kingdom. It must not occur.

As the disciples took their boat to go back to Capernaum they were suddenly engulfed by a great storm. Seeing their distress Jesus left the shore and "came unto them walking upon the sea." This miracle saved them and caused Simon Peter to learn a lesson of faith. As they came again to the western shore of the lake, this time in the vicinity of Gennesaret, they were again greeted by great crowds. Once more "They sent unto all that region round about, and brought unto him all that were sick; and they besought him that they might only touch the border of his garment: and as many as touched him were made whole."

The next day in the synagogue at Capernaum a real crisis developed. (John 6:22-71.) The same fickle people which he had fed with the loaves and fishes were present again. The time had now come for a test of his followers. Jesus therefore boldly asserted that they were following him because of the bread which he could supply. He stated that he was no political Messiah to furnish material necessities; his mission was spiritual. Unless they were willing to understand his mission and follow him unto death they could not belong to his kingdom. These stern words sifted the crowd. The big majority of the people turned away from him. The Galilean bubble had burst. Only the disciples were left. Jesus gave them an opportunity to leave also, but Peter speaking for them proclaimed their loyalty, "Lord, to whom shall we go? thou hast the words of eternal life. We have believed and know that thou art the Holy One of God."

This was the Galilean crisis. Henceforth Jesus was to devote his time to these disciples. Everything depended on them. He and they must spend the summer together in a program of intensive work. These disciples must come to a clearer understanding of his mission.

### 4. *Second Retirement* (Mark 7:24-30; Matthew 15:21-28).

Another outburst of opposition, this time from the Pharisees who had come up from Jerusalem, gave evidence of their determination to continue harassing him. They could pervert his teachings and heckle him in the crowds. Because there was no hope of winning them Jesus felt the necessity of escaping them to work with his disciples. His first effort to find quiet and rest had failed. He now determined to go further away to a place where he would not be interrupted. The place selected was on the coast of ancient Phoenicia around Tyre and Sidon, about thirty-five miles northwest of Capernaum. Here the mountains come down almost to the sea, so he would have a cool, restful retreat. It was outside the jurisdiction of Herod Antipas and was a Gentile region. Even here, however, his fame had spread and people recognized him and called upon him. "And he entered into a house, and would have no man know it; and he could not be hid."

We have no way of knowing exactly how long Jesus remained here, nor of his activities. We may safely assume, however, that his time was almost altogether occupied in instructing his disciples. We have only one incident recorded, and this one presents many difficulties to the interpreter. It is the story of the healing of the Syrophoenician woman's daughter. Jesus was not discourteous to this woman, neither was he insensible to her sorrow, nor unresponsive to her plea. The point he seems to be making is that after all he came not to this Gentile community to engage in a public ministry. "If He should engage in extended ministries here He would forever close the door to further effort on behalf of the 'lost sheep of the house of Israel.' This would be to defeat His wider ministry to the world later through the Jews, who were to be His emissaries when enlightened."[1]

5. *Third Retirement* (Mark 7:31 to 8:12; Matthew 15:29 to 16:4).

Leaving the Phoenician territory Jesus and his disciples went eastward toward Mt. Hermon and then journeyed southward through the region east of the Jordan and the Lake of Galilee to the Decapolis. Sometime during this journey he healed a deaf and dumb man brought to him.

Mark and Matthew record the story of his feeding another multitude of four thousand people. Some interpreters indentify this incident with the feeding of the five thousand men earlier in the summer, though there is no good reason for this assumption. Desiring to get away from the crowds in this area he and his company withdrew to Magdala which was on the western shore of the Lake.

They had hardly landed before the Pharisees and the Sadducees "came and tempting him asked him to show them a sign from heaven." This is the first record of the opposition coming from both of the two leading parties of the Jews. Jesus, knowing that such signs would not convince these critics, boldly declared, "there shall no sign be given." Matthew adds that he qualified the assertion with the words "except the sign of Jonah" by which he meant to predict his own resurrection. Naturally these critics did not understand these words.

6. *Fourth Retirement* (Mark 8:13-26; Matthew 16:5-12).

The fourth withdrawal took Jesus across the lake to the eastern shore and thence northward up to the mountainous region of Caesarea-Philippi, an ideal retreat. The events of this fourth retirement are of real significance in his work. During this season he received from his disciples their great confession of faith in him as the Messiah. In this region he was transfigured after which he began to prepare himself and his disciples for his "exodus" which would take place some six months hence. When he was ready to return home he crossed the Jordan valley into northern Galilee and made his way quietly back to Capernaum. This journey was not a public tour of teaching and healing. "And he would not that any man should know it. For he taught his disciples, and said unto them, The Son of Man is delivered up into the hands of men, and they shall kill him, and when he is killed, after three days he shall rise again. But they understood not the saying, and were afraid to ask him." A very definite turn in the ministry had taken place. The shadow of the cross looms large from now on.

7. *Testing the Disciples* (Mark 8:27 to 9:1; Matthew 16:13-28; Luke 9:18-27).

One of the very important events in this fourth retirement was the special testing of his disciples which brought forth their declaration of faith in him. The beautiful region of Caesarea-Philippi was an ideal setting for this examination of his students. "Everywhere there is a wild medley of cascades, mulberry trees, fig-trees, dashing torrents, festoons of vines, bubbling fountains, reeds and ruins, and the mingled music of birds and waters." (Tristram.)

Here in the quiet retreat Jesus spent much time in prayer. When he was ready he called his disciples about him and asked them some questions. The first of these was not hard to answer: "Who do men say that the Son of Man is?" They replied that there were different opinions on this question. "Some say John the Baptist; some, Elijah; and others Jeremiah or one of the prophets." The next question of Jesus was much more probing. "But who say ye that I am?" Simon Peter, who often spoke first, gave the great statement: "Thou art the Christ the son of the living God!" This courageous and sincere declaration stirred Jesus deeply. He commended Peter for it and then declared that this answer had been given to him by revelation from God. Jesus then uttered one of his most famous and significant statements. "And I say unto thee, that thou are Peter (pertros) and upon this rock (petra) I will build my church; and the gates of Hades shall not prevail against it. I will give unto thee the keys of the kingdom of heaven; and whatsoever thou shalt bind on earth shall be bound in heaven; and whatsoever thou shalt loose on earth shall be loosed in heaven."

This profound declaration of Jesus is variously interpreted. Roman Catholic teachers base their papal claims for Peter on this statement. Non-Catholics are not altogether agreed on what Jesus meant by the "rock." In view of all the facts it seems clear that Jesus was talking about the great statement of trust just made by Peter. "What is the rock in the reply of Jesus to Peter? I take it to be the faith shown in Peter's confession of trust."[2]

Jesus began at once to prepare the disciples for his forthcoming death on the cross. He told them distinctly that this was to occur.

Impulsively and foolishly, Peter now spoke. "And Peter took him, and began to rebuke him, saying, Be it far from thee, Lord; this shall never be unto thee." Jesus then rebuked Peter for his ignorance and boldness. Following this Jesus stated the cost of discipleship with him. "If any man would come after me, let him deny himself, and take up his cross, and follow me. For whosoever would save his life shall lose it: and whosoever shall lose his life for my sake shall find it." (Matthew 16:24-25.)

8. *The Transfiguration* (Mark 9:2-32; Matthew 17:1-27; Luke 9:28-45).

Six days after the testing of the disciples and Peter's great confession Jesus went up into a high mountain, probably Mt. Hermon, to pray. With him he took Peter, James and John, leaving the other nine disciples behind, probably to keep watch. As he prayed "he was transfigured before them; and his face did shine as the sun, and his garments became white as the light. And behold, there appeared unto them Moses and Elijah talking with him." Peter's impulsiveness again asserted itself in his request that they be allowed to remain indefinitely on this glorious mountain with him. This was both unwise and impossible. Such mountain-top experiences have their place in the life of a disciple, but his real place is down in the valley where the people are. The divine approval of Jesus is expressed in an audible voice: "This is my beloved Son, in whom I am well pleased; hear ye him."

Without yielding to the temptation to interpret in detail this significant experience we may say that its chief purpose was to prepare both Jesus and his disciples for his forthcoming death. We should remember that the disciples did not know of the necessity of the cross as we now know it. Putting ourselves in their place we may feel some of the surprise and shock which they must have felt when they were first told of this. With all reverence we may say also that this experience of renewed fellowship with God the Father would also strengthen Jesus and assure him that the cross was a part of the divine plan for his work.

9. *Closing Days in Galilee* (Mark 9:33-50; Matthew 18:1-55; Luke 9:46-62).

After these momentous happenings the disciples followed Jesus back into Galilee, though they did not yet understand all that they had heard about his crucifixion. Back in Capernaum they engaged in an argument which reveals how imperfectly they understood what Jesus had taught them. Actually they were contending as to who should be greatest in this new kingdom of God. Jesus came among them and sensing the situation, inquired into their argument. He taught them the meaning of true greatness in a manner which they should never forget. "And he called to him a little child, and set him in the midst of them, and said, Verily I say unto you, except ye turn, and become as little children, ye shall in no wise enter into the kingdom of heaven. Whosoever therefore shall humble himself as this little child, the same is greatest in the kingdom of heaven."

Continuing his teaching he explained the infinite worth of human personality and the necessity for the deepest concern over all the poor, lost sheep of the world. The relation of his subjects to one another was tremendously important. The necessity for forgiveness of one who sinned against them, and the demand for purity and perfection in their own lives was indelibly impressed upon them. He closed with the declaration that his followers must give up everything for his service. "No man having put his hand to the plough, and looking back, is fit for the kingdom of God."

*10. Ready for Jerusalem* (John 7:2-10).

It was now September, the time for the Feast of Tabernacles in Jerusalem. Jesus recognized the necessity of his going to this feast because of the crisis now developing. "He steadfastly set his face to go to Jerusalem," knowing well what awaited him. He went privately from village to village through Samaria. With his arrival in Jerusalem we enter upon the next phase of his ministry which is known as the Later Judean Ministry.

[1]Shepard, *The Christ of the Gospels,* pp. 286-287.
[2]Robertson, A. T., *Class Lectures.*

*Chapter VI*

## LATER MINISTRY IN JUDEA

# Later Ministry in Judea

## 1. Extent of This Ministry.

This phase of Jesus' public ministry took place in the fall and early winter before his crucifixion the next spring. It began with the Feast of Tabernacles in September and closed about the time of the Feast of Dedication in December. It opened with the experiences of Jesus in Jerusalem around the temple area, but it included a ministry in various parts of the province of Judea. As we have seen Jesus had already visited Jerusalem and Judea nearly two years earlier. In the city itself he did not get much of a hearing. Out in the country of Judea he was received with popular favor. The second visit proved to be a repetition of the first. In Jerusalem he clashed with the Jews in bitter controversy. Their hostility was so strong that again he was unable to accomplish much. He went then to the villages whither he had sent his seventy disciples in pairs to prepare the way for him. In this brief but effective campaign which closed in December he seems to have covered much of the province of Judea. He remained in Jerusalem for the Feast of Dedication when his enemies openly tried to stone him. He then withdrew to Bethany beyond the Jordan where he remained until his Perean ministry. In considering the activities of these three months we shall have to be content to follow the main course of events without attempting to interpret many interesting experiences.

## 2. In Jerusalem Again (John 7:11-52).

The Feast of Tabernacles, which came in the autumn, was a sort of Thanksgiving occasion to express gratitude for the blessings of the year and to acknowledge the leadership of God in the years of their history. While not as old as the Passover feast and without its historic significance, this feast was usually an important event which brought to the city many thousands of pilgrims. It provided an occasion for the gathering of religious leaders and the discussion of religious developments.

The work of Jesus had spread his fame over all Palestine. He was the chief topic of conversation, particularly since the leaders themselves had challenged him. The main question at this particular feast was, Would Jesus appear? When he did not arrive for the first three days of the feast the Jewish leaders began to seek for him. "And there was much murmuring among the multitudes concerning him. Some said he is a good man; others say Nay, but he leads the multitude astray. Yet no one spoke openly concerning him, for fear of the Jews."

Suddenly, in the midst of the feast Jesus appeared in the temple, probably on Solomon's porch, and there began to teach. The student will read carefully the account of his teaching. We should note that he spoke boldly, that his critics challenged him, that he answered them, usually to their discomfiture, and that he had friends even in this hostile crowd. This was a lively session, a "give and take" affair, when tempers clashed, the sparks flew and the feeling was tense and bitter. Jesus could fight when the occasion demanded it. Had he refused to meet his enemies, stand his ground and expose them his cause would have been lost.

It was on the last day of the feast that Jesus issued his great invitation, "If any man thirst, let him come unto me and drink. He that believeth on me, as the scripture hath said, out of his belly shall flow rivers of living water." This caused a division in the crowd. Some declared him to be a prophet; others said that no prophet could come from Galilee.

The officers who were commissioned to arrest him reported to the Sanhedrin, but they didn't bring Jesus, giving as their reason "Never man so spoke." Nicodemus, with whom Jesus had talked on his first visit to Jerusalem, now declared that he could not be arrested without a charge. The only answer these fanatical Jews could make to this was the sneer, "Art thou also of Galilee?"

### 3. Forgiveness and Light (John 7:53 to 8:11).

After this stormy session the crowds went home but Jesus repaired to the Mount of Olives, on the hillside across the brook Kedron east of the city. Again next day he came to the temple and taught the people who came to him. The Pharisees and Scribes now sought to entrap Jesus. They brought a woman taken in adultery and asked him what he had to say about this. When they insisted on a reply, he said, "He that is without sin among you let him first cast a stone at her." They did not know how to deal with this and began one by one to slink away until all were gone. Then Jesus said to the woman, "Neither do I condemn thee: go thy way; from henceforth sin no more."

Resuming his discourse Jesus announced, "I am the light of the world: he that followeth me shall not walk in darkness, but shall have the light of life." What a claim — either it was true or it was the most conceited utterance ever made by a man. Such a claim infuriated the Pharisees who had now regathered with the crowd after their failure to entrap him. Defending this claim he asserted that he was the Son of God, but he added, "Ye neither know me nor my Father: if ye knew me ye would know my Father also." He was indeed the Son of God, and the light of the world, but these angry, blind religious leaders would not or could not see it.

### 4. Further Clashes (John 8:21-59).

Continuing his discourse Jesus announced that he was "going away" that they would some day seek him, but would die in their sin because "whither I go, ye can not come." He devoted the remainder of his discourse to an unanswerable exposure of the Scribes and Pharisees. "Everything he says to them has a whipcracker on the end." He asserts that the truth would make them free, but that they now are slaves. They are not really the spiritual sons of Abraham, indeed they are not the sons of God, but of the devil. He closes his discussion by making three great claims for himself: he has power over death, he asserts that Abraham knew his (Jesus) day and was glad, and that he was in existence before Abraham. The Pharisees could not answer this. In anger they picked up stones to stone him!

### 5. The Man Born Blind (John 9:1 to 10:21).

The story of the healing of this man who was born blind is vivid, moving and revealing. Jesus used it to expose the untenable position of the Pharisees against him.

The disciples and others were concerned about whose sin was responsible for this man's blindness. Jesus denounced such theological speculation and healed the man. This created a sensation among the people. How could this be? Bringing the man to the Pharisees they asked these authorities to explain what had happened. They tried but would not give Jesus credit for doing it. The man himself asserted that Jesus who healed him must be a prophet. They then appealed to the man's parents but they evaded the issue — let the boy speak for himself. Again turning to the man whose sight had been restored they demanded an answer. The man then replied: "whether he be a sinner, I know not: one thing I know, that whereas I was blind, now I see!" In anger the Jews cast the poor man out. Jesus then sought him out and told him that it was the Son of God who had healed him. The man then exclaimed, "Lord, I believe," and he worshiped Jesus.

Jesus had won another disciple, but had angered and humiliated the Pharisees again.

Following this experience Jesus gave the familiar story of the Good Shepherd. The point of this parable was to draw the picture of the hostile Pharisees, and to intimate that the Good Shepherd would die for his flock and would then come to life again. Not many understood the significance of these words, but some believed on him. "Many of them said, He hath a devil, and is mad; why hear ye him? Others said, These are not the sayings of one possessed with a devil. Can a devil open the eyes of the blind?"

Realizing now that he could not accomplish much in the hostile atmosphere of Jerusalem Jesus left the city to go out into the province of Judea.

## 6. The Seventy Disciples (Luke 10:1-24).

This ministry in Judea lasted about three months. The first step in this period was a new venture. Jesus selected seventy men and sent them out into the villages and towns of Judea. They were to go two by two to the places where he himself was to come. We do not have the names of these men, nor any personal facts about them. It is to be noted that Jesus had a following sufficiently large to furnish this number who were carefully selected by him. He gave them rather detailed instructions as to their equipment, their work and their behaviour. Naturally these were quite similar to those given to the twelve who went out into Galilee. It was understood that he was to come after them in order to · evaluate their work.

Just how long their ministry lasted we do not know. We are told however, that they "returned with joy, saying, Lord, even the devils are subject to us in thy name." Was this a bit of conceit or were they genuinely stirred by the experiences of this mission? Jesus rejoiced also in their success. Some one has pointed out that the only time we are told of the joy of Jesus is over the conversion of sinners (here and at Jacob's well). Jesus congratulated these disciples upon the privilege they had in participating in his mission: "many prophets and kings desired to see the things which ye see, and saw them not; and to hear the things which ye hear, and heard them not."

## 7. The Good Samaritan (Luke 10:25-37).

One of the best known of all the parables of Jesus is that of the Good Samaritan. To understand it we should know the circumstances under which it was given. It came forth in response to a "catch question" asked by a tricky lawyer who represented religious authorities and not civil law. "A man like me, what will he have to do to get into the kingdom?" The lawyer's purpose was not to get light but to expose Jesus. Jesus asked him to state the law, which he was able to do. He then commended him and added: "do this, and thou shalt live." But the lawyer desiring to justify himself said unto Jesus, "And who is my neighbor?" Then Jesus told the story which we call the "Good Samaritan." This story was a terrible condemnation of this lawyer and the Scribes and Pharisees. Only one — and he a despised Samaritan — was willing to do what was right. Without mercy Jesus made the lawyer admit this. This beautiful story unwittingly called forth by an insincere questioner has done more to build hospitals and other elee-mosynary institutions than any other words ever spoken.

## 8. *Jesus' New Home* (Luke 10:38-42).

While in Galilee Jesus seems to have had his home in the house of Simon Peter in Capernaum. From now on he appears to have enjoyed the hospitality of a good home in Bethany. In this little town, which was some two or three miles southeast of Jerusalem, Lazarus and his sisters, Mary and Martha, welcomed Jesus into their home where he could find comfort and rest. These two sisters, both of them devout followers of Jesus, represent two types of Christians. Martha was exceedingly practical, a good hostess, "cumbered about much serving." She always "set a good table," and was conscious of her obligations as a hostess. Mary was meditative and responsive to spiritual things. She was an alert and eager disciple of Jesus. These sisters made the home for Lazarus and later were to call on Jesus in their sorrow at the death of their beloved brother. One likes to think of Jesus spending much time in this home where he was so cordially welcomed and where he found stimulating friendship and support.

## 9. *A Lesson in Prayer* (Luke 11:1-3).

There are frequent references to the times Jesus spent in prayer. We may think of him doing much of this in the night time. Certainly he prepared himself for the crises in his ministry by long seasons of fellowship with his Father. His disciples no doubt had seen him pray many times and had seen the peace and strength which came to him after such periods of devotion. This had impressed them so that on one occasion they besought Jesus to teach them to pray. He responded by teaching them again the model prayer, often erroneously called the "Lord's Prayer," which he had taught them many months earlier in Galilee. This was not meant to be their only prayer, but would serve as a guide in their praying.

He then taught his followers persistence in prayer by the use of a story which is now familiar. Jesus does not mean to represent God as selfish, indifferent and heartless, one to tease his children by withholding. God is loving, tender, fatherly. His ear is always open to the petitions of his children who come to him in faith and humility. However, oftentimes for good reasons our prayers are not answered at once. The experience of genuine prayer ennobles the life of a Christian and a delay in answering should cause us not to give up and lose hope, but to persist in faith that God will do for us what is best.

### 10. Further Clashes With Pharisees (Luke 11:14-54).

There were many different kinds of Pharisees but all of them were opposed to Jesus. Luke recounts several fresh clashes which Jesus had with these at this time.

The first was brought about by healing a dumb man. This raised afresh the question of how Jesus could do it. The Pharisees answered that he did it through Beelzebub, the Prince of devils. Jesus showed the fallacy of their argument by stating that Satan is not divided against himself. Beelzebub would not cast out his own kind.

As the multitudes gathered about him he answered his critics who demanded a "sign," by saying that no sign would be given, because already they had abundant evidence and did not accept it. The only sign should be that of Jonah, by which he predicted his resurrection from the dead on the third day. However, no one, not even the disciples, understood what he meant. He then asserted that their wicked generation was blind, because a greater than Solomon and Jonah was among them and they could not see him.

His next clash with the Pharisees came in the home of one of these who had invited him to dine with him. Jesus accepted the invitation but to the amazement of his host did not engage in the elaborate ablutions which the Pharisees observed before a meal. Seeing their surprise he explained that they were very careful to cleans the outside of the cup, but that it was far more important for them to be inwardly clean. He enforced his point by pronouncing three woes upon these Pharisees for their hypocrisy. At this one of the lawyers remarked to Jesus that in his words to the Pharisees he was reproaching the lawyers also. To this Jesus replied by pronouncing three woes upon them. The degree to which these words stung both groups is seen by the fact that both turned on him as he came out of the house. "They began to press upon him vehemently, and to provoke him to speak of many things: laying wait for him to catch something out of his mouth."

*11. Further Discourses* (Luke 12:1-13:21).

The extent to which Jesus succeeded in these months in Judea is indicated by the multitudes who attended his ministry; "the many thousands of the multitude were gathered together insomuch that they trod one upon another." He had the crowds. In jealousy and anger the Pharisees grew even more daring in their efforts to ensnare him. Nevertheless he taught boldly, frankly denouncing the hypocrisy of these religious officials and warning his own followers that their faith must be deeper and more genuine than that of their leaders. In view of the crises which was coming he warned his followers to be ready to endure persecution and suffering for his sake. At the same time he stressed the spiritual aspect of the kingdom. This kingdom was not one of splendor and worldly character but was in the hearts of men. They should trust in God who feeds the fowls of the air and clothes the lilies of the field. They should be busy and should be prepared for the coming of the King. "For in an hour that ye think not the Son of man cometh."

On a subsequent occasion Jesus entered into a synagogue on the Sabbath and healed a poor "woman which had a spirit of infirmity eighteen years." This caused an uproar and the ruler of the synagogue severely rebuked Jesus. He defended his action by quoting from their scriptures and denouncing the Pharisees for their hypocrisy in saving their cattle on the Sabbath while protesting the healing of the poor woman. "And as he said these things, all his adversaries were put to shame: and all the multitude rejoiced for all the glorious things that were done by him."

*12. Closing Scenes in Jerusalem* (John 10:22-39).

It was the time of the Feast of Dedication in December and Jesus was again at Jerusalem, having completed his journeys out in Judea. This was the last of the great feasts to be instituted. It was to commemorate the dedication of the temple after Judas Maccabeus had gained possession of Jerusalem from the Seleucids in 165 b.c. The feast lasted eight days and usually was attended by large crowds.

Jesus went to the temple and on Solomon's porch the Jews gathered about him and requested that he tell them plainly whether or not he was the Messiah. Jesus replied, "I told you, and ye believe not: the works that I do in my Father's name, these bear witness of me." He explained that they did not believe in him because they were not willing to believe. He then declared that he and the Father were one. Such a bold claim of deity they could never accept. In anger they "took up stones again to stone him." Having asked for a statement they refused to believe him and would have killed him, but "he went forth out of their hand."

Once more Jerusalem had closed its doors to him. He knew that his work here was done, at least for the present. Leaving the city he went down the valley, crossed the Jordan and came to Bethany where he had been baptized and proclaimed the Messiah by his great fore-runer, John the Baptist. This spot was for our Lord one of hallowed memory. Here almost three years ago he had been called to begin his ministry which was now so near to completion. Here he must await the call that would issue in his supreme sacrifice.

What about Jerusalem? Was there any hope for this great city? Even though she had defied the Saviour she was to have yet another chance. He would spend another week there, his last days in the flesh, when these conceited and bigoted religious leaders might have the final opportunity to receive the Son of God. Discouraging as it appeared, his labor had not been altogether in vain. Even though he had been rejected by the rulers his words had found entrance into the hearts of many lowly people. At least he had been faithful and could trust the final results to his heavenly Father.

*Chapter VII*

## THE MINISTRY IN PEREA

1. Extent of This Ministry. 2. Around Bethany (Betha-bara). 3. Another Sabbath Controversy. 4. The Cost of Discipleship. 5. A Group of Parables. 6. Raising Lazarus From the Dead. 7. Journeys Away From Jerusalem. 8. Further Discourses in Perea. 9. Preparing His Disciples. 10. Jesus in Jericho.

# The Ministry in Perea

## 1. Extent of This Ministry.

The ministry in Judea closed in December, some four months before the crucifixion of Jesus. Having left Jerusalem and gone to Bethany beyond Jordan, Jesus was to spend some three and a half months, January to early in April, in the region east of the Jordan known as Perea. This province extended from the Decapolis in the north down to the region just east of the Dead Sea. It was under the rule of Herod Antipas and was quite different politically and religiously from Judea and Galilee. It was predominantly Jewish in population but was so exposed to Gentile influences that the ideas of the people were much more liberal than in the strictly Jewish areas.

The work of Jesus in this region is given almost wholly by Luke, who himself was a Gentile. The exact order of events and places visited is not given, though Jesus probably covered much of this territory. His travels included a trip to Jerusalem and Ephraim in Judea, a journey north through Samaria into Galilee, and the long journey from there through Perea on the way to Jerusalem for the Passover feast. This ministry closed with his arrival at the home of Mary and Martha in Bethany on Friday before his crucifixion one week later.

## 2. Around Bethany (Bethabara) (John 10:40-42).

Jesus did not retire to Bethany to rest, but rather to continue his work unmolested by his enemies, hence his days here were busy ones. "And many came unto him; and they said, John indeed did no sign: but all things whatsoever John spake of this man were true. And many believed on him there." The brave words of the Forerunner were vindicated. Jesus was demonstrating beyond question that he was the Messiah. Evidently he lingered here for several days and performed many miracles and taught great numbers of people.

Some time later, just when is not clear, Jesus made a brief trip to Jerusalem. As he journeyed "through cities and villages" the crowds followed. On one occasion some one asked him "if those being saved were few." This question, seemingly harmless, was really a keenly debated theological one. The answer of Jesus was to all his hearers, "strive to enter in by the narrow door." It is useless to speculate on the number who might be saved; the important thing is for each one to see that he himself is in right relation to God.

On the same occasion certain Pharisees said to Jesus, "Get thee out and go hence: for Herod would fain kill thee." Jesus' reply was that he had no fear of Herod.

### 3. Another Sabbath Controversy (Luke 14:1-24).

Again Jesus accepted an invitation to dine in the home of a Pharisee on the Sabbath. Seeing among the group a man who had the dropsy, Jesus this time took the initiative by addressing a question directly to the Pharisees, "Is it lawful to heal on the Sabbath or not?" They hesitated to answer so Jesus boldly "took him, and healed him, and let him go." He based his act of mercy on the provision of the law for relieving the distress of an ass or an ox on the Sabbath. This left the critics in embarrassment.

Observing the practices common to such a formal meal Jesus then addressed three parables to those who were present. (1) To teach the lesson of humility he advised them not to seek the chief places at a dinner, but to wait until they were invited to occupy these. (2) The lesson on hospitality was enforced by his suggestion that in giving a dinner one should invite not his choice friends and kinsmen, but the underprivileged ones who could not recompense him by giving a dinner in return. (3) To show them the privilege which they enjoyed in being able to enter his kingdom he told the story of the Great Supper. He meant for them to understand that the place which they were invited to occupy would some day be filled by people from the "highways and hedges."

### 4. The Cost of Discipleship (Luke 14:25-36).

Great crowds swarmed around Jesus and he realized that they might easily misunderstand what was involved in being his disciples. They must not be misled; so he urged the necessity for careful consideration of this by the illustrations of the man counting the cost before erecting his tower and the king taking into account all the possibilities before going to war. One who would follow Jesus must know the facts, count the cost and then decide upon his course. After the fashion of Orientals he would use strong language to startle his hearers. So he boldly asserted that "If any man cometh unto me, and hateth not his own father, and mother, and wife, and children, and brethren, and sisters, yea, and his own life also, he can not be my disciple." We do not understand, of course, that Jesus commands his followers to hate their kinsmen. Christ must have the first place in the hearts of his disciples. He must come ahead of the dearest family ties. Should one have to make the final decision between his loved ones and Christ, he must be loyal to Christ his master.

On no occasion did Jesus make the terms of discipleship easy or alluring. He purposely made them hard, because he would deceive no one. It has never been easy to be a real disciple of Jesus. It calls for sacrifices and self-denial and hardship of one kind or another. But the rewards of faithful discipleship far outweigh the difficulties and sacrifices entailed.

### 5. *A Group of Parables* (Luke 15:1-17:10).

During these weeks in Perea some of the most notable of Jesus' parables were given. Six of these were spoken on one occasion. In order to appreciate them we must understand the circumstances under which they were related.

Publicans and sinners, outcasts in the eyes of Jewish religious teachers, were attracted to this strange teacher and were cordially received by him. On this occasion a number of them were present to hear him, and responded as he spoke. Pretending astonishment at the interest which Jesus displayed in these undesirable people the Scribes and Pharisees murmured, saying, "this man receiveth sinners and eateth with them." To justify his position Jesus told the stories of the Lost Coin, the Lost Sheep, and the Lost Boy (Prodigal Son). Resisting the temptation to discuss these memorable stories we must point out that Jesus had one great purpose in telling them. He intended to show God's concern and love for unworthy sinners, but also to condemn the attitude of these selfish, conceited religionists who assumed that they were the elect and that God had no business showing any interest in other people. In the story of the Prodigal Son the elder brother, with all his despicable behavior, represents the Scribes and Pharisees.

The next three parables deal with possessions. The first of these, the Unjust Steward, was spoken to the disciples. The point was to teach his disciples how to use material wealth so as to make eternal friends and to lay up treasures in heaven.

The parable of the Rich Man and Lazarus was directed to the Pharisees. Men are trustees of the wealth committed to them by God to use for the benefit of needy people. The rich man here, representing the Pharisees, was not necessarily a vicious sinner. He was selfish, conceited and unconcerned about the misery of unfortunate people.

He did not have the spirit of a Christian. He could never be at home with God or Christian people.

The parable of the Unprofitable Servants was addressed to his disciples. He introduced the story by statements about the sin of causing others to do wrong, the duty of forgiveness and the power of faith. The point of this story is that the disciples were to maintain at all times a spirit of humble dependence on him, and to be ready to serve him as faithful servants.

### 6. *Raising Lazarus From the Dead* (John 11:1-54).

While Jesus was in the vicinity of Bethany beyond Jordan (Bethabara) word came to him of the grave illness of his friend Lazarus, the brother of Martha and Mary in Bethany of Judea. He was separated from Lazarus by the distance of more than a day's travel, and in view of the urgency of the call we should expect Jesus to make all haste to reach the home of these friends. Instead, however, he said to his disciples, "This illness is not unto death, but for the glory of God, that the Son of God may be glorified thereby." He loved Lazarus and was not belittling his illness. But he delayed two full days before starting to their home. Jesus explained to his disciples his purpose in going: "Lazarus our friend has fallen asleep; but I go that I may awake him out of his sleep." Since Lazarus had died by the time Jesus received word of his illness, and since he could reach there only on the second day after starting, it would be four days after his death when Jesus arrived. He had been buried and all hope was gone out of the hearts of these sisters who were at home surrounded by many prominent friends who had come to be with them. Unable to understand Jesus' delay in coming they said again and again, "If the Lord had been here our brother would not have died!"

Martha upon learning of Jesus' approach, hurried to him and cried, "Lord, if thou hadst been here my brother had not died. And even now I know that whatsoever thou shalt ask of God, God will give thee." Jesus assured her that he would be raised — even now. "Believest thou this?" he asked of her. To this she replied: "Yea, Lord: I have believed that thou art the Christ, the Son of God, even he that cometh into the world." Martha then told Mary that Jesus had come. Hopefully Mary hurried to Jesus, using the same plaintive words of Martha, as she fell down at his feet. The Jews and the sisters were weeping as they conducted Jesus to the burial place of Lazarus. We are told at this point that Jesus himself wept. Why did Jesus weep? Various answers have been given to this question. Surely he loved Lazarus and would grieve at his death. Surely he sympathized (suffered with) these sisters, Perhaps the real reason is the one given by the ancient teacher, St. Isidore of Pelusium: "He was about to raise him for his own glory. He wept for him (Lazarus) saying in effect: 'One who has entered within the haven I am calling back to the billows; one who has been crowned I am calling back to the lists.'"

When they had reached the tomb Jesus commanded them to remove the stone from the door. Jesus had already prayed as is indicated by his word, "Father, I thank thee that thou heardest me." Then with a loud voice he cried, "Lazarus, come forth." To the amazement of all Lazarus came to life. "He that was dead came forth, bound hand and foot with grave-clothes; and his face was bound about with a napkin. Jesus saith unto them, Loose him and let him go."

Suppose Jesus had failed. Here were his enemies ready to broadcast such a failure. Jesus risked his claims on this test. But his Father did not let him fail! "It was by the power of God that this miracle was wrought; and why indeed should it be judged a thing incredible that God should raise the dead — that the power that fashions the embryo in the womb, makes it live, brings the child to birth, and makes him grow in stature and understanding, should re-animate a lifeless form and repair in a moment the wastage of decay?"[1]

The effect of this unheard-of miracle would be sensational. Many of the Jews who saw it now believed on Jesus. Cost what it might they would follow this man who could raise the dead. The effect on the Pharisees was even more far-reaching. This man whom they had often challenged, always to their dismay, and about whom they were so uneasy, had openly entered their domain and had defied them by performing a miracle which had discredited them and put them on the defensive. The extent of their distress is revealed by the fact that they hurriedly asembled the Sanhedrin to consider what they could do. Their panic is indicated by their excited cries, "What are we doing? This man is doing many miracles. If we let him thus alone, all men will believe on him; and the Romans will come and take away both our place and our nation." It was a helpless, frantic cry in a strange meeting. The general result of the conference was the resolve to do away with Jesus at the very earliest moment. "So from that day forth they took counsel that they might put him to death." The die was cast; in raising Lazarus from the dead Jesus had committed the final and unpardonable act. For this they must kill him. This experience had a direct result in the changing of the plans of Jesus. He was not safe in Jerusalem and his hour had not yet come. "Jesus therefore walked no more openly among the Jews."

### 7. Journeys Away From Jerusalem (Luke 17:11-37; 18:1-14).

Since the issue was now joined it was necessary for Jesus to get away from Jerusalem to a place where he would not be molested. He elected to go to Ephraim, a town in northeast Judea about twenty miles from the city. It would be a safe retreat since a part of the wilderness of Judea separated it from Jerusalem and it was on the borders of Samaria so that in the event the Sanhedrin should find him here he could easily cross into Samaria. After a brief stay here he entered Samaria on his way for a short visit to Galilee. Jesus was always friendly and kind to the Samaritans and while passing through their province he performed another miracle of healing. Ten men afflicted with the dread disease of leprosy "stood afar off and lifted up their voices, saying, Jesus, Master have mercy on us." The Master commanded them to go show themselves to the priests according to law. (Leviticus 13:49.) As they went they were made clean. One of the ten returned to Jesus to thank him for his cleansing. The other nine did not return. Jesus used this experience to teach the lesson of gratitude and appreciation which this "stranger" had exhibited. Jesus was doing what he could to break down the "middle wall of partition" between races.

Among those who followed Jesus and his disciples in this journey were some Pharisees. As Jesus approached his death he taught much concerning his kingdom. These Pharisees were interested in the time when this kingdom would be set up. To their question he answered that his kingdom should not come "with observation." It was not an earthly rule to be set up with pomp and ceremony. It should come quietly in the hearts of men. Continuing his discourse he stressed again the necessary ideal in the purpose of his followers: "Whosoever shall seek to gain his life shall lose it; but whosoever shall lose his life shall preserve it."

Stressing again the necessity for prayer he told two stories to illustrate the nature of genuine and effective prayer. The parable of the Importunate Widow was given "to the end that they ought always to pray, and not to faint."

For the benfit of the Pharisees he told the story of the two men who went up into the temple to pray. One was a Pharisee, proud and self-sufficient, who "stood and prayed thus with himself, God, I thank thee that I am not as the rest of men, extortioners, unjust, adulterous, or even like this publican." This was not a prayer, but a soliloquy of self-congratulation. The other who prayed was a poor publican, who, "standing afar off, would not lift up so much as his eyes unto heaven, but smote his breast, saying, God be merciful to me a sinner." God approved this publican because of his humility, his self-abasement and his sincerity. He disapproved of the Pharisee because of his self-complacency, self-praise, snobbery and insincerity. Effective prayer depends on the character of the one praying, the nature of the request and the spirit of the prayer.

8. *Further Discourses in Perea* (Mark 10:1-31; Matthew 19:1-20; Luke 18:15-30).

Matthew and Mark give the incident in which the Pharisee propounded to Jesus the question of divorce. This was a very troublesome and divisive question and the Pharisees were seeking to embarass Jesus. The two great theological schools of the Jews, Hillel and Shammai, debated this question with fervor. Hillel took the liberal side, Shammai the conservative. The Pharisees sought to get Jesus to line up with one or the other and thus cause him to alienate a part of the crowd.

Hillel held that divorce should be granted for even the most trivial offense. This view had gained popular support with the result that there was great moral laxity. Women had become a mere chattel of man, and was subject to unjust and cruel treatment.

As always, Jesus perceived their purpose, and instead of taking sides, immediately pointed to the real fundamental law of marriage given in Genesis. "Did you never read that the creator from the beginning made them both male and female?" "The strong cohesive force of sex was purposed by God to be the basis of an inseparable unity. The union, in a true marriage is one of body, mind and spirit. In the Hebrew conception, body stood for all three. Therefore this yoke of God by which he bound two souls together, 'let no man try to separate.' Thus Jesus soars far above the fog of controversial opinions and bears the question to the open skies of God's establishment of law of marriage in the beginning. . . . Jesus was deeply moved by the wrongs suffered by womanhood among the Jews, and all over the world, and here lays down the eternal law of God for marriage which has never been changed since the beginning of the race."[2]

It is significant that the incident of the parents bringing their children to Jesus should come in connection with his teaching on marriage. It is difficult for us who are so accustomed to the respect accorded children today to understand the setting of this experience. We shall have to remember that children did not have the consideration and standing which we accord them. Indeed, the great attention and appreciation which is given childhood today can be attributed directly to the teachings of Jesus Christ. The simple truth is that Christianity has enfranchised childhood.

It is worthy of note that children were always attracted to Jesus and felt instinctively that he was their friend. Even the disciples shared the common feeling toward children and looked upon their coming to Jesus as an intrusion. "But when Jesus saw it he was moved with indignation, and said unto them, suffer the little children to come unto me, and forbid them not, for of such is the kingdom of God." He went further to explain that all his followers must be child-like in spirit. "Whosoever shall not receive the kingdom of God as a little child, he shall in no wise enter in." The kingdom belongs to people of child-like nature — trusting, simple and teachable. He does not say that children are in the kingdom of God because they are children. He makes the child the model of those who come into the kingdom. There is no more revealing or touching picture of Jesus than this. "And he took them in his arms, and blessed them, laying hands upon them."

Another revealing experience occurred as Jesus went his way toward Jerusalem. The student will do well to read carefully the entire account of Jesus dealing with the rich young ruler. We should note the fine qualities exhibited in this young man — his humility and honesty, his genuine desire for help. He was wealthy, knew the law and evidently was a good man. He had good intentions but had wrong ideas about how to become a disciple. Note also the gentleness which Jesus displayed toward him. He wanted to help him and had finally to prescribe a shocking remedy to him. One thing — his possessions — stood between him and eternal life. He must surrender all these things and put Jesus Christ first. The young ruler had not anticipated such an answer. He was seeking some counsel from the great teacher, but not such radical measures that would affect his whole life. Thus the young man "went away sorrowful; for he was one that had great possessions."

This incident raised the whole question of wealth in its relation to the kingdom. "And Jesus said unto his disciples, Verily I say unto you,

It is hard for a rich man to enter into the kingdom of heaven." The disciples who held the common notion that wealth was an evidence of God's approval on men and hence the wealthy could not be ungodly, were amazed at his words. He then interpreted this for them with the statement, "Children, how hard is it for them that trust in riches to enter the kingdom of God."

Jesus assured the disciples in response to their question that everyone who has left all to follow him shall be fully recompensed. The sacrifices entailed do not compare to the reward which shall be theirs.

9. *Preparing His Disciples* (Mark 10:32-45; Matthew 20:17-28; Luke 18:31-34).

Jesus had now steadfastly set his face toward Jerusalem and was in haste. He walked ahead of his disciples who were "terrified and they that followed were afraid" at the determined and solemn appearance of Jesus. Little did they realize what was ahead for all of them. Sensing their anxiety Jesus took the disciples apart and told them frankly what was to come. "The Son of man shall be delivered unto the chief priests and the scribes; and they shall condemn him to death, and shall deliver him unto the Gentiles; and they shall mock him, and shall spit upon him, and shall scourge him, and shall kill him; and after three days he shall rise again." How could they believe this! It seemed so utterly unreasonable. Luke adds that "they understood none of these things."

At this point in their journey toward Jerusalem they were joined by Salome the mother of James and John by Zebedee. She went immediately to Jesus for a special favor. When asked what her request was she replied, "Command that these my two sons may sit, one on thy right hand, and one on thy left hand, in thy kingdom." This request revealed the thinking of all the disciples about the nature of the kingdom. To them it was to be one of worldly nature where men would occupy places of honor. Each wanted to have an honorable place when the appointments were made. They were presumptuous and irreverent in making such a request of him. His answer was that they knew not what they asked. "To sit on my right hand or on my left hand is not mine to give; but it is for them for whom it is prepared." What did Jesus mean to say? "Suppose there is an umpire, and many gallant athletes entering the lists. Two of these who are intimate with him approach him and say: 'Arrange that we be crowned and proclaimed victors,' relying on their good will and friendship with him. But he answers: 'This is not mine to give; it is theirs for whom it has been prepared by their efforts and sweat.'" (St. Chrysostom.)

Then Jesus pointed out the nature of greatness in his kingdom. "Whosoever would become great among you, shall be your minister; and whosoever would be first among you shall be servant of all." How hard it is, even today, for Christians to accept this truth.

*10. Jesus in Jericho* (Mark 10:46-52; Matthew 20:29-34; Luke 18:35-19:28).

At last the company of Jesus moved down into the Jordan valley and crossed the river over into Judea. Coming up on the western side they entered the ancient city of Jericho where two important events took place. Immense crowds had already formed as they worked their way to the great Passover feast, now only a few days away. A blind beggar known as Bartimaeus sat by the roadside and learned that the famous teacher was passing by. In a loud voice he called, "Jesus, thou son of David, have mercy on me." The crowd rebuked him but he cried even more loudly and piteously. Standing still Jesus commanded them to bring the poor blind man to him. Upon hearing this Bartimaeus cast off his garment, sprang up and ran to him. He piteously renewed his plea for his sight. In mercy, Jesus healed him. "And straightway he received his sight, and followed him in the way. And all the people when they saw it gave praise unto God."

Zacchaeus of Jericho was a tax collector who had amassed great wealth. He wanted to see Jesus, this famous teacher, but being small in stature was unable to get to him in the dense crowd. Getting ahead of the multitude he climbed up a tree overlooking the road so that he could see him. On came the crowd in the midst of which he discerned this teacher. To his astonishment Jesus stopped under the tree, looked up and calling him by name ordered him to come down "for today I must abide at thy house." He did as commanded, received him joyfully, welcomed him into his home, talked with him and became a disciple of Jesus.

This unexpected acceptance of a hated publican caused a storm of protest among the Jews. They murmured saying, "He is gone to lodge with a man that is a sinner." Zacchaeus then gave unmistakable evidence of his conversion, "Lord, the half of my goods I give to the poor; and if I have wrongfully exacted ought of any man, I restore fourfold." No doubt he, like all publicans, had taken more than his part. But he would now make restitution. Honesty in business is a requirement for the Christian. Jesus closed the matter with his declaration of the purpose of his own ministry, "For the Son of man came to seek and to save that which wast lost."

His travels had now come to a close. "And when he had thus spoken he went on as before, going up to Jerusalem." He would tarry briefly at Bethany, but Jerusalem was his destination.

[1]Smith, *Our Lord's Earthly Life,* p. 307.
[2]Shepard, *The Christ of the Gospels,* p. 453.

*Chapter VIII*

## THE PASSION WEEK

1. Importance of This Last Week. 2. Limits of Study. 3. Order of Events. 4. Jesus in the Presence of Death. 5. The Passover Feast. 6. Resting at Bethany. 7. Sunday. 8. Monday. 9. Tuesday. (1) Efforts to Ensnare Jesus. (2) Denouncing the Scribes and Pharisees. (3) Three Discourses. (4) Anointed for Burial. (5) Plans for the Betrayal. 10. Wednesday. 11. Thursday. (1) The Passover Meal. (2) A Lesson on Humility. (3) Identifying the Traitor. (4) The Lord's Supper. (5) Farewell Discourse. (6) In Gethsemane.

# The Passion Week

## 1. Importance of This Last Week.

Every student of the New Testament knows that the events in the last week or ten days of the earthly life of Jesus are of the utmost importance. As much as we value the other events in the life of our Lord we consider the experiences of this week in Jerusalem the most precious heritage of the Christian faith. It was a week of intense activity, of heart breaking disappointment, of bitter rejection and tragic suffering, and yet one of triumph and victory. We can scarcely over-emphasize its importance.

The gospel writers themselves recognized, perhaps better than we do, its significance. This is indicated by the amount of space given to it in their brief writings. It is not accidental that each of these four writers gave it in such detail. Of the chapters which deal with the actual ministry of Jesus, almost forty per cent are devoted to his experiences in these closing days.

## 2. Limits of Study.

Because of the unusual importance of these events every writer feels the urge to give detailed consideration to each of these happenings. Almost every sentence in these accounts invites discussion. However, the limit of space forbids this. We must resist the temptation to explain and interpret, and must content ourselves with the effort to trace in proper chronological order the more outstanding happenings of these last days in Jerusalem.

## 3. Order of Events.

In the treatment of the events of this week we shall follow their order day by day. These events occurred during the great Passover feast which came in the spring of the year. According to the chronology given by Dr. David Smith (*Our Lord's Earthly Life*), these events took place during the second and third week of April that year. Jesus arrived in Bethany, just outside Jerusalem, on Friday, April 10. He remained here until Sunday morning, April 12, when his triumphal entry into Jerusalem took place. He returned to Bethany Sunday night, and each night through Wednesday. On Monday and Tuesday, April 13 and 14, he went into Jerusalem. On Thursday, April 16, he went to the great city for his last time. Thursday evening and night and Friday morning he ate the Passover meal with his disciples, instituted the Lord's Supper, had his long farewell discourse with his disciples, went to the Garden of Gethsemane, was arrested and endured the harassing experiences of a series of so-called trials until after sunrise Friday, April 17. He was crucified on Friday and was laid in the tomb later that afternoon. He remained in the tomb Saturday; early Sunday morning, April 19, he rose from the dead and appeared on several different occasions to believers that day. His ascension took place forty days later.

By considering these events day by day we shall be able, not only to keep them in proper order, but to interpret the feelings of Jesus as he passed through these crises which culminated in his death.

### 4. Jesus in the Presence of Death.

As we move with Jesus from one experience to another in this tragic week we shall be impressed with his composure, his dignity and his complete self-possession. The grandeur of his character stands out above the cheap and shameless behaviour of those who made him prisoner and did him to death. "Christianity has no more precious possession than the memory of Jesus during the week when He stood face to face with death. Unspeakably great as He always was, it may be reverently said that He was never so great as during those days of direst calamity. All that was grandest and all that was most tender, the most human and the most divine aspects of His character, were brought out as they had never been before.

"He came to Jerusalem well aware that He was about to die. For a whole year the fact had been staring Him constantly in the face, and the long-looked-for had come at last. He knew it was His Father's will, and, when the hour arrived, He bent His steps with sublime fortitude to the fatal spot. It was not, however, without a terrible conflict of feelings; the ebb and flow of the most diverse emotions — anguish and ectasy, the most prolonged and crushing depression, the most triumphant joy and the most majestic peace — swayed hither and thither within Him like the moods of a vast ocean."[1]

### 5. The Passover Feast.

This feast was not only the oldest of the six observed annually by the Jews, but it was also the one most largely attended. Jerusalem was never a large city, but on these special occasions it was host to unbelievably large numbers of people. It is said by some authorities that this particular Passover was attended by more than two million people. These would not demand hotel reservations as in modern life. Many visitors would be the guests of relatives and friends. But by far the largest number would camp in the environs of the city, as was the custom of Oriental peoples.

There was good reason for the large attendance at this particular Passover. The fame of Jesus had gone far. His name was on every lip. His miracles had stirred the entire nation. Furthermore the people were aware of his frequent clashes with the Scribes and Pharisees, and knew that this controversy had grown so bitter that something unusual might occur at any moment. They knew of the courage of Jesus and of the determination of the religious leaders to get rid of him. It was but natural to expect that sensational developments would take place at this particular religious festival. So the multitudes were there, and a feeling of expectancy possessed the crowds. The one big question was, Would Jesus come to the feast? Some said that he would not have the courage to come; others insisted that he would come and face his enemies. At any rate, multitudes were there to see what would happen. None of them knew the depth of disgrace into which their leaders were to take their nation nor the victory which Jesus was to achieve in the tragedy of this week.

## 6. Resting at Bethany.

We shall now go back to follow the experiences of Jesus during these fateful days. He had frequently been a guest in the hospitable home of Lazarus, Martha and Mary in Bethany. On his last visit some weeks previously he had raised Lazarus from the dead. This home would provide an ideal resting place for him before the ordeals of the week ahead. However, his coming to Bethany was soon whispered abroad. Many from Jerusalem would come to this village, only two and a half miles distant, to see both Jesus and the man he had raised from the dead. Lazarus was a living witness of the power of Jesus. Never had people heard of such a miracle. Could one who had power to bring a man back from the embrace of death be less than the Messiah? For this reason many of them believed on Jesus. All this so angered the priests that they now sought to do away with Lazarus as well as Jesus.

Jesus reached Bethany on Friday afternoon. The Jewish Sabbath began at six o'clock Friday afternoon and extended till the same hour Saturday. The gospels do not mention any events on Saturday, but we may imagine Jesus going to the synagogue on the Sabbath as was his custom. We may assume also that he spent the remainder of the day resting in the home of Lazarus.

7. *Sunday* (Mark 11:1-11; Matthew 21:1-11, 14-17; Luke 19:29-44; John 12:12-19).

The first of his visits to the holy city was made on Sunday. His entrance into the city on this occasion is usually called the Triumphal Entry. We often think of his going to the city that day amid the peaceful quiet of our Sunday or Sabbath. However the Jewish Sabbath was the day before and the day of his entry would correspond to our Monday. The city was not quiet. It was densely crowded; the noisy multitude filled all available space. People were expectant and excited. Everybody was talking about Jesus and wondering whether he would dare come to face his enemies. A price was on his head. It would take real courage to come.

He deliberately planned his manner of entering the city. On one or two occasions he had acknowledged that he was the Messiah. His hour had now come. In a symbolic manner he would openly declare his Messiahship. In the prophecy of Zechariah there was a picture of the entrance of the Messiah: "Rejoice greatly, O daughter of Zion! Shout, O daughter of Jerusalem! Behold thy King cometh unto thee. Righteous and victorius He: meek, and riding upon an ass, yea upon a colt, a she ass's foal." (Zechariah 9:9.) Notice that he was to ride, not upon a horse which Jews always asosciated with war, but upon an ass which to them was a goodly creature, highly esteemed and ridden by princes on peaceful missions.

Jesus moved toward the city riding the colt, preceded by a great crowd which had come out from Jerusalem, and followed by his disciples and a multitude of others. The multitudes had caught the significance of what Jesus was doing. Some spread their garments in the way, others tore branches from the trees along the route and spread them on the road. The enthusiasm mounted, the crowds hailed him and burst into a chorus of praise saying, "Hosanna, Blessed is he that cometh in the name of the Lord. Hosanna, in the highest!" This procession approached the city with their shouts reverberating from hill to hill. The multitudes which lined the roadway into the city caught spirit and joined in hailing the Messiah.

As Jesus rounded the point of the Mount of Olives and turned north in the valley of Kedron the holy city burst into view. Every Jew loved this city, and it was dear to the heart of Jesus. As he gazed upon it now and realized the fate that should soon befall it, tears came to his eyes and a lamentation broke from his lips: "If thou hadst known in this day, even thou, the things which belong unto peace! but now they are hid from thine eyes." The day of destruction was not far ahead. The procession swept down the valley, by the golden gate of the temple and then up the incline to the temple area. Jesus was the center of interest to the vast crowds surging on all sides. He was being acclaimed Messiah by these multitudes, though he well knew that many who hailed him Messiah today would be shouting for his death a few days later.

This spontaneous outburst of acclaim stunned the enemies of Jesus. "The Pharisees therefore said among themselves Behold how ye prevail nothing: lo, the world has gone after him." Dr. Robertson pictures their helplessness: "The Pharisees are off on the roadside looking on. Rabbi Smelfungus and the others got up on the walls of Jerusalem and looked. 'Man alive, look! They are coming down the mountainside just like ants.' They are turning on each other and blaming each other for it. The world has gone after him! Why can't you catch him? It is victory for Jesus and we are whipped." (Class lectures.)

Jesus went into the temple and healed the blind and lame who came to him. The children even took up the refrain and sang "Hosanna to the Son of David." Jesus allowed himself to be acclaimed as the Messiah. He had met the challenge of the Jews. "It being now eventide, he went out unto Bethany with the twelve."

8. *Monday* (Mark 11:12-18; Matthew 21:18, 19, 12, 13; Luke 19:45-48; John 12:20-50).

After a night of rest in Bethany he and his disciples again set out for Jerusalem. Conscious of all the things to be done he would get an early start, leaving in all probability before breakfast could be served by Martha and Mary. We are told that he saw on the way a fig tree with leaves already on it. Since in Palestine the fruit appears on a fig tree before the leaves are formed Jesus naturally assumed that he would find figs here to relieve his hunger. Instead he found the tree completely barren of fruit. Immediately he saw in this a symbol of Israel. Though carefully cultivated it bore no fruit. He then said to the fig bush, "Let there be no fruit from thee henceforward forever."

Upon arriving in the city Jesus went immediately to the temple. He found here again a situation which had so deeply angered him

three years earlier. Those who sold animals for sacrifice and those who
changed money had moved again into the forbidden area and were
desecrating the house of God. Again Jesus angrily drove them out and
cleansed the temple.

The reader will want to study carefully John's account of the visit
of the Greeks to the temple on this day. We should remember that
they were Gentiles and had no right to appear here. Notice how
courteously they requested an interview with Jesus, how the disciples
hesitated to introduce them to him, and how deeply Jesus was affected
by this request from these Gentiles. He was soon to be rejected and
killed by his own race and he knew it. Here was an invitation to
escape death and become the teacher of the Gentiles. Unquestionably
Jesus saw all this in this incident and it elicited one of his profoundest
statements: "Except a grain of wheat fall into the earth and die, it
abideth by itself alone, but if it die it beareth much fruit. . . .
Now is my soul troubled; and what shall I say? Father, save me from
this hour. But for this cause came I unto this hour." He affirmed his
purpose to carry out his mission even on the cross. This brought forth
words of divine approbation. The world crisis was on, and the world
would be judged and condemned in a few days because of their
condemnation of him.

9. *Tuesday* (Mark 11:19-14:11; Matthew 21:19-26:16; Luke 20,21).

This day was one of the longest, hardest and most decisive in all
the ministry of Jesus. Coming into the city early in the morning he
was occupied constantly until late at night when he trudged wearily
back to Bethany in the darkness. The day is called by some the great
day of controversy, by others the day of rejection. It was both. He
finished his popular teaching in the temple that day and after leaving
the city did not return until the day before his execution.

(1) *Efforts to Ensnare Jesus* — On Sunday and Monday Jesus had
publicly assumed the office of Messiah. This had precipitated a show-
down with the Jewish leaders who denied all his claims. Accordingly,
they prepared to challenge him, ensnare him and discredit him by
subtle questions. There were four different groups, who with carefully
prepared questions, came to him in the temple in the presence of the
people. They appeared innocent and guileless but their propounders
had planned their attacks so they thought Jesus could not possibly
escape their snares.

The first to appear on this Tuesday morning was a group from the Sanhedrin. They asked him by what (whose) authority he had openly taken possession of the temple and taught the people. Jesus replied by asking them about the baptism of John the Baptist, Was it from heaven or from men? They were caught themselves and were afraid to answer either way. Thus he cleverly outwitted them. Jesus then drove home his argument by three parables, The Two Sons, The Wicked Husbandmen, The Marriage Feast of the King's Son. The point in each was to expose the Jewish leaders themselves. Incensed by his exposure of them they would have killed him by force, but feared the people.

The second to try their hand were the Pharisees and Herodians, a group of students. They first complimented Jesus and then with apparent innocence asked whether it was lawful to pay tribute to Caesar or not. Of course this question was loaded with dynamite. They expected Jesus to take one side or the other and thus defy those who held the opposite view. Again Jesus deftly outwitted his questioners by his oft-quoted reply, "Render unto Caesar the things that are Caesar's, and unto God the things that are God's." Thus he quickly disposed of these youngsters.

The next to ask a question were the Sadducees. Theirs was an old catch-question with which they always silenced the Pharisees who believed in the resurrection. It was a rather far-fetched story, but it had been effective. Surely this trick would get Jesus. But again he answered them so effectively that nothing further could be said. "You do err, not knowing the scriptures nor the power of God." They were supposed to be authorities but they were ignorant. The way he put these critics to rout won the applause of the crowd.

Finally another trial was to be made, this time by an experienced lawyer, who felt that he was keener than all these others. His was the old question as to which was the greatest commandment in the law. No other question was more bitterly debated than this. Surely Jesus would have to take sides here. But again he outwitted the keen lawyer by stating, "Thou shalt love the Lord thy God with all thy heart, and with all thy soul, and all thy mind. . . . Thou shalt love they neighbor as thyself. On these two commandments hangeth the whole law and the prophets."

One after another his questioners had been put to rout. Jesus had been the absolute victor and won the acclaim of the crowds. These groups had subjected him to their questions so now, having vanquished them, he asked them a question concerning his Messiahship. This they could not answer. His victory was complete. "No one was able to answer him a word, neither durst any man from that day forth ask him any more questions."

(2) *Denouncing the Scribes and Pharisees* (Matthew 23:1-29) — These unethical and vicious opponents of Jesus, having been completely descredited in the eyes of the people, would have slunk away to nurse their wounded pride, but Jesus was not yet through with them. He must administer a rebuke or an indictment which they deserved. "It was indeed a stern indictment, surely the most terrible ever spoken: yet it was no mere denunciation. Rather was it 'a commiseration of the Scribes and Pharisees.' Its recurring apostrophe 'alas for you Scribes and Pharisees, play actors!' is a cry of compassion; and we miss its spirit and purpose unless we catch the accent of pity quivering in its sternest sentences. In truth it is the Savior's last appeal to his obdurate enemies, portraying their guilt and presaging its inevitable retribution in the hope that even yet they may repent."[2]

After this deliverance, which must have been a hard and exhausting experience for him, Jesus went over and sat down to rest by the chest or treasury where the worshipers placed their offerings. It was here that he observed the offering which the poor widow made and which he used as an illustration of real Christian giving. These words were the last he spoke in the temple. He never entered it again.

(3) *Three Long Discourses* (Mark 13:1-37; Matthew 24, and 25; Luke 21:5-36) — Late in the afternoon Jesus and his disciples went out of the temple, crossed the brook Kedron and went up to the Mount of Olives. Here he sat down and spoke at length to these close friends. This long discourse dealt with his second coming and with the forthcoming destruction of Jerusalem. In the latter part of the discourse he gave a number of parables, including the Fig Tree, the Porter, the Master of the House, the Faithful Servant and the Evil Servant, the Ten Virgins and the Talents.

When he had finished he again reminded the disciples of his death which would come only two days later. It was probably at the same time that the chief priests and elders were gathered at the court of Caiaphas, "and they took counsel together that they might take Jesus by subtilty and kill him."

(4) *Anointed for Burial* (Mark 14:3-9; Matthew 26:6-13; John 12:2-8) — Jesus left the city late in the afternoon and went back to Bethany where he was entertained in the home of Simon the leper that

night. At this dinner a happening took place which brought great joy to the heart of Jesus. Lazarus and Martha and Mary were present for this happy occasion. The guests were gathered around the table. They did not sit in upright position with feet under the table as Westerners do, but occupied a couch in a semi-reclining position with the head at the table and their feet extending away from it. Mary, the sister of Lazarus, knowing something of the plans of his enemies and of his own need of sympathetic understanding, entered the room with a vase of white alabaster-stone containing twelve ounces of very precious perfume which represented her savings. She broke the neck of the vase and lavishly anointed his head and his feet. The room was filled with the aroma of the perfume. It was a gift usually reserved for a king. But only such a lavish gift could express the love and appreciation which Mary had for Jesus.

She was criticized for this extravagance significantly enough by Judas, whose real interest was not in the welfare of the poor as he insisted. Jesus then defended Mary, approved her expression of devotion, and promised her that this act of love should be known "wheresoever the gospel shall be preached throughout the whole world." Mary showed her love for him while he was alive and could appreciate it.

(5) *Plans for the Betrayal* (Mark 14:10-11; Matthew 26:14-16; Luke 22:3-6) — Judas was cut to the quick by the rebuke which Jesus gave him when he objected to the generous gesture of love Mary made at the dinner in Simon's home. "And Satan entered into Judas who was called Iscariot being of the number of the twelve." His greedy and vindictive spirit now asserted itself. Already he had had misgivings about the outcome of Jesus' kingdom in Jerusalem. No doubt he sensed that it was to collapse as far as any material benefits were concerned. He realized that he had but little to gain by staying with Jesus. He was treasurer of the group and had in his possession the little amount belonging to the company. Since the enterprise was about to collapse he probably reasoned that he would profit best by getting what he could now. Added to this desire for money was the humiliating rebuke he had just suffered. Smarting under this he now decided to sell his Master for the best price he could obtain. So he went back to the city to the chief priests "that he might deliver him unto them." "And they when they heard it were glad." They agreed upon thirty pieces of silver as the price for delivery of Jesus into their hands. This was the price of a slave, and Judas accepted it, and thus sold his honor for the paltry price.

> "Still, as of old,
> Man by himself is priced
> For thirty pieces Judas sold
> Himself, not Christ."

There is no sin held in greater contempt by all mankind than betrayal. And Judas Iscariot will forever remain the arch traitor of the human race. Little did he realize the consequences of his vile deed. Condemn his actions as we must, we can not avoid a feeling of pity for the man whose base deed brought to him death and eternal infamy.

### 10. Wednesday.

With the intensive activities of Tuesday Jesus had finished his ministry in Jerusalem, except for the last experiences which were to come on Thursday and Friday. He had been rejected by his own people and had announced to them in stern but piteous words the awful fate to befall the nation. "O Jerusalem, Jerusalem, which killeth the prophets, and stonest them that are sent unto her! how often would I have gathered thy children together, even as a hen gathereth her chickens under her wings, and ye would not! Behold your house is left unto you desolate!"

Tuesday night, Wednesday and most of Thursday were spent in Bethany. The gospels do not tell of any activities on Wednesday. We may imagine however, that this was an important day both for him and his disciples. He would need quiet and rest after the strenuous days already spent and in view of what was to come. He would need time for prayer and meditation as he prepared "to go unto the Father." He would need also to devote himself to his disciples who were always in his heart, in preparation for the events which they were unable to anticipate and understand. Wednesday would be a busy day even in the peaceful retirement among understanding friends in Bethany.

### 11. Thursday (Mark 14:12-21; Matthew 26:17-29; Luke 22:7-30).

This was the day of unleavened bread in the Passover feast. Late in the afternoon all devout Jews would eat the Passover meal. Jesus and his disciples were to eat together that evening as he had desired, and as he had carefully planned. Their place of gathering was a large upper room in the home of some sympathetic friend, probably Mary, the mother of John Mark. Before leaving the city on Tuesday Jesus had arranged for this. Accordingly on Thursday afternoon he sent his disciples on ahead to this upper room where the last details were to be arranged. "And they went, and found, as he had said unto them: and they made ready the passover."

(1) *The Passover Meal* — This meal consisted of a choice lamb roasted whole, unleavened bread, wine and bitter herbs. At sunset the trumpets would blast, and the meal would begin. Before the sunset hour arrived the disciples would have completed all arrangements and would await the coming of Jesus. In due time he arrived and they were ready to celebrate this memorial of the deliverance of their forefathers from Egyptian bondage.

What must have been the feelings of Jesus as he came among his disciples to find them in a bitter contention among themselves as to which of them was to be the greatest. "There is wrangling among them, when he had told them that after two days he would die, and now the two days were past. Peter wanted to get the seat of honor next to Jesus, for he was the leading talker; John because he knew him best; Judas because he was treasurer. John seems to have got the chief place."[3] How human and yet how far from what their master had taught them! He must teach them even now. He began by stating the world's evaluation of greatness which was based on "lordship" or authority. "But ye shall not be so: but he that is the greater among you, let him become as the younger; and he that is chief, as he that doth serve."

(2) *A Lesson on Humility* (John 13:1-20) — John's gospel gives the beautiful story of Jesus teaching the lesson of humility at this Passover meal. The routine of observing the Paschal meal consisted of some thirteen different steps. The first was a benediction, then the cup of wine, and next the formal washing of the hands of the company. It was at this juncture that Jesus washed the feet of the disciples. It was an object lesson to impress upon them the quality of true greatness. He was their Lord, and yet he became their servant as he laid aside his garments, took a towel and girded himself, poured water into a basin, and stooped to wash the feet of his disciples. This was a menial task usually done by a servant, and this act of Jesus would arouse the interest of his followers. He finished his task, replaced his garments and sat down with them to explain his actions. "If I, your Master, have done this for you ye also ought to wash one another's feet. For I have given you an example that ye also should do as I have done to you." We may understand, of course, that Jesus was not here instituting an ordinance like that of the Lord's Supper, but was giving an object lesson in true humility of spirit.

(3) *Identifying the Traitor* (Mark 14:18-31; Matthew 26:21-35; Luke 22:21-38; John 13:31-38) — As they were eating the Paschal meal Jesus startled them all with the statement that one of the twelve was going to betray him. They were all "exceedingly sorrowful and began every one to say unto him, Is it I, Lord?" Jesus then gave the sign by which they should know. According to John's account: "He it is, for whom I shall dip the sop, and give it him. So when he had dipped the sop, he taketh and giveth it to Judas, the son of Simon Iscariot." John further states that again Satan entered into Judas, and that Jesus told him to do quickly what he was to do. "He then having received the sop went out straightway; and it was night."

All knew then that Judas could not be trusted. When he had left Jesus spoke tenderly to these friends, expressing his love for them and warning them of the danger to which they would be exposed. Peter, in over-confidence, asserted that, though every one else should be offended and desert, he would not. He would go with him to death! Then it was that Jesus announced the sorry deed that Peter would do that very night: "This night before the cock crow thou shalt deny me three times." Again Peter most vehemently asserted that he would not, and that he would die with him. "Likewise also said all the disciples." Little did they know what was ahead.

(4) *The Lord's Supper* (Mark 14:22-25; Matthew 26:26-29; Luke 22:17-20; I Corinthians 11:23-26) — After the paschal lamb had been eaten with the bitter herbs, and the time for the explanation of this ancient feast arrived, Jesus instituted the memorial supper. He took bread, gave thanks, broke it and gave it to them saying: "Take ye, eat it, this is my body which is broken for you; this do in remembrance of me." A little later he took a small cup of wine, gave thanks again and said: "Drink ye all (all of you) of it for this is my blood of the covenant, which is shed for many unto remission of sins. For as often as ye eat this bread and drink the cup, ye proclaim the Lord's death till he come."

"The Supper was a new institution. It, like baptism, is symbolic of the life in Jesus. Christ left us only two church ordinances; but the two cover symbolically the whole Christian life. Baptism stands at the beginning and symbolizes the spiritual transformation which takes place in the new birth — the death to sin and resurrection to a new life. The Memorial Supper represents the means of continuation of the disciple's life through the continuous assimilation of Christ who is our bread of life — our Passover. The Supper commemorates the

atoning death of Jesus, but at the same time symbolizes the life —
flesh and blood — which must be eaten by the disciple for the sus-
tenance of his spiritual life."[4]

(5) *Farewell Discourse* (John 14-17) — The paschal meal and the
Lord's Supper together would consume about two hours or more. But
since it was still early in the night Jesus used the remaining three or
four hours before midnight Thursday for a long farewell discourse
with these friends, who despite their weaknesses, were very dear to him.
This conference began in the upper room and continued informally
as Jesus and his friends walked through the streets out of the eastern
gate, down into the valley of the Kedron and up the slopes of the
Mount of Olives to his place of retreat, the Garden of Gethsemane.

The reader should study carefully this long discourse with these
disciples since it is one of the richest treasures of the Christian faith.
Understanding the situation under which Jesus spoke these immortal
words should give them a new meaning to us. Jesus opened his heart to
his disciples as the great rush of emotions swept over him.

The fourteenth chapter, so familiar to every devout Christian, was
intended to console his disciples in view of his death. They are not to
grieve too much for his death, for it is expedient — and they will have
the Holy Spirit as their comforter, teacher and helper. And this is
better.

Chapters fifteen and sixteen are devoted to exhortation. The disciples
must be true to him; they must love each other; they must follow their
new teacher, they must watch for his return, they must wait for
further light.

Chapter seventeen is the real Lord's prayer. In this deeply moving
experience he prays: first for himself (1-5); for these disciples (6-19);
and for the whole world — all believers in all ages (20-26).

(6) *In Gethsemane* (Mark 14:26, 32-42; Matthew 26:30, 36-46; Luke
22:39-46; John 18:1) — The last event in the life of Jesus on this momentous day was his experience in the Garden of Gethsemane. On the
way to Gethsemane they crossed the brook Kedron, now swollen with
winter rains and tinged red with the blood of animals slain for the
sacrifices of the Passover feast. Gethsemane, a garden of olive trees,
was a favorite retreat of Jesus not more than half mile directly east of
the Golden Gate. The present garden, about seventy yards square, is
enclosed by a wall and contains about seventy-five gnarled olive trees
which present-day guides erroneously claim are the same trees under
which Jesus suffered that night.

Reaching the gate of the garden, Jesus left eight of his eleven disciples (Judas was no longer with them) to watch. He then took Peter, James and John and went a little distance inside. The strange and awful experience awaiting him caused him to be "amazed and sore troubled." "My soul is exceedingly sorrowful even unto death." Commanding these three to abide there and watch, he himself went on a little further and fell on his face and prayed. These disciples could hear his cry of anguish, "O my Father, if it be possible let this cup pass away from me: nevertheless not as I will but as thou wilt." As he suffered his three friends, weary in body, fell asleep. He had counted on them for comfort and sympathy, but they failed him. Arising he went to them and said to Peter, "What, could ye not watch with me one hour?" He went back to his lonely retreat and prayed again. Then he came a second time to find his friends once more asleep. This time they were greatly embarrassed and knew not how to answer him. Still a third time he retreated and prayed again "using the same words." Returning to them he said, "Sleep on now and take your rest: behold the hour is at hand, and the Son of Man is betrayed unto the hands of sinners." He had won his victory, but without their help.

Even as he spoke to them he saw the torches of the company led by Judas coming up the hillside to the garden. He knew the purpose of their coming. He then said to his disciples, "Arise, let us be going: behold, he is at hand that betrayeth me." The four of them went immediately to the gate to join the eight other disciples. It was now midnight or later. His enemies had come to take him.

[1]Stalker, *The Life of Jesus Christ,* p. 116.
[2]Smith, *Our Lord's Earthly Life,* p. 353.
[3]Robertson, *Class Lectures.*
[4]Shepard, *The Christ of the Gospels,* p. 544.

*Chapter IX*

## REJECTION AND DEATH

1. Friday, The Dark Day. 2. Jesus "Tasting Death for Every Man." 3. Victim and Victor. 4. Arrest. 5. Legal Conspiracies. 6. Before Annas. 7. Caiaphas and The Sanhedrin. 8. Peter's Denials. 9. Before the Sanhedrin Again. 10. Illegalities in the Ecclesiastical Trials. 11. The End of Judas. 12. Before Pilate. 13. Before Herod Antipas. 14. Before Pilate Again. 15. Illegalities in the Civil Trials. 16. Further Indignities. 17. The Act of Crucifixion. 18. Via Dolorosa. 19. The First Three Hours on the Cross. 20. The Three Hours of Darkness. 21. All Nature Speaks. 22. The Burial of His Body.

# Rejection and Death

## 1. Friday, The Dark Day.

Friday of the passion week was the last day of the earthly life of our Lord. It was a day of darkness, a day that witnessed the supreme tragedy of the ages. On this day humanity sank to its lowest depths and exhibited a depravity and degradation never approached before or afterwards. On this day the immortal Son of God suffered as no man before or since could ever suffer. It was the "Tragedy of the Ages," and yet this tragedy is the supreme victory of all time.

Thursday and Friday merged into one long day in which Jesus had no rest. His arrest at the gate of Gethsemane took place approximately around midnight. His so-called trials began almost immediately and lasted the remainder of the night. These trials were in six stages and were not completed before six or seven o'clock Friday morning. With the surrender of Pilate, Jesus was in the hands of his enemies, so they began at once the march out to Calvary to consummate their vile deed as early as possible. He was placed on the cross about nine o'clock in the morning. By the middle of the afternoon he was dead. His friends, with the permission of Pilate, removed his body from the cross, bathed it and wrapped it in clean linen for burial. Nearby was a tomb into which he was tenderly placed before six o'clock, which was the beginning of the Sabbath day.

## 2. Jesus "Tasting Death for Every Man."

It will be well to consider briefly the feelings of Jesus as he faced the experiences just ahead of him. Because he was the Son of God we are apt to forget that he was also a man and thus could suffer like all other men. We sometimes hesitate to think that he had any natural shrinking from death. Let us remember that he was still young, only thirty-three years old, and was in the full vigor of manhood. It is not irreverent to assume that he did not want to die. His death was accompanied by terrible experiences. He was betrayed by one of his own intimate friends; he was denied by another; he was not only rejected but was publicly repudiated by his own nation; he was deserted by everyone, even his own disciples. "He was terribly alone. . . . The whole world was against Him — Jerusalem panting for his life with passionate hate. . . . Not one of His apostles, not even John, was in the least aware of the real situation, or able to be the confidant of His thoughts. This was one of the bitterest drops in His cup. He felt, as no other person has ever felt, the necessity of living on in the world after death."[1] Humanly speaking he was utterly alone. And yet he was not alone. His Father was with him, and this fact kept fresh by constant prayer and fellowship, sustained him in his sufferings.

### 3. Victim and Victor.

It is customary for us to think more of what happened to Jesus during these days than what Jesus was achieving in his suffering and death. It is but natural for us to sympathize with him, and this is good, but we must get the full picture. It is easy to look upon him as a poor, defeated, helpless victim circumscribed by the cleverness of his enemies, caught in the meshes, doomed to death — a victim to be pitied. Instinctively we find ourselves wishing we might intervene to rescue him from his cruel fate. In a sense he was a victim, a "sheep led to the slaughter." But this is only a part of the picture. Jesus did surrender to his enemies and allowed himself to be their victim, but he did this consciously and purposefully. He chose this course, he knew fully what he was doing, and he knew that in so doing he was to achieve his divine purpose. He was not only their victim; he was the victor. In all these harrowing experiences he was the only calm composed person in the great throng who participated in this tragedy. He moved through all the scenes with a composure, a serenity and dignity that is the marvel of the ages. He was master of every situation and he achieved his purpose. He surrendered to them voluntarily and played his part knowing that in this he was to be the real victor.

### 4. Arrest (Mark 14:43-52; Matthew 26:47-56; Luke 22:47-53; John 18:2-12).

The official arrest took place at the Garden of Gethsemane after Jesus had gained his victory there. With his eleven disciples he went to meet the crowd which had come to take him. This "great multitude" was a vulgar crowd made up of the Levitical police of the temple, some of the Sanhedrin, a company of soldiers and others who joined them out of curiosity. They came "with lanterns, torches and weapons" to arrest one man who was unarmed and without defenders.

They were led by Judas Iscariot who had left the upper room several hours earlier after he had been publicly identified as the traitor. He had gone to the enemies of Jesus with whom he had already bargained for his delivery into their hands. Being familiar with the habits of

Jesus he had correctly surmised that he would go to his retreat for prayer. Consequently he led the crowd to the place and then, as he had agreed, he identified Jesus for the soldiers. For this foul purpose he used the usual sign of discipleship — the kiss. He approached the Master saying, "Hail, Rabbi" and kissed him repeatedly. Jesus recoiled at this infamy and stepping back cried, "Judas, betrayest thou the Son of man with a kiss?"

In his account John states that Jesus went immediately to this company asking "Whom seek ye?" When they told him, "Jesus of Nazareth," he answered them, "I am he." They stepped backward and fell to the ground. The strength, courage and conquering appearance of such a man overwhelmed them. Even here Jesus was in command.

The disciples were bewildered and behaved badly in this crisis. Peter, remembering the prediction of Jesus, and determined to keep his pledge, had secured an old sword. At this juncture, he rashly attempted to defend the Lord and wounded a soldier. Knowing the danger of a riot Jesus took charge of the situation, reprimanded Peter for his foolish act, healed the wounded man and then surrendered to the mob. He allowed them to bind him and lead him away, but not before stating that he was surrendering voluntarily and purposefully. They could never have seized him except that it was divinely planned. His last word to them was "this is your hour and the power of darkness." Then all the disciples left him and fled. He was alone in the power of his enemies at last!

5. *Legal Conspiracies.*

Before tracing the experiences of Jesus in the six stages of his so-called trials we should comment on the nature of these trials to which he was subjected. There is always the danger that inexperienced students may assume that these trials were legitimate and that Jesus was guilty of some crime which merited punishment. But such was not the case. These trials were not legitimate, honest processes to establish the guilt or the innocence of the defendant. They were never intended to be fair, impartial efforts. They were legal conspiracies engineered by his enemies, not to secure a just verdict, but to secure the condemnation of Jesus. The Jews were determined to kill Jesus and these trials were intended only to provide a legal justification for their designs. As we shall point out later, every trial was filled with glaring illegalities.

The trials of Jesus had two general aspects, ecclesiastical and civil, because the Jews under Roman rule were permitted to hold only trials of a religious nature. All civil trials were handled by Roman authorities. The Jews could not assess the death penalty; this privilege was retained by the Romans. Since Jesus was a religious leader and the charges made against him by the Jews were of this nature, he had to appear before the Sanhedrin. These ecclesiastical trials were before three groups: Annas, the Sanhedrin before daylight, the Sanhedrin again after sunrise. The civil trials likewise were in three stages: before Pilate, before Herod Antipas, and before Pilate the second time. Thus he passed through six hearings.

6. *Before Annas* (John 18:12-14, 19-23).

Strictly speaking the appearance of Jesus before Annas was not a trial. Annas was an ex-high priest and had no authority. Furthermore what took place there was of no special significance. The chief idea seems to have been the notion of the Jews that Annas might say or do something that would help their case before the Sanhedrin, since Annas was the father-in-law of Caiaphas, high priest at the time. Then too, it would take some time to assemble the Sanhedrin. Jesus was arrested around one o'clock Friday morning, evidently earlier and easier than the Jews anticipated, and they had not called the Sanhedrin together. To dispatch messengers to all the seventy members who were asleep in different sections of the city and to get the members of the court together would require about two hours. In order to kill time while these were being assembled they brought Jesus before Annas.

Annas had to recognize Jesus but since he had no plan of procedure he asked him a vague question about his disciples and his teachings. Jesus replied that Annas should ask those who had heard him, and presumably knew what he taught. In anger an officer smote Jesus with his hand. This was both an insult and an indignity to which no defendant should have been subjected.

7. *Caiaphas and the Sanhedrin* (Mark 14:53-65; Matthew 26:57-68; Luke 22:54, 63-65; John 18:24).

It may be assumed that the Sanhedrin assembled and were ready for the appearance of the defendant by three or four o'clock Friday morning. They met in an upper room overlooking an interior court.

The scope of our studies will not permit a detailed account of the proceedings in any of these so-called trials. The student should read carefully the gospel narrative for these details. We should note, however, several important items. They secured false witnesses to testify against him; these disagreed and the Jews were becoming frantic when finally two of them agreed on the statement of Jesus about the temple; Jesus maintained a dignified silence and Caiaphas, sensing that their scheme was about to collapse, put Jesus on oath to state whether or not he was the Christ. Jesus, of course, replied that he was the Christ. Then in jubilation they cried, "We have no need of further witnesses; Ye have heard the blasphemy!" So they condemned him on this count to be worthy of death. After the vote was taken, assuming that he was now in their possession they began to mock him. Now the pent-up sea of hatred burst loose. They spat in his face, struck him with sticks, covered his face and mocked him. "With uncontrolled glee and abandon like a group of hoodlums, these doctors of divinity insulted Jesus. Such a scene of vulgar brutality, enacted by and with the approval of the dignified Sanhedrin, was worthy of the lowest criminals of the underworld."[2] We can not conceive what insult and dishonor this must have been to his pure, sensitive and regal mind.

8. *Peter's Denials* (Mark 14:66-72; Matthew 26:58, 69-75; Luke 22:54-62; John 18:15-18, 25-27).

While Jesus was before the Sanhedrin, a group had gathered in the open court down below to await the outcome of the trial. In this group was Peter who had followed "afar off," and another disciple, John. To relieve the chill of the early morning a fire was built out in the court. Peter warmed himself by this fire and kept company with the enemies of Christ. He was nervous, filled with fear at what might happen, yet he wanted to be there. It was during this period of waiting that he denied his Lord three different times, as Jesus had predicted. The last denial was accompanied by cursing and swearing. "And immediately while he yet spake the cock crew." Overwhelmed by the realization of his great sin Peter was beside himself. In the meantime the trial upstairs had ended and Jesus was brought down through the crowd where Peter stood. Jesus turning looked upon Peter. He said nothing but that look broke the heart of Peter "and he went out and wept bitterly." What must have been his remorse! He had done what he swore not to do. He had denied his best friend, the Son of God. He felt now that it was all over and there was no hope for him!

9. *Before the Sanhedrin Again* (Mark 15:1; Matthew 27:1; Luke 22:66-71).

The Jews must wait till after dawn so the Sanhedrin could meet again. Their first session was illegal since no session of this body could be held except during daylight hours. While they waited Jesus was again subjected to vile mocking and abuse by the Jews. They enjoyed their hour of vengeance, and filled it with insults and injuries to their innocent victim. After daylight the Sanhedrin met again simply to approve formally their decision made during the night. It was a short session and their work was done. This ecclesiastical session had accomplished their purpose.

*10. Illegalities in the Ecclesiastical Trials.*

To understand what a farce this so-called trial before the Sanhedrin was we may note a few of the flagrant illegalities in it. (1) Jesus was arrested without a formal charge. (2) He was rushed to trial without an opportunity to defend his case. (3) They brought paid witnesses who bore false testimony. (4) They asked for no testimony in behalf of Jesus. (5) They put him on oath to condemn himself. (6) They allowed no discussion of the charge of blasphemy. (7) The time of meeting (before dawn) was illegal. (8) They had no authority to pronounce the sentence of death.

*11. The End of Judas* (Matthew 27:3-10; Acts 1:18-19).

It was probably early on Friday morning that the last tragic act in the career of Judas Iscariot took place. He had collected his thirty pieces of silver and had carried out his agreement to deliver Jesus into the hands of the Jews. But this didn't close the case. He was seized with remorse as he saw Jesus mocked and abused by his enemies. Might he not even yet cancel his infamous contract? Waiting for an opportunity he rushed up to the chief priests and elders with the cry: "I have sinned in that I betrayed innocent blood." They brushed him aside with the statement, "What is that to us?" They were satisfied with their bargain and so far as they were concerned the matter was closed. Hoping for some relief of conscience Judas cast the money at their feet in the sanctuary. He then "went out and hanged himself." They gathered up the coins and finally decided, since they were the price of blood and could not be put into the temple treasury, to buy with them a little plot of land south of the city to be used as a burial place for Gentiles. The place came to be known as Akeldama, "the field of blood." Thus Judas came to his tragic end and "went unto his own place."

*12. Before Pilate* (Mark 15:1-5; Matthew 27:2, 11-14; Luke 23:1-5; John 18:28-38).

The Jews having already secured the verdict they wanted from the Sanhedrin, would gladly have proceeded at once to carry out their program of death. But the Roman law did not permit them to do this. They must now get the consent of the Roman governor before they could crucify Jesus. Consequently they must now go before Pilate, the governor of Judea, and persuade him to turn their prisoner over to them for death.

They proceeded at once to the palace of the governor, taking their prisoner and a motley crowd along with them. The trial evidently was held in the open court in front of the palace. We can not deal here with all the details, but we should notice their effort to get Pilate to confirm their sentence without examination; Pilate refused to do this so they gave a long list of charges against their prisoner. Chief among these were that he perverted the nation, he refused to pay tribute and that he set himself up as a king. Pilate was not interested in the first two but would want to know more of his claims to be king. He took Jesus inside and examined him privately. Being persuaded that this man was innocent he brought him back before the Jews and pronounced him not guilty of the charges. This did not satisfy this crowd of angry Jews, and Pilate, knowing their obduracy, was afraid. Then an idea came to him which he hoped might save him from having to yield to the demands of the Jews. Jesus was from Galilee and thus was under the jurisdiction of Herod Antipas, the tetrarch of Galilee and Perea. Herod was in Jerusalem for the Passover and could be made to pass judgment in this troublesome case. Therefore Pilate told the Jews that they must take their prisoner to Herod who was staying at the palace of the Maccabees in the city.

*13. Before Herod Antipas* (Luke 23:6-12).

With growing anger and determination the Jews now rushed their victim to Herod, who had already beheaded John the Baptist and who had often desired to see Jesus. Now he had the opportunity and relished it. He regarded him as a miracle worker, a showman on the level of a singer or dancer. His only concern was to have Jesus perform a miracle for his amusement. He questioned him in many words, but Jesus maintained a dignified silence. Evidently Herod took him to be stupid and unable to perform a miracle, so he ignored all the accusations of the Jews against him, threw an old mantle over his shoulders and sent him back to Pilate. In no sense can this be regarded as a serious trial. It was only one step in the disgraceful treatment of an innocent man.

*14. Before Pilate Again* (Mark 15:6-15; Matthew 27:15-26; Luke 23:13-25; John 18:39-19:16).

It was still early in the morning when the mob got back to the palace of Pilate. Their patience had reached the breaking point. They were in no mood for argument. In dismay Pilate saw them return and knew that he must now meet the issue. The events of this last stage are longer and more important than any of the previous ones.

Pilate remembered that it was customary at this feast to set free some prisoner. He now conceived the idea of releasing Jesus according to this custom. But this failed because they would be satisfied with nothing less than the death of Jesus. They therefore demanded the release of a noted robber, named Barabbas, but the death of Jesus. Taken aback Pilate asked, "What then shall I do unto him whom ye call king of the Jews?" Then came the cry, "Crucify him." Pilate's effort to avert this resulted only in more vehement cries. "They cried out exceedingly saying, Let him be crucified."

John tells us that at this point Pilate again took Jesus inside for a private examination. This interview with Jesus was the real crisis for Pilate. Jesus tried to save him and Pilate recognized the innocence of his prisoner and made one more effort to be a man and do what was right. However, the Jews, anticipating this had saved one last weapon which they knew would prevail. Their reply to Pilate's suggestion of clemency for Jesus was "If thou release this man, thou are not Caesar's friend; every one that maketh himself a king speaketh against Caesar." Pilate could not afford to be reported to Caesar because of his grievous maladministration. It meant that Caesar would depose him. The Jews knew this and with it they clinched their demand for the death of Jesus. Pilate surrendered Jesus to them and in so doing displayed a feebleness of character that has earned for him the contempt of all respectable men. Ascending the judgment seat he pointed to Jesus and tried to taunt them with the words, "Behold your King!" The Jews replied, "Away with him, away with him, crucify him!" "Shall I crucify your King?" asked Pilate. The Jews then reached the depth of their degradation with the assertion, "We have no king but Caesar."

Knowing that he had consented to the crucifixion of an innocent man, Pilate called for a basin of water and washed his hands before the multitude saying, "I am innocent of the blood of this righteous man, see ye to it." Their response was, "His blood be on us and our children." This reply was the "renouncement of their birthright, the abandonment of their destiny." Pilate and the Jews both were guilty of this crime.

### 15. Illegalities in the Civil Trials.

Here again we find numerous violations of all the recognized principles of court procedure. The charges preferred against Jesus before Pilate never mentioned blasphemy, the one on which the Sanhedrin had condemned him. Again no witnesses for Jesus were called. Pilate really acquitted the prisoner at the first trial before him, but instead of releasing him passed him on to Herod Antipas. Likewise Herod found no crime against him. Pilate again found him innocent but turned him over to his accusers. Jesus was never given any sort of protection against indignities, was rushed from one official to the other with inexcusable haste. Finally he was taken immediately from Pilate's last hearing to be crucified. The entire proceedings constitute one of the most disgraceful legal farces in all history.

### 16. Further Indignities (Mark 15:16-19; Matthew 27:27-30).

At last the enemies of Jesus had gained their objective and now could proceed with the plan for his death. As Pilate withdrew after his cowardly surrender the mob shouted in glee. Barabbas, the infamous thief was freed, but Jesus, the innocent victim, was turned over to his enemies. They were now free to do as they pleased. The smell of blood was in the air. Vile passions were released and the scene that followed is one from which every respectable person recoils in horror. This time the brutal Roman soldiers were allowed to abuse and villify the one soon to be crucified. "So the soldiers took Jesus away and scourged Him. The scourge was a whip with several thongs, each loaded with acorn-shaped balls of lead, with sharp pieces of bone or spikes. Stripped of His clothes, His hands tied to a column or stake with His back bent, the victim was lashed with the flagels by six lictors, who plied these instruments of torture with severity almost to the point of death of the prisoner. Each stroke cut into the quivering flesh, until the veins and sometimes the entrails were laid bare. Often the scourge struck the face and knocked out the eyes and teeth. Scourging almost always ended in fainting and sometimes even in death.

"In the case of Jesus, it was made all the worse by the period of mockery which followed. Over His lacerated body, they cast a purple robe — provided by Herod — and pressed down on His head a plaited crown of thorns. In His right hand, they placed a reed for a sceptre, and then made Him the subject of jesting, striking Him insultingly with rods on His thorn-crowned head, and with the palms of their hands in His face, and on His lacerated body. Kneeling down to Him, they exclaimed in derision: 'Hail, King of the Jews.' Most nauseating of all the insulting treatment, they repeatedly spat in His face."[2]

## 17. The Act of Crucifixion.

It will be well at this point to consider briefly the act of crucifixion as a means of killing criminals. This horrible form of capital punishment was not invented by the Romans. It had been devised and employed by the Egyptians, Babylonians, Phoenicians and other Oriental people for many centuries. When the Romans conquered Palestine they continued the use of this form of punishment, but only in the case of slaves and the most vicious criminals. Thus crucifixion carried with it a stigma. It was a part of the humiliation of Jesus that he should be made to suffer this particular form of death. It identified him with the lowest class of criminals.

Crucifixion was an unspeakably horrible means of death. Cicero in condemning it said, "Let it never come near the body of a Roman citizen; nay, not even near his thoughts, or eyes, or ears." Victims of crucifixion were suspended on a cross placed well above the ground. The cross was then a crude and cruel implement invested with horror and disgrace. Today we employ it as a symbol of honor and adoration because Jesus has transformed it. It consisted of two rough beams or logs nailed together near the top of the upright beam which was placed in the ground. The victim was usually stripped of all clothing, these garments falling to the lot of the executioners. The upright was placed securely in the earth standing some ten feet above the ground. The horizontal beam was placed on the ground, the victim was laid down with arms extended on this crossbar to which they were fastened with cords and afterwards by nails driven through the palms. The bar was then raised to its appointed place near the top of the upright where it was securely fastened. The body of the victim was left suspended by the arms. The feet were then fastened to the upright by the use of long spikes driven through the balls of the feet. Thus suspended the victim was left to hang in physical agony until death mercifully released him from suffering. This fact constituted its horror. Since no vital organs were affected the poor victim lingered in the throes of the most excruciating pain. Death came slowly; the victim often lived as long as two or three full days. Throbbing with pain, burned with fever and tortured by thirst, these unfortunate men often prayed for the relief which only death could furnish. This was the form of death awaiting the Son of God.

*18. Via Dolorosa* (Mark 15:20-23; Matthew 27:31-34; Luke 23:26-33; John 19:16-17).

One of the added indignities of crucifixion was the custom which permitted the exhibiting of the victim in a public procession out to the place of death. Naturally the Jews would insist on this as it would add to the humiliation of Jesus. This march out to Calvary is known as the Via Dolorosa (the way of sorrow).

The place of the crucifixion was a hill outside the walls of Jerusalem about a quarter of a mile north of the Damascus gate. It was long held that the death of Jesus took place inside the city walls at a site on which the Church of the Holy Sepulchre now stands. It is generally agreed now however, that the little hill to the north of the city, known as Gordon's Calvary, is the spot which meets all the requirements of the gospel records. The route of this procession would lead from the heart of the city where Jesus was surrendered by Pilate, out the Damascus gate, then to Calvary. This site, Golgotha (the place of a skull), can be recognized today because of the crude rock formation which viewed from a little distance bears an unmistakable resemblance to a skull.

The Jews had anticipated a victory over Pilate and thus were ready to proceed with their plans. A crude cross had been secured and the Roman soldiers were there to do their work. The procession formed. It would be led by Jesus and the two thieves who were to be crucified with him, each bearing his cross. Immediately behind the victims were the Roman soldiers, then the Jews followed by a great mob of people who delighted in such a scene. John the Apostle seems to have been there and reported to a company of women followers of Jesus among whom were Mary the mother of Jesus and Mary Magdalene. Seeing what was to take place these friends joined the procession out to Golgotha.

Two incidents of the journey to the place of death are recorded in the gospels: the commandeering of Simon to carry the cross of Jesus, and the lamentation of the women. Tradition asserts, though it is not stated in the gospels, that Jesus, exhausted by all the harrowing experiences of the past two days, and having had no sleep or rest during the long night, sank down under the weight of his cross. The soldiers recognized his condition and looking for some one to bear his cross, spied a man named Simon from Cyrene, a province of Africa, coming in the gate on his way to the temple for morning prayer. Upon orders from the soldiers Simon, perhaps reluctantly, took up the cross of the Saviour. At the moment these orders were annoying and humiliating to Simon and yet later he could be thankful since this was his introduction to the Saviour. He could never forget his walk with him, and no doubt counted this service a high honor all his life.

Probably at the point when the procession had stopped for Simon to assume his burden for Jesus some of the women in the company bewailed and lamented the fate of Jesus. The reply of Jesus to them was that they should not weep for him because his suffering would soon be over, but rather to weep for themselves and their children since their sufferings were hardly begun.

At last they reached the appointed place. In order to stupefy and dull the senses the poor victims to be crucified were offered a drink of wine which contained a drug. It was given to Jesus and he tasted it but would not drink it. There was but one reason for this refusal. He wanted to do his work on the cross in full possession of all his faculties.

*19. The First Three Hours on the Cross* (Mark 15:24-32; Matthew 27:35-44; Luke 23:33-43; John 19:18-27).

Jesus was placed on the cross about nine o'clock in the morning. During the three hours before noon a number of events transpired: Jesus uttered three sayings, the soldiers cast lots for his garments, the inscription was placed on the cross, the multitudes scoffed, the soldiers and others derided Jesus, and the penitent thief was saved.

Pilate, as an act of revenge on the Jews, had an inscription made to be placed on the perpendicular bar of the cross just above the head of Jesus. The words, "This is Jesus the king of the Jews" written in Hebrew, Greek and Latin were thus displayed so that all could read them. Angrily the Jews protested and besought Pilate to change this inscription to read, "He said I am King of the Jews." With a sneer Pilate answered, "What I have written I have written."

The cross on which Jesus was placed stood between the two crosses bearing the thieves. "And they that passed by railed on him, wagging their heads and saying, Thou that destroyest the temple and buildest it again in three days, save thyself: if thou art the Son of God come down from the cross." Then it was that one of the elders unwittingly uttered one of the profoundest truths in all the scriptures. "He saved others;

himself he can not save." The mocking multitude made sport of him as he hung there.

The gospel writers have recorded seven sayings of Jesus on the cross. The first of these came in the early stages of the crucifixion. As the nails were driven through the hands of victims they usually shrieked and cursed. Not so with Jesus. Not a word of complaint, no plea for mercy, but instead the prayer, "Father, forgive them for they know not what they do." In his life time he had taught his disciples to pray for those that despitefully used them. He practiced his precept in his first words on the cross. His heart went out to these poor, ignorant, sinful men who were committing the crime.

Having finished their job the soldiers now exercised their right of casting dice for the garments of Jesus (turban, sandals, cape, girdle and his seamless robe made and presented to him by devout friends). Even the soldiers did not want to rend this beautiful robe so they cast lots to see who should own it.

One of the thieves joined in the jeering of the crowd as they derided Jesus, "Art not thou the Christ? Save thyself and us." The other thief recognizing the innocence of Jesus, rebuked his fellow-thief and defended Jesus. As the Saviour heard these words, he caught the eye of his friend and smiled his appreciation. The poor thief then piteously cried out, "Jesus, remember me when thou comest in thy kingdom." It was in response to this plea that Jesus spoke the second words from the cross: "Today, shalt thou be with me in Paradise."

The company of several faithful women had come in the procession to the place of execution. "At the foot of the cross they took up their station in the ministry of waiting love. Here was the courage of abandon, and devotion stronger than death. They came to minister to him in his dying hour."[3] Disregarding his own physical anguish, Jesus with infinite tenderness gave his attention to Mary, his mother. With these good women was John "that disciple whom Jesus loved." Speaking first to his mother he said, "Woman, behold thy son!" Then to John, "Behold, thy mother." He wanted his mother in good hands when he was gone. John in his gospel says that "from that hour the disciple took her to his own home." To save her from the horror of these last hours John took her immediately from the scene.

20. *The Three Hours of Darkness* (Mark 15:33-37; Matthew 27:45-50; Luke 23:44-46; John 19:28-30).

The first three hours ended at noon. It was then that a thick darkness settled down over the earth, though the Syrian sun should have been at its brightest at this hour. As this strange darkness came the multitudes were startled and fear possessed them. This must be the power of God.

This supernatural darkness lasted until three o'clock in the afternoon when the last of the agony on the cross had ceased and Jesus was dead. During these last three hours Jesus uttered four other sayings. As the awful darkness came over the scene a cry of desolation broke from his lips. "My God, My God, why hast thou forsaken me?" Jesus felt he was deserted. His race had rejected him, his disciples had fled, nature had left him in darkness and now apparently his Father also had forsaken him. The spiritual presence of God seemed to have gone. God had turned his face and Jesus felt it. The answer is John 3:16. In truth it was necessary for Jesus to suffer alone to do his redemptive work. In this heartbreaking cry he reached the depths of his suffering, desolation and death. This suffering was not physical; it was his redemption of the race. He descended to the depths, met Satan and conquered him. This was the climax of all his sufferings. Did God forsake him? Didn't he love him any more? Truly the Father was never so near to him nor so well pleased in his beloved Son as in this hour of supreme suffering and devotion. Jesus had "tasted death for every man" and had conquered.

The fifth cry of Jesus, "I thirst," was one of physical anguish. One of the horrible accompaniments of crucifixion was the awful thirst which tortured the victim. The Saviour was human and like any other man suffered this anguish.

The sixth cry was one of victory. The suffering was over. He had overcome the devil and was not afraid. Victoriously he cried out, "It is finished."

As the hours dragged on the darkness began to dissipate. In peaceful resignation Jesus calmly repeated the words of the Psalmist, "Father, into thy hands I commend my spirit." At last having finished his work "the unresting Saviour took his rest." Life had left his body. His spirit had returned to the Father.

The "Tragedy of the Ages" was finished. We may now reverently ask, What caused the death of Jesus? Within six hours after he was placed on the cross he was dead, whereas victims usually lived for two or three days, dying by degrees. The answer is that he died of a broken heart or a ruptured blood vessel. Since no vital organs were affected crucifixion did not result in immediate death. In an experience of intense emotional suffering the blood vessels rupture and death ensues. Nearly a century ago Dr. Strauss advanced this explanation of the death of Jesus, which is all but universally accepted today. The burden of the sin of the world — past, present and future — broke his heart. He bore the sin of the world, and it killed him.

*21. All Nature Speaks* (Mark 15:38-41; Matthew 27:51-56; Luke 23:45-49).

In addition to the darkness which enveloped the scene from noon until three o'clock there were other phenomena which accompanied the death of Jesus. The beautiful and exquisite veil which separated the Holy Place from the Holy of Holies in the temple was rent from top to bottom. This miracle symbolized the fact that whereas up to this time only the priests could enter the Holy of Holies into the actual presence of God, now all men could come to him. There is no longer any veil to intervene.

The records tell also of the earthquake, "And the earth did quake; and the rocks were rent; and the tombs were opened; and many bodies of the saints that had fallen asleep were raised; and coming forth out of the tombs after his resurrection they entered into the holy city and appeared unto many."

These portents made such a deep impression on both the disciples and others that they were filled with great fear. Never had such things occurred. Surely God was in this. The Roman Centurion, who probably was the officer in charge of the crucifixion, expressed his own feelings, "Truly this was the son of God." Luke adds that "all the multitudes that came together to this sight, when they beheld the things that were done, returned smiting their breasts." Mark and Matthew state that a large company of disciples and women who had followed him in Galilee were there, beholding from afar what had taken place. These were deeply grieved and sorrowful. So far as they could see this was the end!

*22. The Burial of His Body* (Mark 15:42-46; Matthew 27:57-60; Luke 23:50-54; John 19:31-42).

The Jews had a law that the victims of crucifixion could not remain on the cross on their Sabbath day. Since the Jewish Sabbath began at six o'clock on Friday afternoon, it was necessary for the body of Jesus and those of the two thieves to be removed by this hour. In case the men were not dead by this time the usual practice was to crush their

bones with a heavy mallet to bring death at once. This probably was
done in the case of the thieves. But this was not necessary with Jesus
since they found upon examination that he was already dead. However,
to be absolutely sure a soldier pierced his side with a spear. As he withdrew the spear it was followed by a gush of "blood and water," —
clotted blood and clear fluid — proving the theory that he died of a
broken heart. The disposal of the bodies of those who were crucified
was an old problem. In most instances these victims were outcasts and
had no friends or loved ones to claim their bodies for honorable burial.
A special field for the burial of such victims had now been secured and
but for the intervention of friends the body of Jesus would have been
placed in this field. Joseph, a friend of Jesus, a rich man who lived
in the nearby village of Arimathea, and who was a devout man "who
was looking for the kingdom of God" asked Pilate for the body of
Jesus. Pilate, being convinced that Jesus was dead, granted this request.
Joseph had a new tomb "wherein no man had yet lain" — his own
family tomb. This was near the place of crucifixion and evidently was
one of unusual elegance.

John tells us that another also came to assist in this gracious errand.
He was Nicodemus, the man who first came to Jesus by night for his
memorable conference three years earlier. He had never forgotten Jesus
and at this time wanted to show his loyalty and his devotion to him.
Joseph and Nicodemus, therefore, took possession of the body of Jesus.
After the custom of the Jews, they bathed the body, embalmed it in
spices which Nicodemus had furnished, wrapped it in a clean linen
cloth, and laid it in Joseph's new tomb. This tomb "which had been
hewn out in the rock" was a vault or small room excavated in one of
the hillsides nearby. The door leading to the room was suspended on
sockets so that it would swing outward. To insure privacy the door
could be fastened or "sealed," and for added protection a stone could
be rolled up against the door. In this tomb the body of Jesus was placed
on late Friday afternoon. Though Jesus was dead and buried there
was a lingering fear and anxiety among both the Jews and the Roman
soldiers. To be sure that nothing should happen they took extra pre-
cautions. A guard was stationed by the tomb, the door was sealed with
the Roman seal and a large stone was rolled against the door. As the
Sabbath came the mob scattered, the soldiers went their way, the
Jews returned to the city probably to celebrate their triumph, and a few
timid believers slipped away bewildered by all that had happened
that day.

All the synoptic gospels tell of the faithfulness of the group of women who had come out of Galilee and had seen the crucifixion. Mary Magdalene and Mary the mother of Jesus were two of these who watched carefully and perhaps assisted in the burial of the Saviour. "They followed after, and beheld the tomb, and how his body was laid." Matthew states that "they sat over against the sepulchre." These devoted followers were faithful to the end.

[1]Stalker, *Life of Christ*, p. 119.
[2]Shepard, *The Christ of the Gospels*, p. 577.
[3]Ibid., pp. 589-590.
[4]Ibid., p. 600.

*Chapter X*

## VICTORY OVER DEATH

1. Close of Jesus' Earthly Life. 2. Despondency of the Disciples. 3. Importance of the Resurrection. 4. Happenings at the Tomb. 5. Visit of the Women. 6. The First Task of the Risen Lord. 7. Appearances the First Day. (1) To Mary Magdalene. (2) To the Other Women. (3) To the Two Disciples Enroute to Emmaus. (4) To Simon Peter. (5) To the Disciples at Night. 8. Subsequent Appearances. (1) To the Disciples Next Sunday Night. (2) To the Seven at the Lake. (3) To the Five Hundred in Galilee. (4) To James, the Brother of Jesus. (5) To the Disciples Again. (6) To the Disciples the Last Time. 9. Attempted Explanations. (1) The Swoon Theory. (2) The Fraud Theory. (3) The Mistake Theory. (4) The Vision Theory. 10. Positive Proofs. (1) Documentary Evidence. (2) The Testimony of Witnesses. (3) The Change in the Disciples. 11. The Significance of the Resurrection.

## CHAPTER X
# Victory Over Death

### 1. Close of Jesus' Earthly Life.

This chapter will be devoted to the closing scenes in the earthly life of our Lord. Most of these scenes were enacted in Jerusalem or its environs, though some reached up into Galilee. Our Lord was crucified on Friday, was buried Friday afternoon, and remained in the tomb until his resurrection early Sunday morning. He appeared to his disciples several times this "first day" and appeared to believers again at intervals for a period of forty days. Finally he ascended from the presence of his followers on the mount opposite Jerusalem, to end his earthly career. All four gospels give accounts of the happenings of these forty days. These records constitute one of the most valuable possessions of the Christian faith. Without these we would know nothing of the victory over death which was achieved by our Lord.

### 2. Despondency of the Disciples.

We should begin our study of these events by trying to place ourselves in the position of the disciples. Fortunately we know already that Jesus was raised from the dead. It is hard, therefore, for us to visualize the experiences of his followers after his arrest, crucifixion and death. We must remember that they did not understand all that was taking place. They watched as he died on the cross; they saw his limp body taken from the cross and placed in the sepulchre; they grieved at his death. But not one of them even dreamed that he would come forth alive from the grave. He was dead, and "dead men stay dead." Theirs was a double sorrow. They grieved in the tragic rejection and death of their best friend whom they really loved. But more than this they were bewildered by it all, their faith was in eclipse. If he were the Son of God how could this happen? He had failed. Death had conquered him. The kingdom was at an end. This meant that they were now the objects of derision and scorn. Friday, Saturday and part of Sunday were days of darkness and desolation for all who had believed on Jesus.

### 3. Importance of the Resurrection.

The supremely important question is, Was Jesus raised from the dead? Is the resurrection a fact? Everything depends on this. This is the fundamental tenet of Christianity. Other doctrines are important, but this one is absolutely essential.

The resurrection is the most amazing of all his miracles. Important as were all his other supernatural works this stands forth as the one of greatest significance. Frankly, Jesus staked everything on this. He asserted on several occasions that no sign should be given except this. If he did not rise again, he had failed; it was complete defeat and repudiation. If he did triumph over death, then he was all that he claimed to be, he and all his claims were vindicated. Because of the tremendous issues involved no other miracle has been so exhaustively considered and studied.

*4. Happenings at the Tomb* (Mark 16:1; Matthew 28:1-4).

Late Saturday afternoon the two Marys made a visit to the sepulchre where the body of Jesus was laid. Though they knew not what was to come, they remained loyal to him. They could be faithful even in the darkness. In two or three brief statements Matthew tells us what occurred on early Sunday morning. "And behold, there was a great earthquake; for an angel of the Lord descended from heaven, and came and rolled away the stone, and sat upon it. His appearance was as lightning, and his raiment white as snow: and for fear of him the watchers did quake and became as dead men." As the angels announced the appearance of Jesus in the flesh at the time of his birth, it is fitting that an angel should minister at his resurrection from the dead. Before daylight Jesus was brought forth from the tomb by the power of God. The guard and others were to come to the tomb at sunrise or afterwards only to find it empty.

At this point it may be well to speak briefly of the length of Jesus' stay in the tomb. There is much difference of opinion on this question and the arguments are long. Suffice it to say that it seems logical, in view of all the stated facts, to hold that he was in the tomb from late Friday afternoon until early Sunday morning. This view meets all the requirements made in the gospels.

*5. Visit of the Women* (Mark 16:2-8; Matthew 28:5-8; Luke 24:1-12; John 20:1-10).

The group of women came to the sepulchre before sunrise on Sunday morning, the first day of the week. Mary Magdalene hurriedly ran ahead, reached the tomb first and finding it open ran back to tell Peter and John. The other women came a little later, after sunrise. An angel appeared to them with a message to the disciples. Still later another party of women came and saw "two young men" dressed in white, who said to them, "Why seek ye the living among the dead? He is not here, but is risen." It must have been about 6:30 A.M. when Peter and John, having received the message, hurried to the sepulchre. John outran Peter and having reached the place stopped at the door, looked inside and considered what had taken place. Peter came, and with his usual impulsiveness, entered the tomb and saw "the linen cloths lying, and the napkin that was upon his head, not lying with the linen cloths, but rolled up in a place by itself." John then followed Peter inside "and he saw and believed." Apparently these two were the first upon whom the reality of the resurrection dawned. They then went back to their home.

### 6. The First Task of the Risen Lord.

It is customary, and perhaps natural, for students who have not placed themselves in the position of the disciples, to assume that they were expecting Jesus to be raised from the dead. But such was not the case. John states specifically, "as yet they knew not the scripture, that he must rise again from the dead." (20:9.) The truth is that no one expected this. The first great task of the risen Lord was to convince his own disciples that he was alive again. Once the Sanhedrin was skeptical; now the disciples are the skeptics. With this in mind we shall understand better the appearances of Jesus on this first day.

### 7. Appearances the First Day.

A careful study of all the records would indicate that Jesus appeared on five different occasions on that Sunday.

(1) *To Mary Magdalene* (Mark 16:9-11; John 20:11-18) — Mary Magdalene from whom Jesus had cast out the demons earlier in his ministry, proved to be one of his most loyal followers. She witnessed the crucifixion, watched as he was buried, came to the tomb on Saturday afternoon, and early Sunday morning came again. The tomb was empty and she wept, thinking that the grave had been robbed. Upon looking, however, she saw two angels who said, "Woman, why weepest thou?" Her reply was, "They have taken away my Lord, and I know not where they have laid him." Turning aside she saw a man standing there who also asked her why she wept. Supposing he was the keeper of the garden she bravely uttered words of great devotion and courage, "If thou hast borne him hence, tell me where thou hast laid him, and I will take him away." What words for a poor, frail woman! Jesus then spoke only one word — "Mary." The voice was

familiar! This was Jesus! He told her to go and tell his disciples. She did this with great enthusiasm, but they "disbelieved."

(2) *To the Other Women* (Matthew 28:9-15) — Another group of women came to the sepulchre, unaware of what had happened, and met the risen Lord who greeted them with the words, "All hail." They were convinced of his resurrection and worshiped him and at his command they went to tell "his brethren."

Matthew relates that by this time some of the guard had reported to the chief priests all the things that had happened. Forthwith a council was held to consider this distressing news. Their decision was to bribe the guards with large gifts of money to explain it all with the statement "his disciples came by night, and stole him away while we slept." This was a weak statement; how could they know this if they were asleep? Then the guards took the money and told the story as agreed.

(3) *To the Two Disciples Enroute to Emmaus* (Mark 16:12-13; Luke 24:13-32) — The student will want to read carefully this classic story for its beauty and significance. Cleopas and his companion lived in Emmaus, a little village not far from Jerusalem, and were now on the way home after the disappointing outcome of Christ's ministry. Note the sadness in their hearts, the tactful approach of the "stranger," how he led them to tell their story of heartbreaking disappointment in the fact that Jesus was dead and that his body had been stolen. Note also how Jesus "interpreted to them in all the scriptures the things concerning himself," how they recognized him only when he broke bread with them, and how they hurried back to Jerusalem immediately to tell that Jesus was risen from the dead and had talked with them.

(4) *To Simon Peter* (I Corinthians 15:5; Luke 24:33-35) — The gospels do not tell this story fully, though Paul wrote of it to the church at Corinth. It was an event of great importance however, since a special meeting of the disciples was called to discuss it that Sunday evening. When Cleopas and his companion came in to tell their story those at the door triumphantly announced that "the Lord is risen indeed, and hath appeared to Simon." Simon was still a leader and his word carried weight. The testimony of these two from Emmaus was then added. The proof is accumulating and the disciples are convinced.

We wish we had the full story of Jesus' appearance to Peter that Sunday afternoon. Apparently Peter had not seen Jesus since the dark hours early Friday morning when, after denying his Lord, he had gone out and "wept bitterly." He thought then that it was all over. He had disgraced himself and had failed his Lord. So far as he knew that was the end. Friday, Saturday and Sunday must have been dreadful days for him. Then the Lord appeared to him, forgave him, restored him and commissioned him for yet greater work in the kingdom.

(5) *To the Disciples at Night* (Mark 16:14; Luke 24:36-43; John 20:19-25) — Reference has already been made of this special meeting of the followers of Jesus on the evening of this eventful day. It may have been in the same upper room in the home of Mary the mother of John Mark. They closed the doors "for fear of the Jews" and were eagerly listening to the reports of the appearances of Jesus. For some reason Thomas, one of the twelve, was not present. Suddenly Jesus himself appeared in their midst with the greeting, "Peace be unto you." They were frightened and "supposed that they beheld a spirit." To convince them he showed them his hands and his feet. "Handle me, and see; for a spirit hath not flesh and bones, as ye behold me having." To add further proof he asked for food and in their presence ate the broiled fish which they gave him. Having convinced them that he was alive he then gave them the commission 'to go forth to bless all the world.

## 8. *Subsequent Appearances.*

In the forty days yet remaining before his ascension Jesus appeared to five or six other groups in different sections of Palestine.

(1) *The Disciples Next Sunday Night* (John 20:24-31) — After the passing of a full week the disciples decided to meet again on Sunday night. Thomas who had been told of their gathering on the first Sunday night, was present this time. We do not know just how he was persuaded to come, though he had stated to the disciples earlier in the week his unwillingness to accept their story. "Except I shall see in his hands the print of the nails, and put my finger into the print of the nails and put my hand into his side, I will not believe." He was in the group tonight, when Jesus again appeared to them. He challenged Thomas with the invitation to examine his hands and his side. Be it said to the credit of Thomas that he did not carry out his declaration, but reverently made his noble confession of faith in the deity of Christ.

(2) *To Seven Disciples* (John 21) — John alone tells this beautiful story of Jesus meeting these seven disciples on the shore of the Lake of Galilee. For some reason they had returned to the familiar scenes of earlier days. Peter and the others had gone back to their fishing with

no intention of deserting Jesus. "That night they took nothing" and at daybreak they saw a man on the shore who told them to cast their net on the other side of the boat. They did so and were amazed at the size of their catch, one hundred and fifty-three big ones! John was the first to realize that it was Jesus who had spoken to them. The group then had breakfast on the shore after which Jesus gave his searching examination to Peter. To get the full force of this the student should understand the Greek verbs which Peter and Jesus used in their conversation. Peter was grieved when Jesus the third time used the verb which Peter had used all along. In other words he was not offended because three times Jesus interrogated him. This examination humbled Peter who remembered all too well his tragic failure after his confident boast that he would never do such a thing. Peter was fully restored and now understood what his work was to be.

(3) *To the Five Hundred in Galilee* (Mark 16:15-18; Matthew 28:16-20; I Corinthians 15:6) — This meeting had been prearranged and so the great company came together on some undesignated mountain in Galilee. As the company waited Jesus appeared. Of these the majority evidently were from Galilee. They had known him before his death, had heard that he was alive, and now they saw him, heard him speak and were convinced of his resurrection. Matthew adds, however, "though some doubted." It was on this occasion that Jesus gave what we usually call the "Great Commission." These were his followers, and they must now be his witnesses and assume responsibility for telling the story. He was soon to go back to the Father. These were commanded to take his good news all over the world. They were to "make disciples, to baptize believers, and to teach them to observe all that he had commanded." These and all who shall follow them are undergirded with the promise of his presence to "the consummation of the age." In Galilee he won his largest following and in Galilee he sent forth the largest number of disciples.

(4) *To James, the Brother of Jesus* (I Corinthians 15:7 — The gospels do not speak of this appearance; Paul knew of it and states it in his first letter to the Corinthian Christians. We do not know the time nor place of its occurrence. It is believed by many that this appearance resulted in the conversion of James who was the brother of Jesus who, after joining the ranks of the disciples soon became a leader of great influence.

(5) *To the Disciples Again* (Luke 24:44-49; Acts 1:3-8) — Only Luke tells of this appearance to the disciples near Jerusalem. Jesus

spoke briefly identifying his work with the Old Testament scriptures. He then "opened their mind that they might understand the scriptures." It was written that "the Christ must suffer, and rise again from the dead the third day; and that repentance and remission of sins should be preached in his name unto all nations, beginning from Jerusalem." These disciples were to be witnesses of these things. They were to "tarry in Jerusalem until they should be clothed with power from on high."

(6) *To the Disciples the Last Time* (Mark 16:19-20; Luke 24:50-53; Acts 1:9-12) — Jesus led his disciples out to Mount Olivet where they had often been. He spoke briefly and as he gave them his blessing, "as they were looking he was taken up; and a cloud received him out of their sight." In amazement the disciples continued gazing upward until two angels spoke to them assuring them that "this Jesus, which was received up from you into heaven, shall so come in like manner as ye behold him going into heaven." These returned to Jerusalem "with great joy." They then "went forth and preached everywhere."

The work which he came to the earth to do has been finished; his mission has been completed. The future of the kingdom is in the hands of his followers.

9. *Attempted Explanations.*

Because of the tremendous issues involved in the question of the resurrection of Jesus this miracle has received more exhaustive and critical study than any other event recorded in the New Testament. If it is true, as we believe, the consequences are far-reaching. However, from the first century to the present day there have been people who refuse to accept the miracle.

To deny the reality of the resurrection one must discredit the documentary evidence. The documents (the gospels and Acts) were written by competent, reputable men and they still stand. However, some scholars who recognize the validity of these records will not accept the resurrection, holding that what the records say can be interpreted otherwise. In other words, there are various theories which attempt to get rid of this supernatural event. These are not new; in fact, they were offered early in the history of Christianity. These are frequently classed under six headings, but since some of them are quite similar we may put them under four headings.

(1) *The Swoon Theory* — This theory holds that Jesus was not really dead; that he had only swooned or fainted and that when he was

placed in the cool, quiet tomb he revived, pushed open the door and joined his disciples. In reply we may answer that it is specifically stated that he was already dead. (John 19:33.) The soldiers pierced his side with the spear. Furthermore, Pilate himself examined him and pronounced him dead. Moreover, his weakened physical condition would have prohibited this. Then too, he certainly would have been apprehended by the guards.

(2) *The Fraud Theory* — Those who hold this view assert that the disciples of Jesus furtively slipped to the tomb at night and stole his body, hid it somewhere and then circulated the report that he had risen from the dead. The guards who reported the empty tomb to the Jewish authorities were told by the Jews to circulate just such a tale, with the explanation that the disciples stole his body "while we slept." How would they know it if they were asleep? What good would the body of Jesus have done them? The disciples were not trying to prove anything; in fact they were reluctant to believe in him after they saw him alive again. Such a view is a reflection on the character of these men. Whatever their weaknesses they were neither deceivers nor thieves. Furthermore they would have been seen by the guards or some of the great crowds of people who were present. This theory is refuted by the several appearances of Jesus in which he was recognized by his friends.

(3) *The Mistake Theory* — These who hold this view claim that the women made a mistake and went to an old deserted tomb, and thinking this to be the burial place of Jesus, hurried away to circulate the report that Jesus had risen. There is no parallel to this in all history. People do not forget a place so indelibly impressed on their minds and hearts. Matthew states that the women were there when he was buried. Luke says that "they beheld it and saw how he was laid." They visited the tomb Saturday and Sunday. They could not be as stupid as this theory would necessitate.

(4) *The Vision Theory* — According to this theory these agitated disciples and hysterical women did not see what they saw. They had hallucinations. All this was only in their minds; it was purely visionary.

This theory changes every known fact in the record. It assumes that the disciples expected him to rise, which certainly was not the case. It makes Jesus guilty of deception since he told his followers that he would rise again. The records all indicate that this resurrected Jesus had a body. The disciples recognized his features; Mary recognized his voice; he ate fish with his disciples; he invited Thomas to examine his

# PART THREE

*The Early Expansion of Christianity*

*Chapter I*

## THE NEW ERA

1. A Continued Story. 2. The Book of Acts. 3. Prayer and Power. 4. Matthias. 5. The New Era. 6. Peter, the Leader. 7. The New Force. 8. The Church in Jerusalem. 9. Persecution. 10. A Social Problem. 11. Popularity and Renewed Persecution. 12. Seven Assistants. 13. The Testimony of Stephen. 14. The First Appearance of Saul. 15. Work of Philip. 16. Peter in Sharon. 17. Christians in Antioch. 18. Persecution by the State.

CHAPTER I

# The New Era

## 1. A Continued Story.

It is customary to think of a rather definite break or interval between the ascension of Jesus and the beginning of the work of the apostles as related in the book of Acts. This, however, was not the case. It was one movement which Jesus inaugurated and which his followers took up immediately. In fact, Luke takes particular pains to show that it was a continued story. In his gospel which he addressed to Theophilus, he told the story up through the ascension. In writing Acts, which he likewise dedicated to Theophilus, he repeats the story of the ascension and links up what followed directly with the story which had preceded. In his prefatory word in Acts he brings the two together by referring to the preceding events which Jesus *"began* both to do and to teach." He means to say that what is to be done and taught is to be through Jesus. We shall do well, therefore, to think of these events as one continuous story.

## 2. The Book of Acts.

Without considering any of the critical questions connected with the book of Acts we shall assume that it was written by Luke, the only Gentile writer in the Bible. He was probably a Greek and a freedman who had become a Christian. He was not only an eminent and reputable historian, but also a physician. He was actively identified with the Christian movement, was a close friend of Paul's and traveled with him on some of his missionary campaigns as his "beloved physician." He did thorough research to secure facts for his book and was an eyewitness of much what he relates in the book.

Since this book is the only record we have of the early expansion or development of Christianity its value is easily apparent. It seems to have been the purpose of Luke to record some of the leading incidents in this growth as it was carried on by the apostles after the ascension of Jesus. All but the first few chapters are devoted to the spread of the gospel among the Gentiles. The book does not claim to be a complete account of the labors of all the early apostles. It is not the work of all of them since some of the leaders are not even mentioned; neither is it the complete record of the work of any one of them. It does give specific and representative developments to show how Christianity

238 THE HEART OF THE NEW TESTAMENT

was propagated after the death of Jesus and how it was received by those to whom it was preached. To chronicle all the events of these early years would have been a task too great for any man.

The book, after the brief introduction (1:1-3), falls naturally into three well defined sections. First is the story of the development in Jerusalem itself. (1:4-8:1.) The next section (8:2-12:25) tells the story of the spread of the faith in the land of Palestine. The third section (13:1-28:31) is devoted to the work of the apostles among the Gentiles in other parts of the Roman empire.

### 3. Prayer and Power (Acts 1:3-14).

After the resurrection and ascension of Jesus the disciples had the facts of the gospel story which included the sinless life of Jesus, his incarnation, his teachings, his wondrous works, his atoning death, his resurrection and ascension, his promise to return, the commission to win the world for him, and the assurance of his presence. But they were not yet ready to begin their work. They needed a better comprehension of these momentous facts and the power or skill to use them.

For this reason Jesus commanded them to tarry in Jerusalem for a while, they did not know how long. The kingdom was not to be a worldly one but a spiritual one. In their work they would need the presence and the leadership of the Holy Spirit. They were to tarry until they should be "endued with power." Accordingly this company of believers "continued with one accord in prayer and supplication." Altogether the number was one hundred twenty, which included the eleven disciples, the faithful women including Mary the mother of Jesus, the "brethren," and the other disciples. Their meeting place was the upper room where several significant gatherings had already taken place. They prayed fervently and remained together in close fellowship. They had a "common love, common mission, common joy, common hope."

### 4. Matthias (Acts 1:15-26).

There was one matter which all felt should be attended to while they waited. Judas, one of the twelve, had betrayed his Lord and had committed suicide. At the suggestion of Peter, who was already beginning to assume leadership, they agreed to select one to take the place of Judas. There was one necessary qualification for this one — he should be one who had been with Jesus from the baptism of John to the ascension of Jesus. Two men were nominated, and after prayer the "lot fell on Matthias." In this way Matthias was numbered with the apostles. It so happens that his name is not mentioned afterwards. This, however, does not mean that he was not an active and able leader since other apostles like Bartholomew and Matthew are not mentioned again.

5. *The New Era* (Acts 2:1-40).

By reading carefully the account of this remarkable event the student will be impressed with the unusual importance of what took place. Evidently these believers were in an attitude of expectancy. They did not know just how or when the revelation would be made known. Ten days passed bringing them to the time for the observance of the annual feast of Pentecost, which interestingly enough was the feast of first fruits. It came fifty days after the Passover when Jesus, the real Paschal Lamb, had been slain.

The company was "all together in one place" when suddenly they were startled by supernatural happenings — "a sound as the rushing of a mighty wind" which filled all the house, "tongues parting asunder, like as of fire: and it sat upon each one of them." Then the believers "were all filled with the Holy Spirit, and began to speak with other tongues, as the Spirit gave them utterance." We should not confuse these supernatural phenomena with the Holy Spirit. They were not the Holy Spirit; they were miracles, outward signs as evidence that the promise of the Father had been fulfilled.

Naturally this caused a sensation and "the multitudes came together" to see what had happened. Luke says that in the multitude were "Jews, devout men from every nation under heaven." He then mentions fourteen different nations represented. They wanted an explanation of the happening. "Behold, are not all these that speak Galileans? And how hear we, every man in our own language wherein we were born." The miracle was that every one of them, regardless of his language, could understand what the disciples were saying.

There were different explanations. Some quickly and erroneously, concluded that these men were drunk. Of course, this was no answer. Peter then came to the front, got the attention of the multitude and gave the real answer. This was the fulfillment of the prophecy of Joel. (2:28ff.) It was the word and work of God. Having secured their attention he then delivered a memorable sermon. He asserts that Jesus had fulfilled this prophecy. The Holy Spirit has been poured out, the day of power is at hand. He interprets the meaning of the life, death and resurrection of Jesus. The death of Jesus atones for sin; the resurrection of Jesus is victory for all who believe on him. This was the first sermon after the ascension of Jesus and it dealt with these great doctrines. On numerous other occasions Peter delivered messages, and usually he repeated these important truths.

The effects of the sermon were immediate. Under conviction men cried out, "What shall we do?" They were to repent and then be baptized. About three thousand people repented, believed and were baptized and were added to the number of believers that day. The results continued, "and fear came upon every soul; and many signs and wonders were done through the apostles."

### 6. Peter, the Leader.

The leader in the experiences of these first days was Simon Peter. He seems to be the directing force of the group as well as its spokesman. He is now coming to be the *rock* which Jesus predicted he would become. On the night of the trials of Jesus he was a shrinking, cowardly follower. Now he speaks with unbelievable boldness. He is no longer afraid of the Jews, but openly asserts that they were guilty of killing Jesus, "the prince of life." He defies the Sadducees and announces his intentions of continuing his work despite the warnings and threats of the Jews. Peter is unconquerable. With boldness he leads from one achievement to another until the Jews were in despair.

### 7. The New Force.

It is quite evident that a new force was at work in Jerusalem. The disciples had become a dynamic, courageous and aggressive company using every occasion for the propagation of their faith. Great numbers of people believed and were baptized. Miracles occurred with frequency and the whole city was stirred. The Jewish leaders who had thought when they crucified Jesus that they had stopped this movement discovered to their dismay that their difficulties had multiplied a thousand-fold. They didn't know how to cope with the situation, except with the use of physical force, but this did not stop these men. In vain the Sanhedrin met and deliberated and tried one measure after another, and still the movement swept on.

### 8. The Church in Jerusalem (Acts 2:41-47).

The large number of believers were not left to drift apart, but were kept together and shaped into a unit of fellowship and faith. "They continued steadfastly in the apostle's doctrine, in fellowship, in the breaking of bread and the prayers." Members were carefully instructed in the doctrines of Christ; they maintained communion with each other; they consecrated their daily meals with the spirit of the Lord's Supper; they were unwavering in their attendance at prayers. They added others to their number through their personal witnessing. "The notes of a happy church were here — unity, instruction, fellowship or partnership, liberality, praise, prayer, gladness, singleness of heart."[1]

9. *Persecution* (Acts 3:1-4:31).

It was to be the lot of the disciples of Jesus to suffer severe persecution, and this at the hands of their own countrymen, the Sadducees. This began with Peter and John and ultimately reached great numbers, especially in the reaction after the martyrdom of Stephen when thousands of them were scattered abroad.

Peter and John started up to the temple at the third hour of prayer (3:00 P.M.), but at the Beautiful Gate were stopped by a poor, lame beggar asking for alms. To the amazement of all the crowd Peter healed him. The man leaped up and went with them into the temple, "walking and leaping and praising God." A great crowd quickly gathered and Peter used this opportunity to preach as he had done on the day of Pentecost. This was much like his first sermon. He stressed the death and resurrection of Jesus and called on the people to repent. The Sadducees had gathered in time to hear Peter charge the Jews with the death of Jesus and then proclaim his resurrection. Since they did not believe in the resurrection of anyone they were thus incensed on two counts. They arrested Peter and John and kept them in the ward during the night. But many men believed; the number was now five thousand.

Next morning the Sanhedrin with Annas, Caiaphas and others, came together for the trial. Then Peter "filled with the Holy Spirit" spoke boldly using much the same sermon as on former occasions. The Sanhedrin were amazed at the boldness of the apostles, but could say nothing against it "seeing the man that was healed standing with them." They held a private consultation and decided to reprove the apostles, and warn them "not to speak at all nor to teach in the name of Jesus." Peter boldly replied that he would obey God and not man, "for we can not but speak the things which we saw and heard." The issue was now joined.

Peter and John reported to their company the things that had happened. In a service of prayer and thanksgiving these disciples dedicated themselves anew to their work. They rejoiced in their opportunities and prayed, not for exemption from suffering, but for courage: "grant unto thy servants to speak thy word with all boldness while thou stretchest forth thy hand to heal." A group like this could not be stopped by persecution.

## 10. A Social Problem (Acts 4:32-5:11).

In Acts 2:43-45, and 4:32-35 we have a number of statements which are used by some as a basis for the argument that a form of communism is taught in the New Testament. However, we should remember that the situation here described was an emergency. In the rapid growth of the company a great many poor people were included. There were also many visitors in the city whose funds had been exhausted. It is possible also that in the increasing opposition to the Christians a sort of boycott of the disciples in business had taken place. At any rate, there was acute need, and the disciples met that need by sharing generously their possessions. Certain competent men were put in charge of these matters and gifts were made to be distributed by these brethren. It may be noted, therefore, that this was an emergency, a situation which was temporary, and that there is no teaching of this as a policy by any other group in the New Testament. It was not taught or practiced by Paul or any other New Testament teacher. We should remember also that it was altogether voluntary.

There were two general effects of this. Naturally it brought the group into close and happy fellowship with each other. It also tempted some to donate their possessions because of the honor and distinction which was accorded these generous givers. An illustration of this desire for credit is seen in the story of Ananias and Sapphira who wanted to gain the praise of the people and at the same time not make a sacrificial gift. They were punished instantly, not because they did not bring all their possessions, but because they acted as if they had, and thus were guilty of lying to the Holy Spirit. If their penalty appears too severe, let us remember that theirs was a grievous sin and that this practice might have had very disastrous consequences in the life of the church. Severe measures were justified. The death of these two stopped this evil practice.

## 11. Popularity and Renewed Persecution (Acts 5:12-42).

The apostles acquired still greater reverence and prestige as many signs and wonders were wrought. It appears that the apostles stood daily in Solomon's porch to teach and heal. The crowds grew until "they even carried out the sick into the streets, and laid them on beds and couches, that as Peter came by at least his shadow might overshadow some of them." From the cities round about "they came bringing sick folk, and them that were vexed with unclean spirits: and they were healed every one."

Such excitement aroused the Sanhedrin who now saw that more stringent measures must be adopted. They seized the apostles and put them in prison, and called a meeting for the next morning. As the Sanhedrin assembled to await the bringing in of their prisoners, the officers who were sent to conduct them to trial came to report that the apostles were released from prison by an angel during the night and even then were in the temple where they had been teaching since daylight.

Other officials were sent to the temple to bring these men before the Sanhedrin. The apostles without resisting went before the court. Upon being charged with disobeying the charge formerly given them, Peter again spoke for the apostles. Once more he reiterated the chief points in his previous sermons. This bold defiance of their commandment and Peter's justification of their behaviour infuriated the Jews. Some of them were ready and even eager to execute these men at once. Then the aged and influential Rabbi Gamaliel took the floor and gave his advice. He urged caution and insisted that they do nothing rash. "Refrain from these men, and let them alone: for if this counsel or this work be of men, it will be overthrown: but if it is of God, ye will not be able to overthrow them: lest haply ye be found even to be fighting against God." Of course, this policy of Gamaliel will not always do as a working principle, but it did save the apostles. The Sanhedrin followed Gamaliel's advice, but before releasing the apostles, called them in, beat them and charged them not to speak in the name of Jesus. The disciples left "rejoicing that they were counted worthy to suffer dishonor for the name." However, they did not obey the orders of the council. "And every day in the temple and at home, they ceased not to teach and to preach Jesus as the Christ."

The number of disciples continued to grow. It started with one hundred twenty; three thousand were added on the day of Pentecost; a little later they numbered five thousand; now "multitudes both of men and women" were added to the number of believers.

## 12. Seven Assistants (Acts 6:1-6).

As time passed and the number of Christians increased other problems arose. One of these difficulties was within the church itself. The membership now included not only Jews from Palestine, but

Hellenists, Jews from Greek settlements. These Hellenists protested that in the distribution of funds raised for needy Christians they were discriminated against. Evidently the issue became serious and was brought to the apostles. However, these men declined to abandon their proper duty of ministering the Word in order "to serve tables." In this they were wise since their work of preaching could be done only by those who were especially qualified for it while the other work could be done by others. They recommended that the brethren select seven other men for the handling of the distribution of relief. These men were to be "men of good report, full of the Spirit and of wisdom." Accordingly the group elected Stephen, Philip, Prochorus, Nicanor, Timon, Parmenas and Nicolaus. It is to be noted that all these bore Greek names. Two of them later became famous, Stephen as the first martyr and Philip as the first missionary outside Jerusalem.

While these men are not called deacons in this instance it is generally held that this is the origin of the office of deacon. The fact that seven were elected in this situation does not imply that the number seven is obligatory; the number may be smaller or larger as the situation may demand.

### 13. The Testimony of Stephen (Acts 6:7-7:60).

While all seven were good and worthy men Stephen seems to have been the leading one. He assumed a place of prominence as the church grew. Luke states (Acts 6:7) that "the number of the disciples multiplied in Jerusalem exceedingly: and a great company of the priests were obedient to the faith." The fact that the priests were usually Sadducees made the Sadducaic party all the more bitter. Stephen's work was so effective that renewed persecution broke out. "Stephen, full of grace and power wrought great wonders and signs, among the people." His opponents "were not able to withstand the wisdom and the Spirit by which he spoke." He was definitely charged with hostility to Judaism which was a charge not hitherto brought against the other disciples. But in the debates the Jews were no match for Stephen. Even Saul had gone down before the matchless argument of this man. Being outwitted by him they resorted to force. They hired witnesses who swore that "we have heard him speak blasphemous words against Moses and against God." Then "they seized him and brought him into the council" where they again used false witnesses against him. The high priest then asked Stephen if these things were true. In reply Stephen delivered a lengthy address to refute the charges against him.

"Stephen, in his defense before the Sanhedrin, gave a sketch of the history of Israel in such a way as to reply to the charges of (a) disloyalty to the temple, (b) rejection of Moses. God's appearance was never confined to one place. He appeared to Abraham in Mesopotamia; He was with Joseph in Egypt; He revealed Himself to Moses in the wilderness of Sinai. The temple was not built till the days of Solomon, for the Most High *dwelleth not in temples made with hands.* As to the rejection of Moses, Israel had been guilty of this from the first: in Egypt, in the wilderness, and to the Law given *by the disposition of angels* they had been equally unfaithful. Moses had foretold Christ; and the betrayal of Jesus, *the Just One,* was only in keeping with all Israel had done before."[2] The Sanhedrin could not endure this mighty argument and the severe rebuke which it carried. "They were cut to the heart, and they gnashed on him with their teeth." Stephen perceiving what was coming, calmly looked up to heaven and exclaimed, "Behold, I see the heavens opened, and the Son of man standing on the right hand of God." They then rushed upon him with one accord and forced him outside the gate to stone him. The stones were quickly collected, the witnesses who threw the stones cast off their outer coats, and as the cruel deed took place Stephen turned his gaze heavenward and prayed, "Lord Jesus, receive my spirit." As they beat him down he cried with a loud voice, "Lord, lay not this sin to their charge." He then "fell asleep." Thus Stephen, the first of the Christians to seal his testimony with his blood, came to the end. He gained that crown of which his name Stephen (the crown) had been an unwitting prophecy.

### 14. The First Appearance of Saul (Acts 8:1-4).

The death of Stephen brings to our notice for the first time a young man who was destined to play a very large part in the early history of the Christian movement. This young man was Saul of Tarsus who stood guard over the garments of these who stoned Stephen. (Acts 6:58.) Since our next chapter will be devoted wholly to Saul, it will be sufficient here simply to state that he immediately became a vigorous leader in the opposition to the Christians in Jerusalem and elsewhere.

The effective testimony of Stephen and his martyrdom was the signal for an organized persecution of the Christians far larger and more severe than any heretofore experienced. Pharisees and Sadducees were now united in their program of destroying Christianity. Up to this time only the disciples had been arrested; but now all believers, laymen and women, were subjected to brutal treatment. They were committed to prison and sentenced to death by the Sanhedrin, as in the case of Jesus. Terror reigned as unjustified indignities and brutal punishment were inflicted upon believers. In this Saul was the ring leader. "Saul did not hesitate to enter into private homes to make arrests. He hunted the church like a flock of partridges that fluttered as they flew. Those not caught flew far and wide and told of Jesus as they went. Thus were the lay preachers forced to go out of Jerusalem to carry the good news to Judea, Samaria and the uttermost part of the earth. Too long they had tarried in Jerusalem."[3]

Despite all the sufferings which this involved, there were good results to issue from this persecution. These Christians were scattered to various parts of the Roman empire. However, instead of this resulting in the destruction of the church as the Jews anticipated, it proved to be the means of spreading Christianity in a way which none had anticipated. Wherever they went they gave their testimony, won others to Christ and established little communities of believers. These things "have fallen out rather unto the progress of the gospel."

*15. Work of Philip* (Acts 8:5-40).

To Philip, one of the seven, belongs the honor of being the first missionary out of Jerusalem. As a result of the terrible persecutions he "went down to the city of Samaria and preached the Christ." He was heartily received and many responded to his message and were baptized. He was able also to perform many miracles "and there was much joy in that city." One of those who heard Philip and professed to believe in Christ was a noted sorcerer known as Simon Magus. He had won great renown with his sorceries and when he claimed to be a follower of Jesus it occasioned considerable comment.

In the meantime the church in Jerusalem heard of the successful mission of Philip in Samaria and sent Peter and John to confirm his work. They came and approved the work which was done among these people by laying their hands on these new converts who "received the Holy Spirit." Simon saw this and immediately sought to buy from Peter this gift of imparting the Holy Spirit. Indignantly Peter denounced Simon Magus declaring that he was not a Christian, "thy heart is not right before God." He then urged him to repent since he was still "in the gall of bitterness and in the bond of iniquity." Then Simon besought Peter to pray for him "that none of these things which ye have spoken come upon me."

This experience has perpetuated the name of Simon Magus who came to be regarded as the father of heresy. One of the legends is that Peter traveled all over the world to refute him and finally overtook him in Rome where Simon attempting to escape, was struck down by an angel. In later years the corrupt traffic of buying and selling church offices was given the name "Simony."

Upon the completion of their mission in the city of Samaria Peter and John returned to Jerusalem, "and preached the gospel to many villages of the Samaritans."

Philip later returned to Jerusalem where he again received a commission to go outside the city for work. He went southward on the desert road that led to Gaza where he met the Ethiopian eunuch "of great authority under Candace, queen of the Ethiopians." The eunuch was sitting in his chariot reading from the fifty-third chapter of the prophecy of Isaiah. Philip asked him if he understood what he was reading and the eunuch replied, "How can I except some one guide me?" Thereupon he invited Philip to sit with him in the chariot. Philip "beginning from this scripture, preached unto him Jesus." The eunuch believed and as they came to a lake by the roadside he requested baptism at the hands of Philip. When the eunuch had resumed his journey Philip turned northward, "and passing through he preached the gospel to all the cities till he came to Caesarea."

*16. Peter in Sharon* (Acts 9:32-10:38).

Since our next chapter is to deal with Paul, we omit the references to him made in Chapter 9, and consider the work of Peter who had left Jerusalem for a visit to the region of the Mediterranean coast anciently known as the plain of Sharon. Here he visited the cities of Lydda and Joppa and performed two notable miracles; healing Aeneas who had been ill eight years with palsy, and restoring to life the good woman Dorcas, known afar for her good works. As a result "it became known throughout all Joppa, and many believed on the Lord."

The most notable event in his ministry in this region was the conversion of Cornelius, the Roman centurion, and the consequent meeting in which great numbers were won to the Christian faith. Space does not permit an exposition of this important series of events in the spread of Christianity in Palestine. We may call attention to the obvious leadership of the Holy Spirit, both in the life of Peter and among the people in Caesarea, the home of Cornelius. Note the eagerness with which they received Peter and his message, and the quick response to his message. It is of special significance that this was in a Gentile home and that these believers were Gentile people. Peter has stepped over the "middle-wall of partition" with his message and the gospel has entered the lives of people outside the Jewish race. It was like a Gentile Pentecost.

Just how long Peter tarried in Caesarea is not told, though they had besought him to tarry certain days. The report of the large number of Gentiles who became Christians soon reached the ears of the Christians in Jerusalem. So when Peter returned to Jerusalem "they that were of the circumcision contended with him" and reproved him for receiving people who were uncircumcised. Peter then related to them what had occurred and defended his action which he insisted was under the leadership of the Holy Spirit. They heard him to the end and "held their peace, and glorified God, saying, Then to the Gentiles also hath God granted repentance unto life." Apparently this closed the matter for a time, though this divisive question was to rise again to become one which threatened the very life of the early church.

*17. Christians in Antioch* (Acts 11:19-30).

At this point in his narrative Luke tells of the spread of the gospel among the Gentiles in another community which was soon to become a center from which the whole foreign mission enterprise was to be launched. It was in Antioch of Syria. This city was the seat of the ancient Seleucid monarchy and was the capital of the East. It is now a poor Turkish city of only a few thousand population, but then it was the metropolis of Syria, and the third city of the Roman empire. It was fifteen miles inland from the shore of the Mediterranean Sea on the Orontes river. It had a population of some two hundred thousand people made up of four general classes; the native Syrians, the invading Greeks, a large colony of Jews, and the Roman element. It was widely known for its learning, but even more notorious for its licentious character, probably because of the location nearby of the infamous "Groves of Daphne" known afar for the immorality practiced there.

When the furious persecution after the death of Stephen occurred some believers went up to Antioch to live. At first they spoke of Christ only to Jews, but later arrivals boldly proclaimed their faith to Greeks living in Antioch. Again the results were amazing because a great number believed and were baptized. From this beginning a mighty Christian church, predominantly Greek, was to grow. They were active and aroused such opposition among the native people that they earned a nickname, a "derisive epithet," which has come to be a designation honored and respected by the whole world. "The disciples were called *Christians* first in Antioch."

### 18. Persecution by the State (Acts 12:1-24).

As we come to the close of this epoch in the history of the early church we see the Roman state taking a hand in the persecution of the Christians. Herod Agrippa I was king of all Palestine at the time. On a visit to Jerusalem he had James, the brother of John, killed with the sword, though the reasons for this are not given. Because this act pleased the Jews Herod, in order to gain further favor with the Jews, reached out and committed Peter to prison. This was the first time the government had taken a hand in the persecution of believers and the situation was so crucial that the disciples met in the home of Mary, the mother of John Mark, to counsel together and to pray. God heard their prayers. Peter was miraculously delivered during the night, and hurried to the home where the Christians were gathered. They were amazed at his delivery from prison, but when he had related in detail the manner of his escape, he departed and went to another place. Herod, learning of Peter's escape, examined the guards and commanded that they be put to death. Herod then left Jerusalem for Caesarea where he tarried for a while. Luke gives the brief story of the strange death of Herod, who was smitten by an angel of the Lord, "because he gave not God the glory." He then adds that "he was eaten of worms and gave up the ghost."

We may close this first chapter in the new era of Christianity with the revealing words of Luke. "But the word of God grew and multiplied." Already there were strong Christian settlements in Jerusalem, Samaria, Sharon, Damascus and Antioch of Syria. No doubt there were large numbers also in Perea and Galilee, and perhaps in other regions, though we are told nothing of them.

---

[1]Robertson, *Studies in the New Testament*, p. 137.
[2]Foakes-Jackson, *A Brief Biblical History*, p. 137.
[3]Robertson, *Studies in the New Testament*, p. 145.

*Chapter II*

THE NEW APOSTLE

1. Paul's Place in History. 2. Elements of Greatness. 3. The Need for Paul. 4. His Ancestry. 5. His Family. 6. Survey of His Life. 7. Birth and Boyhood. 8. His Education. 9. Persecuting the Christians. 10. His Conversion. 11. His Baptism. 12. Testifying in Damascus. 13. In Arabia. 14. Back in Damascus. 15. In Jerusalem as a Christian. 16. In Tarsus Again. 17. In Antioch of Syria.

CHAPTER II

# The New Apostle

## 1. Paul's Place in History.

Our studies have now brought us to the most important man in all Christian history, except of course, Jesus Christ himself. Many unprejudiced scholars rank Paul as one of the greatest men who ever lived. "He was naturally of immense mental stature and force. He would have been a remarkable man even if he had never become a Christian. The other apostles would have lived and died in the obscurity of Galilee if they had not been lifted into prominence by the Christian movement; but the name of Saul of Tarsus would have been remembered still in some character or other even if Christianity had never existed."[1]

When we understand the situation in which he worked, follow him in long and varied labors, see him as he displayed his matchless gifts in his devotion to the cause of Christ, and survey his accomplishments at the day of his martyrdom, we shall agree that he was unquestionably one of the great men of all history. "His name today is the great name in Christian history after that of Jesus. It is not enough to say that he stood at the source of Christianity and put his impress upon it in the formative period. This is quite true, but a great deal more is true. Real Christianity has never gotten away from Paul. I do not believe that it ever will. He was the great thinker in this important era. He blazed the way in doctrine and in life. He caught the spirit of Jesus and breathed that spirit into Gentile Christianity."[2] "Passing by Jesus himself, Paul stands forever the foremost representative of Christ, the ablest exponent of Christianity, its most constructive genius, its dominant spirit from the merely human side, its most fearless champion, its most illustrious and influential missionary, preacher, teacher, and its most distinguished martyr."[3]

## 2. Elements of Greatness.

It is not always easy to analyze the life of a great man and determine just what made him great. However, in the career of Paul we may discern certain elements of character which we believe were responsible for some of his magnificent achievements.

In the first place he was endowed by nature with many unusual qualities. His mind was naturally keen, alert and inquisitive. Intellectually few men in history were more generously endowed. He was a trained and logical thinker, as his writings attest. He had an unusual command of language for expressing his thoughts with effectiveness. Though he seems to have been unprepossessing in physical appearance, which sometimes embarrassed him, he was a man of rare personal magnetism. Though he was capable of great indignation and was an uncompromising contender for what he knew to be right, he had a warm heart. He loved people and his followers were bound to him by almost unbreakable ties.

He was a man of unimpeachable character; he was genuine. He was a Christian who embodied in his own personal behaviour the noblest qualities of Christian character. First, last and always he strove to be true to Christ.

He was fortunate in his cosmopolitan background and sympathies. He was a Roman citizen, was familiar with Greek culture, knew and loved life in the great cities, and knew how to approach men of all classes.

He was a man of balanced powers. With all his gifts he had unusual balance in judgment and action. He was neither an extremist nor a specialist.

As a theologian his rank is pre-eminent; he has interpreted Christ for all the world. His writings, though never intended by him to be masterpieces in literature, still rank among the most notable contributions to scholarly writing.

As a missionary statesman he occupies a place of pre-eminence. Not only did he preach to win converts and teach the churches for the accomplishment of their missions; he determined matters of policy among the churches. He steered them in difficult relations with opponents and with other Christians. The policies which he inaugurated for the conquest of the Roman world still serve as a guide to all Christian groups in their missionary endeavors. He was a statesman of the first rank.

*3. The Need for Paul.*

It is no reflection upon any of the apostles to say that at the time Paul came upon the scene there was a very great need for a man such as he to take the leadership of the church in its world-wide mission. We certainly should not regard the disciples as simple-minded, incompetent or ignorant. The writings of Peter, James, John and other apostles should convince any one that these men were not intellectual weaklings. For example, after reading the gospel of John we can understand why he is regarded as a Christian philosopher of the first rank. Nevertheless these men did have limitations that precluded their doing what needed to be done. They were not trained in the schools of the time. In this sense they were unlettered. They were not acquainted with the world outside the confines of their own little land. They knew but little, so far as we know, of Greek philosophy, or Roman culture, or pagan literature and history. They knew nothing of life as it was in such Gentile cities as Ephesus, Corinth and Rome. If Christianity was to be introduced to the Roman world and win a place of recognition in competition with all the other philosophies and religions of the Gentile world it must be done by a man like Paul.

*4. His Ancestry.*

Saul was a Jew and was proud of it. He called himself a Hebrew of the Hebrews. His ancestry went back to the tribe of Benjamin which furnished the first king of Israel, another man by the name of Saul. Surely there was enough of good in the history of the Jews to give Saul a right to be proud. Israel was the chosen race "whose is the adoption, and the glory, covenants, and the giving of the law, and the service of God, and the promises; whose are the fathers." (Romans 9:4-5.) This proud Jew was honest when he exclaimed, "If any other man thinketh to have confidence in the flesh, I yet more." His ancestry was noble, his race a proud and worthy one. He had good blood in his veins. This was a good start then, even as now, for making a distinguished career.

*5. His Family.*

While we may not have the full picture we are able to get a very good idea of the family of which this young man was a part. We do not know the name of his father or his mother. His father was a strict Jew since Saul was "instructed according to the strict manner of the law of our fathers." (Acts 22:3.) He was also a Hellenist since he lived in Tarsus, one of the great Greek cities of the world, though he was a loyal Jew at heart. It is generally agreed that he was a native of Galilee. Some scholars contend that he was from Gischala in northern Galilee, that he was driven from his home by some disturbance and had to find refuge in a Gentile city. We assume that he was a Roman citizen since he later declared, "But I am a Roman born." (Acts 22:28.) It is possible that this man may have secured his Roman citizenship by some deed of valor. Sir William Ramsay shows that Jews lived in Tarsus, the boyhood home of Saul, as early as 171 B.C. and that Saul's father was a man of high standing in this city. The tone of Paul's language in speaking of his birthplace indicates that his family was one of influence and position.

We know but little of his mother, though it may be safely assumed that she was of a good family, and was a devout woman who took special care in the training she gave her son. We know of one other member of the family, a daughter, the sister of Saul. Luke tells the story of "Paul's sister's son," who heard of the plot of the Jews to kill Paul while he was a prisoner in Jerusalem. (Acts 23:16.) There may have been other members of this family though we have no mention of them.

6. *Survey of His Life.*

There are several points at which scholars disagree in a chronological arrangment of the events in the career of Saul, though the general outline is clear. It will be advantageous to the student to get a preview of the main events in the life of this, the greatest apostle, before taking up the details of his career.

| | |
|---|---|
| Birth in Tarsus | A.D. 1 |
| Conversion in Damascus | 33 |
| Stay in Damascus and Arabia | 33-36 |
| Visit to Jerusalem | 36 |
| In Tarsus and Syria — Cilicia | 36-45 |
| Call to Antioch (Syria) | 45 |
| First Missionary Campaign | 47-49 |
| Great Jerusalem Council | 50 |
| Second Missionary Campaign | 50-53 |
| In Antioch (Syria) | 53 |
| Third Missionary Campaign | 53-57 |
| Back in Jerusalem | 57 |
| In Prison at Caesarea | 57-59 |
| Enroute to Rome | 59 Winter |
| On Island of Melita | 59-60 Winter |
| Arrival in Rome | 60 Spring |
| Roman Imprisonment | 60-62 |
| Release from Prison | 62 Spring |
| Ministry in Empire | 62-64 |
| Mission to Gaul and Spain | 64-66 |
| Evangelization of Crete | 66 |
| At Nicopolis | 66-67 Winter |
| At Rome Again | 67 Fall |
| Trial and Execution | 67 Fall |

### 7. Birth and Boyhood.

Paul tells with pride that he was born in Tarsus of Cilicia "no undistinguished city." (Acts 21:39.) This city was the western capital of the united province of Syria-Cilicia. It was located on a fertile plain only three quarters of a mile from the Mediterranean Sea. The river Cydnus, which rose in the mountains above the city, flowed through Tarsus to the sea. The city was famous for her commercial enterprises, and no less so for intellectual pursuits. Indeed, she was the principal seat of learning in the Roman world. Students from her famous schools went out into all parts of the Roman empire. This proud city was the birthplace of many sons who later became famous and brought pride to her. The greatest of these was Saul.

It is generally assumed that Saul was born after his sister. After the custom of the time, his parents gave him the honored Jewish name Saul *(asked for)* and also the Roman name Paul. In Christian history he is known as Saul up to the time of his visit to Paphos on the island of Cyprus during his first missionary campaign, after which he is called Paul.

The year A.D. 1 is generally accepted as the date of the birth of Saul. Certainly this date could not be far wrong. "There is no straining of the facts if we imagine the boy John in the hill country of Judea, the boy Jesus in Nazareth and the child Saul in Tarsus at the same time. Each faced the same world, but from a different point of view, these boys who were to revolutionize the world."[4]

John the Baptist grew up in the wilderness, Jesus in the Jewish town of Nazareth, but Saul in a great Gentile city. And this city was the ideal place for the training of the man who was later to become the missionary to the world. Here he would see merchants and traders from all parts of the Roman world busily engaged in the exchange of goods. Here his eager mind would be stimulated by the intellectual atmosphere of the city. Here too, in this cosmopolitan center, the Jew had a freedom and a standing which must have given Paul a background for his later vision of a world in which both Jew and Gentile would live together as brothers in the spirit of Christ.

### 8. His Education.

According to custom every Jewish boy was given a thorough schedule of education. Without attempting to go into details we may give the general outlines of his training. As the son of a devout Jew he would receive careful training in the home, as commanded in the laws of Moses. When he reached his sixth or seventh year he was expected to enter the elementary school which was connected with the synagogue where the Old Testament scriptures would be the basis of his studies. He would become familiar with these in the original Hebrew language and also in the Greek. He used as a text the famous Septuagint, which was employed by all Greek-speaking Jews. As he advanced he would memorize much of the Law so as to be able to quote it accurately. The synagogue training would continue up to the early teen age. When he attained the age of thirteen he became "a son of the commandment" and was then ready for the preparation for his life work. Since Saul was destined for the Rabbinate, he would follow a prescribed course. This started with the learning of a "trade" which would provide a means of livelihood since a rabbi was not permitted to accept a salary or even a voluntary gift. Saul thus learned to be a maker of tents, which trade stood him in good stead as a Christian missionary later on.

Upon reaching the age of thirteen to fifteen these students for the Rabbinate would go to the city of Jerusalem for their further study in the Rabbinical college — "The House of Interpretation." The course of study here was well planned and thorough. Upon completion of the requirements of study here a young rabbi was well equipped to do his work. Without discussing the details of this prescribed course of instruction we can assume that young Saul was not only adequate for it but that he stood far ahead of his fellow students. He sat at the feet of Gamaliel, the most learned and distinguished of all Jewish teachers of the time. We may also assume that this wise and experienced teacher at once took notice of this brilliant student, that he gave special attention to him and as he marked the development of this young man he began to plan for him. He would be an able successor to Gamaliel. The great teacher knew that here was a young man who was destined for achievement and fame.

Upon completion of his studies in Jerusalem Saul returned to his native city of Tarsus. He was now ready for his work. He was the pride of his parents and of his teachers. It is generally held that he devoted himself to his chosen profession in his home city. We do not have any mention of him during these years until he later went to Jerusalem again, probably just before the death of Stephen. This brilliant, accomplished, ambitious young man heard of the challenge to his faith which the Christian movement was now imposing and was eager to get into the fierce struggle and lend his brilliant powers to the defense of the faith of his fathers. He was with his brethren at the trial of Stephen and while he threw no stones to kill this heretic, he consented to his death and shared the sentiments of his people in removing this troublesome and effective opponent of Pharisaism. He watched Stephen die, and though he did not realize it at the time, this event was destined to play a decisive part in his career.

9. *Persecuting the Christians* (Acts 9:1-2, 3-5, 26:4-11; Galatians 1:13-14).

The brilliant young Pharisee who returned to Jerusalem to devote himself to the defense of Pharisaism against the new sect seems to have come rapidly to a place of leadership. Older leaders stepped aside and Saul took command of the forces to destroy Christianity. It appears that he was in Tarsus during the years of Jesus' ministry and had come back to Jerusalem after the resurrection and ascension of Jesus. Thus it would seem that he had never seen Jesus. At any rate, this new movement was threatening the very existence of the faith which Saul cherished. The Sadducees had failed to stamp it out; the Pharisees must now try their hand. It is probable that he was already a member of the Sanhedrin since he speaks of voting with them.

His own words are the best description of his activities against the Christians. "I persecuted this way unto the death, binding and delivering into prisons both men and women." "And I both shut many of the saints in prisons, having received authority from the chief priests, and when they were put to death I gave my vote against them. And punishing them oftentimes in all the synagogues, I strove to make them blaspheme; and being exceedingly mad against them, I persecuted them even unto foreign cities." "For ye have heard of my manner of life in time past in the Jew's religion, how that beyond measure I persecuted the church of God and made havoc of it." No wonder that Luke the historian speaks of this young zealot as "breathing threatening and slaughter against the disciples of the Lord."

10. *His Conversion* (Acts 9:4-9, 22:6-11, 26:12-19; I Corinthians 15:8-10; Galations 1:15-16).

With the conversion of Saul to the Christian faith we have to do with one of the most significant and far-reaching events in the history of the early church. There are three detailed accounts of this remarkable experience given in the New Testament. Luke records it as a historical fact (Acts 9:4-9) and Paul gives two accounts in his own words. (Acts 22:6-11, 26:12-19.) A careful reading of these accounts will reveal some minor differences in details. However, these minor differences serve not to discredit them but rather to give strength to their validity. One would not expect three independent reports of an event to agree exactly in every detail; in fact such agreement would raise questions about its validity.

The scope of these studies will not permit a full exposition of Saul's conversion. We may be content to trace the main current of the story. Saul had succeeded in making his name a terror to all Christians in Jerusalem. Temporarily at least, he had scattered or silenced most of these heretics in the holy city. Having succeeded here, as he thought, he began to look into other regions for work to be done. He got reports of a strong group of believers in Damascus, the old city of Syria about one hundred fifty miles north of Jerusalem, so he determined to go there to carry on his crusade against these believers. He secured the proper papers for the arrest of any Christians in Damascus so that he might bring them in bonds to Jerusalem. With these matters settled he and his company started the long journey to this ancient city. It would require some six or seven days of travel, and during the journey this brilliant and zealous young man would have time to think. Unquestionably some doubts assailed him. He couldn't get out of his mind the calm manner in which Stephen died, nor could he forget Stephen's prayer as he peacefully "fell asleep." Some one has aptly said, "Had Stephen never prayed Paul had never preached." Thus Saul, fired with zeal for a cause which he conscientiously believed to be right, and yet troubled by questions which he could not answer, made his way toward Damascus.

The news of his coming had reached Damascus before his arrival. The disciples there no doubt prayed that in some way his coming should be arrested. "The Good Shepherd had heard the cries of the trembling flock and went forth to face the wolf on their behalf."[5] His conversion took place on the last stage of this journey as he drew near to the city. At mid-day suddenly a blinding light shone around Saul and his company. He fell prostrate to the earth in complete blindness. He then heard a voice saying unto him, "Saul, Saul, why persecutest thou me? And he said, Who art thou, Lord? And he said, I am Jesus whom thou persecutest: but rise and enter into the city and it shall be told thee what thou must do." Saul arose from the earth, and discovered that he was blind. Some of his company led him by the hand and brought him to Damascus. For three days he remained without sight and "did neither eat nor drink." In a few moments a thing had occurred which changed the course of Saul's life — and indeed the life of the church. "What a change was there! Instead of the proud Pharisee riding through the streets with the pomp of an inquisitor, a stricken man, trembling, groping, clinging to the hand of his guide, arrives at the house of entertainment amidst the consternation of those who receive him and, getting hastily to a room where he can ask them to leave him alone, sinks down there in the darkness."[6]

What had taken place in the life of Saul is of tremendous significance. Unquestionably he himself regarded this appearance of Jesus to him on the Damascus road of the same rank as the appearance of the Saviour to the disciples and others after his resurrection. On this vision he bases his claim to apostleship on a level with Peter, James, John and the others. For the church it meant the virtual collapse of the program of organized persecution. The opposition had no leader to take the place of Saul. It meant that Christians could pursue their work with a free hand. Christianity had gained a leader who could do for it what none of the twelve could do. He can "cross swords with any one." He can bridge the chasm between Greek and Jew. He can dream and plan for the conquest of the Roman empire for Christ. Christianity would soon be on the world stage.

Because of the significance of his conversion this experience will continue to be studied. Like the resurrection of Jesus its implications are inescapable. "All sorts of theories have been advanced to explain away the inevitable meaning of the whole story that Saul saw the risen Jesus and heard his voice. No epileptic fit, no sunstroke, no swoon, no flash of lightning can explain what occurred. The career of Saul as persecutor is stopped, and at once. No possible motive for a voluntary change on Saul's part can be imagined. He was seized upon by Jesus, to whom he surrendered on the spot, and his whole life turned about in exactly the opposite direction. It is an epoch in the history of Christianity."[7]

*11. His Baptism* (Acts 9:10-19, 22:12-16).

After reaching Damascus Paul stayed in the home of a man named Judas on the street called Straight. Another disciple there, named Ananias, received in a vision the command to go to the house of Judas and ask for Saul of Tarsus "for he prayeth." Ananias demurred, fearing that this was a scheme on the part of Saul, the fierce persecutor of the Christians, to do harm to him and other Christians. However, upon being assured that Saul was now "a chosen vessel unto me, to bear my name before the Gentiles and kings and the children of Israel" Ananias went to see Saul. He laid his hands upon the head of the young Pharisee, addressed him as Brother Saul, then proceeded to tell him that he (Ananias) was the one Saul had seen in his vision. Thereupon Saul's eyes were opened and he received the gift of the Holy Spirit. After this "he arose and was baptized," presumably by Ananias, "For thou shalt be a witness for him unto all men of what thou hast seen and heard." Saul was now an apostle and must find himself in the fellowship of these people whom he had so bitterly persecuted. It is not strange that it would take these disciples a while to get used to him in his new role.

### 12. Testifying in Damascus (Acts 9:20-22).

We are not surprised that this new apostle should begin at once his new work. "He proclaimed Jesus, that he is the Son of God." He started where he was and at once. He knew this much — Jesus was the Son of God — and this was basic. From that point he could proceed. Naturally all who heard him were amazed that this noted enemy of Christianity was now preaching Christ. Paul developed rapidly, "increased the more in strength" and soon became more than a match for the Jews with whom he debated. These who formerly were his allies were now "confounded" by his proof that Jesus was the Christ.

### 13. In Arabia (Galatians 1:16-17).

There is no mention in Acts of this next step in the career of Paul, but in his letter to the Galatians he tells this part of his career as a Christian. In reality he faced a crisis in Damascus. While he was successful in his work with the Christians he must consider the commission which he had received. He might remain in Damascus for a while, but he knew that sooner or later the Jews would drive him out. He could return to Jerusalem, but there were good reasons for not doing this. He could find a new field for his endeavors. He decided upon the last course and withdrew to Arabia. He knew that he must have time to think through his new faith. How could all that he knew of Judaism be reconciled to Christianity? This question could not be settled in a day. It would require a long period of study, meditation and prayer. "He must have time to put his theological house in order before he sought to tear down what he had so lately sought to build up." He had been most deeply committed to Judaism. He had now seen it rudely shattered. The new truth was so revolutionary that he could not take it in at once. By nature he was a thinker. He must comprehend this new faith and fit it into the structure of his convictions.

We know none of the details. He tells us that he went away into Arabia and later returned to Damascus. Some scholars hold that he went as far down in Arabia as Mt. Sinai where Moses received the Law. This may be true, and we should like to think so, but we have no facts on which to base the claim. We know that he used this period for deep meditation and honest study, and that when he returned he was ready for his work.

*14. Back in Damascus* (Acts 9:23-25; Galatians 1:17; II Corinthians 11:32-33).

After his stay in Arabia he returned to Damascus where his work met with instant success. He was so effective that the Jews planned to kill him. He was now to face the cruel treatment which he had so often inflicted on others. To prevent his escape the Jews watched the gates of the city day and night. Word of the plot came to Paul and some of his disciples arranged for him to escape. He was placed in a basket and was let down outside the wall at night. In this humiliating manner Paul got out of Damascus despite the plans of the Jews. He was to have other such experiences in the years ahead.

*15. In Jerusalem as a Christian* (Acts 9:26-29, 22:17-22; Galatians 1:18-19).

After his escape from Damascus Paul went to Jerusalem which he had not seen since his departure for Damascus three years earlier. It may be that he decided to go to Jerusalem because no other place was open to him, or it may be that he went purposely. He was now a Christian and an Apostle, and certainly he would want to visit Peter and other leaders in Jerusalem. No doubt he knew the difficulties he would face there. Because of his activities against the church he could not expect the Christians to receive him; in fact it seems that many of them did not know of his conversion. Certainly neither the Sanhedrin nor any of his former associates there would receive him. He knew that they would regard him as a renegade and a traitor. When he reached Jerusalem he found the Christians suspicious and unfriendly. Barnabas, the generous disciple, accepted him and vouched for him so that the Christians later accepted him. He spent two weeks with Peter, not to get authority from him, but to have fellowship with him. These days were memorable ones for both men. He saw James, the Lord's brother also. He preached with such great power in the synagogues that the Jews now plotted to kill him. Yet Saul was so eager to remain in the city that it was only by a direct command of the

Lord that he finally left. His work was to be in the far-off places among Gentile peoples. Some of the brethren accompanied him as far as Caesarea on his journey. His break with the Jews in Jerusalem was complete; he had yet to prove himself as a Christian.

*16. In Tarsus Again* (Acts 9:30; Galatians 1:21-23).

In Caesarea on the coast of Palestine he took ship and sailed for Tarsus, his boyhood home. Once he had come back home as a brilliant young rabbi; he came back this time as a Christian. We do not have the record of his experiences here but we may safely assume that his close friends, his family and even his parents, if they were still living, would be bitterly disappointed, even to the extent of renouncing him for his acceptance of the Christian faith. He may not have preached in Tarsus itself, though he was active in his work in Syria and Cilicia. His work was so successful that reports of it reached the churches back in Judea. These nine years (A.D. 36-45) were busy ones. He refuted the Jews, won converts to Christ and laid the foundations for a strong work there later.

*17. In Antioch of Syria* (Acts 11:19-29, 12:25).

Back in the days of the great persecution at the death of Stephen some of the Christians who were scattered abroad came to Antioch of Syria. Saul was responsible for this. The church at Antioch was now flourishing under the leadership of Barnabas. The opportunities were so great and the labors so heavy that Barnabas was forced to seek help in his ministry. In thinking of the men who might be able to assist he remembered Saul whom he had befriended in Jerusalem and in whom he had such confidence. This man was now in Tarsus not so far from Antioch. Saul thus came to join hands with Barnabas in the work of a large Gentile church. From this center the great Foreign Mission enterprise of the church, with Saul and Barnabas as leaders, was soon to be launched.

[1]Stalker, *Life of St. Paul*, p. 8.
[2]Robertson, *Epochs in the Life of Paul*, p. 318.
[3]Ibid., p. 4.
[4]Robertson, *Epochs in the Life of Paul*, p. 11.
[5]Stalker, *Life of St. Paul*, p. 38.
[6]Ibid., p. 39.
[7]Robertson, *Studies in the New Testament*, p. 154.

*Chapter III*

## THE FIRST MISSIONARY CAMPAIGN

1. Preparatory Steps. 2. The Church at Antioch. 3. The Work of the Holy Spirit. 4. Extent of the First Campaign. 5. The Island of Cyprus. 6. To the Mainland. 7. Antioch of Pisidia. 8. In Iconium. 9. In Lystra and Derbe. 10. The Return Home. 11. Report to the Church. 12. Paul as a Missionary. 13. His Methods of Work. 14. Threatened Disruption. 15. The Council at Jerusalem.

CHAPTER III

# The First Missionary Campaign

## 1. Preparatory Steps.

In this chapter we are to consider the first real foreign missionary effort in the Christian church. This was not a sudden or unexpected venture; it was the outgrowth of certain stages of preparation. To begin with, we do well to recall that Jesus always conceived of his work as world-wide in nature. His gospel was for all races and for all mankind. "And I, if I be lifted up from the earth, will draw all men unto myself." He instructed his disciples as to this universal mission. The so-called "Great Commission" was to "all nations." Naturally it was difficult for his followers, even after his resurrection and ascension, to begin on this world-wide program. Apparently these early disciples would have been content to remain in Jerusalem, but the severe persecutions inflicted upon them at the death of Stephen scattered them abroad and they became missionaries of their faith without having planned to do so. But these Christians needed a leader who could organize them, plan their program and lead them in their mission to Gentile peoples. No such leader was available before the conversion of Saul. Some ten years after his conversion when he had become sure of himself he was at last ready to lead in this real mission of the church. After years of waiting the time had now arrived for the launching of this worthy enterprise.

## 2. The Church at Antioch.

Reference has already been made to the city of Antioch in Syria and the beginning of the church there. From the first the church was dynamic. It was largely Gentile in membership and was constantly growing in numbers and influence. Under the leadership of Barnabas the growth was so great that he needed assistance in meeting the opportunities offered there. When Saul was brought over from Tarsus to assist in the work even greater developments took place. Naturally such a church would feel an obligation to Gentile people in other regions. Under the ministry of Barnabas and Saul the church came to realize its obligation to take the gospel to other peoples. This strong church was to have the honor of serving as a center from which three great campaigns for the proclaiming of the gospel to Gentile people were launched.

*3. The Work of the Holy Spirit* (Acts 13:1-2).

In this new environment, far away from Jewish exclusiveness, the call came to engage in the new work of foreign missions. To five of the leaders in the church at Antioch — Barnabas, Symeon, Lucius, Manaen and Saul — during their regular ministrations came the clear call to this new undertaking. It was under the leadership of the Holy Spirit that the enterprise was begun. The Holy Spirit said, "Separate me Barnabas and Saul for the work whereunto I have called them." Under the direct command of the Holy Spirit these two men were to begin their new work. There is no mention of any formal action by the church on this matter though they did approve it and prayed for these brethren. The loss of these two strong leaders in the church at Antioch would be great, but evidently they were willing to spare these men for what was regarded as a greater work.

*4. Extent of the First Campaign.*

Before going into the details of this first campaign it will be helpful to get a glimpse of it as a whole. There were three men to make the journey, Barnabas, Saul, and a young man from Jerusalem named John Mark. The campaign lasted from the spring of the year A.D. 47 to the summer or fall of A.D. 49. They departed from Antioch of Syria, went down to the port of Seleucia where they took ship and sailed to the island of Cyprus. Their first stop was at Salamis on the east coast of the island. They worked westward through the island to the city of Paphos. From this port they sailed north to the mainland of Asia, landing at Perga in Pamphylia. Here John Mark deserted the company and returned to Jerusalem. Paul and Barnabas went up in the highlands to Antioch of Pisidia. After a period here they went eastward to Iconium, then south a few miles to Lystra and thence later to Derbe a short distance eastward. Retracing their steps they returned to Lystra, Iconium, Antioch, to Perga, to the port of Attalia whence they sailed to the north of Cyprus to Seleucia. The trip from Seleucia up to Antioch of Syria completed their campaign. This was the shortest of the three missionary campaigns, but it was a notable start in the evangelizing of the Gentile world.

*5. The Island of Cyprus* (Acts 13:4-12).

After the approval of the church in Antioch this company of three was now ready to embark upon the great venture. Barnabas being the older, was regarded as the leader and so his name heads the list at the start. Saul and he were close friends with deep appreciation of each

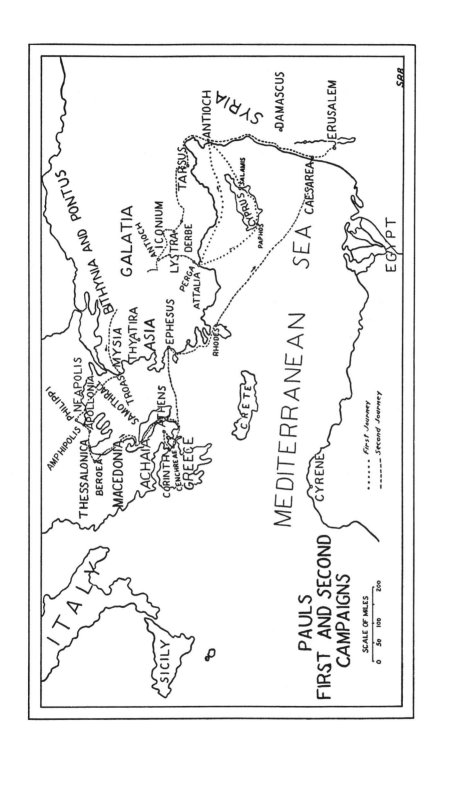

ITALY

SICILY

MEDITERRANEAN SEA

PAULS
FIRST AND SECOND
CAMPAIGNS

SCALE OF MILES
0    50   100   200

BITHYNIA AND PONTUS

GALATIA

THESSALONICA
AMPHIPOLIS
NEAPOLIS
PHILIPPI
APOLLONIA
BEROEA
MACEDONIA
SAMOTHRACIA
TROAS
MYSIA
THYATIRA
ASIA
EPHESUS
ATHENS
ACHAIA
CORINTH
CENCHREAE
GREECE

CRETE

RHODES

ANTIOCH
ICONIUM
LYSTRA
DERBE
PERGA
ATTALIA

TARSUS

CYRENE

CYPRUS SALAMIS
PAPHOS

ANTIOCH

SYRIA

DAMASCUS

CAESAREA
JERUSALEM

EGYPT

········· First Journey
--------- Second Journey

SRB

other. John Mark is the third member and went along as "an attend-ant." He was the son of Mary, a devout and active Christian in Jerusalem. He was a cousin of Barnabas and had come up to Antioch with Saul who had gone to Jerusalem with the offering of the Antioch church for the needy brethren in Jerusalem. He was young and probably was interested in this journey as a sort of adventure, though he was genuinely interested in serving. What his duties on the trip as "an attendant" were is not certain. It is probable that he served acceptably as a helper to the two older men in the details of travel. At any rate he went with enthusiasm and stayed with them for a while.

They set sail from Seleucia and traversed the short distance of seventy miles to Salamis, a port on the eastern coast of Cyprus. It was logical for the company to go first to this island. They had to start somewhere; Cyprus was nearby, and it was the old home of Barnabas. At this time it was a populous and prosperous territory. Its coast line measured three hundred and ninety miles and the island had some fifteen strong cities. It was known for its fruits and agricultural products as well as for its forests of good timber. It was well known in intellectual circles and was a Roman Province. Among the people were large numbers of Jews who had emigrated there for various reasons. They had established their synagogues where they maintained regular worship. Already some Christians had fled to this island to escape persecution.

Luke gives but few details of their work on the island. He states only that they proclaimed the gospel in the synagogue in Salamis, "and when they had gone through the whole island unto Paphos." At Paphos, the seat of the licentious worship of Aphrodite, they met two prominent men, a sorcerer named Elymas Barjesus and Sergius Paulus, the proconsul of the island. Sergius Paulus was "a man of understanding" though was under the influence of Elymas the sorcerer. In their effort to win Sergius Paulus to Christ the apostles encountered the determined opposition of Elymas. Finally Paul challenged this "son of the devil" and caused him to be blinded for a season. Sergius Paulus was deeply impressed and "believed, being astonished at the teaching of the Lord."

It is worthy of note that from this time Luke refers to these missionaries as "Paul and his company" or Paul and Barnabas. At last the leadership of Paul has asserted itself. It is now no longer "Barnabas and Saul" but Paul (Gentile name) and Barnabas. Apparently Barnabas had no feeling about the matter and recognized Paul as the natural leader.

## 6. To the Mainland (Acts 13:13).

The company now left Paphos and came by boat to the mainland of Asia, landing at Perga in the province of Pamphylia. Only one incident is given. John Mark had evidently discovered that this campaign was not as romantic and as easy as he anticipated. They had faced hardships in Cyprus, but these were not to be compared to what apparently awaited them in the rough country ahead. It may be that John was homesick also. At any rate, he decided to give up his part in the venture and return home to Jerusalem. No doubt Barnabas and even Paul tried to reason with him, but he was determined to go back. Luke states it very briefly: "And John departed from them and returned to Jerusalem." It is a disappointing picture of a young man who deserted in the face of hardship. We cannot minimize his failure; but we must not be too severe in condemning him. He is to learn his lesson and later will "come back."

## 7. Antioch of Pisidia (Acts 13:14-52).

Probably they had planned to work in Pamphylia, but for some reason no actual work was done there. They moved northward to Antioch in Pisidia which was in the Roman Province of Galatia. This city was in the highlands some thirty-six hundred feet above sea level. It was a large city whose population was made up of four elements: the natives, the Greek colony, a Jewish settlement and a Roman colony. It was a strategic center, a busy city which served a great territory of central Asia. Thus it offered an opportunity for Paul and Barnabas to reach a wide area through their ministry there.

Just how long they were in the city before Paul's address in the synagogue we do not know. He and Barnabas went to the synagogue on the Sabbath and when the invitation was issued to give "a word of exhortation" Paul arose and spoke. Luke gives a digest of this sermon which created a sensation in the city. The address, which we cannot interpret at length, stresses the main points in Paul's theology as expressed in later addresses and in the Epistles. He emphasized the fact that Jesus was the Messiah, the atoning death of Jesus, his resurrection from the dead, remission of sins through Jesus, and justification by faith in Jesus Christ. This message made a profound impression and caused the people to ask for more. The next Sabbath Paul was again at the synagogue and "almost the whole city was gathered together to hear the word of God." Paul had succeeded too well; the jealousy of the Jews had been aroused. They now interrupted

Paul "and contradicted the things that were spoken by Paul, and blasphemed." The Jews fiercely opposed these two Christian teachers by the use of questionable tactics. Paul then announced that they had given the Jews the first opportunity to receive the message but since they were rejecting it he and Barnabas would turn to the Gentiles. "And as the Gentiles heard this they were glad, and glorified the word of God; and as many as were ordained to eternal life believed. And the word of the Lord was spread abroad throughout all the region." The Gospel had made a start in the heart of a great Gentile community.

Angrily the Jews turned against Paul and Barnabas. They managed to arouse the chief men of the city and some pious women to oppose these Christian teachers. The persecution became severe and they were chased out of the city.

8. *In Iconium* (Acts 14:1-6).

About eighty miles southeast of Antioch lay the ancient city of Iconium. It was a fine and prosperous city in a fertile region. At Iconium Paul and Barnabas went first to the Jewish synagogue where Paul preached. The results were gratifying since a large number believed. However, as at Antioch, there were bitter opponents. The apostles wrought many signs and wonders and "tarried a long time there speakly boldly in the Lord." Finally the opposition took the form of a mob who threatened violence and death. Paul and Barnabas were convinced that discretion was the better part of valor, so they left.

9. *In Lystra and Derbe* (Acts 14:7-20).

The apostles now turned south to go to Lystra, a city in Lycaonia some twenty miles away. This city had attained a place of prominence under Roman rule, though it never became distinguished. The population consisted of native Lycaonians and some Roman families. Strangely enough there were but few Jews in the city and no synagogue. At least one Jewish family resided here and it was a pious home. The mother was a widow named Eunice who had a son, Timothy. The husband had been a Gentile and Timothy, the son, had never been circumcised. Lois, the mother of Eunice, lived in the home. Paul and Barnabas quickly became acquainted with this family and all three were won to the faith.

The event which caught the attention of the indifferent Gentiles of the city was the healing of the poor crippled man by Paul. The reaction was instant. The fickle crowd assumed that Paul and Barnabas were gods "come down to us in the likeness of men." They called them Jupiter and Mercury and instantly began preparations for a great celebration to honor them. The apostles, knowing the consequences of such a movement, immediately sought to dissuade the populace. They disclaimed being gods, and used this as an occasion to explain their mission to the people of the city. They succeeded in breaking up the plan of the crowd and the people dispersed. However, a reaction soon set in. Enthusiasm soon gave place to resentment. At this point a company of Jews from Antioch and Iconium came to the city and hearing Paul speak they recognized him, branded his words as lies and led a revolt against the apostles. The crowd was soon in an uproar. They rushed upon Paul and stoned him until they were certain that he was dead. Realizing that they were in danger because of this unlawful act they dragged the body of Paul to the gate of the city and left it lying outside the walls. Paul's friends now went to the gate and to their great relief discovered that he was still alive. After resting during the night Paul was able to join Barnabas in flight from the city of Lystra.

They made their way to Derbe, the exact location of which is not known. Evidently it was not an important place and the apostles did not tarry here long since there is no mention of their ministry at this place.

*10. The Return Home* (Acts 14:21-27).

It was now time for the apostles to conclude their first campaign and to begin the journey home. For good reasons they decided to retrace their route back to Lystra, Iconium, Antioch and Perga. They wanted to see again their converts in these cities, to give them further instructions, to counsel with them in their work and to organize them into churches, and secure responsible officers for these churches. They established a church in each city and had an elder installed as the pastor and teacher. Gentile churches had now been set up in the heart of Asia.

*11. Report to the Church* (Acts 14:24-28).

On the journey home they followed the order of going except upon arrival at Perga they sailed directly for Seleucia and did not visit Cyprus. When at last they reached home they "gathered the church together and rehearsed all things that God had done with them, and that he had opened a door of faith to the Gentiles." What a wonderful story they had to tell of their two long years of labor among the Gentiles. Evidently the church heard with great satisfaction the report of these apostles. "The work among the Greeks had been launched upon a great scale and God had set the seal of his blessing upon it. Paul and Barnabas deserve some rest with the disciples. The missionary work with Paul is now not a theory merely, but a glorious fact. The Gentiles know the love of Christ and they will not forget him. One of the greatest revolutions in human history has come about. Jews and Greeks are now members of the body of Christ."[1]

*12. Paul as a Missionary.*

In following the experiences of the apostle on this first missionary campaign we have had opportunity to observe Paul at work in his great mission. The work of Paul and Barnabas took at least four definite forms. (1) They were preachers of the gospel. They addressed various groups, stating the central facts of the Christian message in persuasive language. These deliverances were effective in winning many to the Christian faith. (2) They must serve also as teachers. Many important questions could not be answered in public assemblies. We may think of Paul and Barnabas spending an enormous amount of time day and night in the instruction of individuals and groups of Christians. (3) Their work naturally called for much counselling with individuals and groups. They served as pastors to the people who needed this ministry. (4) They must act also as statemen or advisers to the Christians on all matters of church organization and programs. Paul was not only a pioneer in this; his methods were so successful that they have received the sanction of inspiration and still serve as a guide to church workers. The versatility and the genius of Paul are revealed in this first campaign. Even greater triumphs will come in his subsequent campaigns.

*13. His methods of Work.*

It will be well at this point also to note the general plan which Paul followed in his work to establish Christianity in the Roman world. A study of his activities will reveal that he had a plan which he followed regularly. He would begin his work where a real opportunity presented itself. Thus he started at Cyprus. He then went on to harder fields. Usually he worked in the large cities since he could reach the surrounding territory from these strategic centers. He followed the Roman roads to the great cities where there were Roman army posts and Greek colonies. These cities were selected with a view to reaching the province as a district of the Roman empire. He planned to reach all of the Roman empire ultimately, and each province was a part of his plan of conquest.

## 14. Threatened Disruption.

After Paul and Barnabas returned to Antioch they rested and enjoyed the fellowship of their brethren there. Before long, however, they learned of a situation which had arisen during their absence and which was now so serious as to threaten the very life of the church itself. The issue was the question of Gentiles becoming Christians. We have seen that Philip and Peter worked among the people of Samaria and accepted converts there. Peter had openly defended his work in winning Cornelius and other Gentiles at Caesarea. The church had even approved the Greek Christians in the church at Antioch of Syria. But during the absence of Paul and Barnabas from Antioch the issue had been keenly debated. Certain brethren from the church at Jerusalem had taken it upon themselves without authority, to go up to Antioch to debate the issue. These were of the Pharisaic party and had insisted that a Gentile man could not become a Christian without first submitting to the rite of circumcision. In other words he must virtually become a Jew first. The situation in Antioch now was tense and feeling between the groups was bitter.

Paul learned of this and saw at once the grave danger in it. This issue could not only split the churches; it could be the means of putting shackles on Christianity itself. He entered the fight at once and vigorously insisted that circumcision was not essential. He went so far as to reprove Peter and Barnabas for their apparent duplicity in the matter. In this crisis Paul proved his mettle as a great statesman. Without a man of his courage and wisdom the fight might have been lost. He saved the situation in Antioch, but it must be won at Jerusalem also.

## 15. The Council at Jerusalem (Acts 15:1-35).

Paul resolved to take the issue to Jerusalem, not to get authority from the church there since this church had no authority over any other church, but because the brethren from Jerusalem had raised the question at Antioch. Furthermore Paul was eager to have the influential leaders at Jerusalem and elsewhere take a positive stand on the issue so that all the churches would be free.

Luke gives a full account of this momentous conference in Jerusalem which the student should read carefully. Upon arriving in the city Paul called the influential men together for a private conference. This was not unethical; it was essential for these leaders to have an understanding beforehand so that they could give direction to this important discussion. In the meeting Paul was not conspicuous. The Judaizers (those who insisted on circumcision) spoke freely, and were followed by Peter and Barnabas who now boldly joined Paul in telling of their witness of the work of God among the Gentiles. The final decision was an overwhelming victory for Paul. It was decided to send a letter to the churches stating that circumcision and ceremonial acceptance of Judaism were not necessary for the Gentiles. The letter did urge, however, that "they abstain from the pollutions of idols, and from fornication, and from what is strangled, and from blood."

Certain brethren, Judas and Silas, were then selected by the group to return with Paul and Barnabas to Antioch to bear the decision. Upon arriving in Antioch the church was assembled to hear the letter read. "And when they had read it, they rejoiced for the consolation." Judas and Silas remained for awhile exhorting the Christians there. After the completion of their ministry, they "were dismissed in peace." Paul and Barnabas remained in Antioch.

[1]Robertson, *Epochs in the Life of Paul,* p. 120.

*Chapter IV*

## THE SECOND CAMPAIGN

1. Separation of Paul and Barnabas. 2. Survey of the Second Campaign. 3. The New Route. 4. Revisiting the Churches. 5. Hindered by the Holy Spirit. 6. In Philippi. 7. In Thessalonica. 8. In Berea. 9. In Athens. 10. In Corinth. 11. The Pauline Epistles. 12. Purpose and Style. 13. The General Pattern. 14. Some Problems of Early New Testament Churches. 15. I Thessalonians. 16. II Thessalonians. 17. The Homeward Journey. 18. Arrival in Antioch.

# The Second Campaign

*1. Separation of Paul and Barnabas* (Acts 15:31-40).

It appears that within a short time after Paul and Barnabas came again to Antioch from the great conference at Jerusalem the dissension in the church there was healed. The mission of Silas and Judas who had been sent by the Jerusalem church to help in the situation had been very effective. When the work of Silas and Judas was over they prepared to return home. It appears however, that Silas decided to remain in Antioch. Some ancient manuscripts insert verse 34 in Acts 15, which states that "it seemed good to Silas to abide there."

The crisis now over, Paul would turn his thoughts to their work among the Gentiles. So he suggested to Barnabas, "Let us return now and visit the brethren in every city wherein we proclaimed the word of the Lord, and see how they fare." This was entirely agreeable to Barnabas who added the suggestion or request that they take with them John Mark who had come up to Antioch with them from the Jerusalem conference and was eager now to go again with the great apostles. Evidently he had seen his mistake, had repented and was anxious to prove his worth. Barnabas, always generous, was favorable to his going. However, Paul bitterly opposed this on the ground that he had once deserted them, and probably would do so again. There was strong contention, even bitter argument, which ended in the separation of these two friends who had worked so well together. Fortunately we do not have to decide who was right. Certainly we share the feelings of Barnabas in his desire to give this young man another chance. And yet one can see Paul's point. He was devoting himself with complete abandon to the great cause and could not condone halfhearted service on the part of anyone.

They did what was best under the circumstances. Paul chose Silas to go with him on his second campaign while Barnabas took John Mark and went back to the island of Cyprus. The work of Barnabas and Mark is not recorded, not because it was unimportant but because Luke was primarily concerned with the progress of the great mission program under the leadership of Paul. Barnabas does not appear again in the record. Tradition affirms that the Jews burned him at the stake in Salamis and then scattered his ashes in the sea. John Mark is to be heard from again.

## 2. *Survey of the Second Campaign.*

This second campaign was much longer than the first. It covered a greater distance and lasted longer. The members of the party were Paul, Silas, Timothy and Luke, although these were not together at all times. The campaign started in the spring of the year 50 and lasted approximately three years. Paul and Silas started from Antioch, the home base, went overland to Tarsus from whence they traveled to Derbe, Lystra, Iconium and Antioch (Pisidia). From Troas on the coast they went across the strait to Philippi. From here they went to Thessalonica, Berea, Athens and Corinth. The mission ended at Corinth, so Paul embarked at Cenchreae, stopped briefly at Ephesus and went to Jerusalem. Leaving Jerusalem he returned to Antioch three years after setting out on this campaign.

## 3. *The New Route* (Acts 15:41).

The first objective of the second campaign was to visit the places where they had previously worked. With the plans of Barnabas to go to Cyprus, Paul would not be expected to include this in his route. So he and Silas went overland through Syria and Cilicia. Details are not given except the brief statement that they "confirmed the churches." To Paul this would be a happy experience since these were the churches he had founded during his stay in Tarsus some years earlier. Silas would be sympathetic and helpful so we can imagine a journey filled with activities and achievements. No doubt they would tarry some time in Tarsus before leaving that province to go to the four cities in which Paul and Barnabas labored on their first campaign. The route would take them through the famous Gates of Cilicia, the natural pass leading to Lycaonia.

## 4. *Revisiting the Churches* (Acts 16:1-5).

They arrived first at Derbe. There is no mention of what they may have done at this place. They hurried on to Lystra where they were gratified to find that Timothy, the young convert, had made great progress in the Christian faith and showed real promise of leadership. He being half-Gentile had not been circumcised. Paul arranged for Timothy to accompany them in this campaign, and to forestall any criticism on this troublesome question had him circumcised. Paul was not compromising in this action; he was trying to be expedient and wise. This very action, however, brought him great criticism later on. Paul had brought with him a copy of the letter giving the decision of the Jerusalem conference so as to give encouragement to all the Gentile

Christians. The report of their work as they left Lystra and went on to Antioch is very brief, "So the churches were strengthened in the faith, and increased in number daily." This program of visitation by Paul, Silas and Timothy was proving to be very profitable to these Gentile churches.

5. *Hindered by the Holy Spirit* (Acts 16:6-10).

We come now to one of the most baffling incidents in the New Testament. This concerns the plans that Paul had for his work after completing his visit at Antioch of Pisidia. He was hindered by the Holy Spirit from carrying out his intentions. To the west lay the great province of Asia with its magnificent city of Ephesus. Evidently Paul wished to go at once to this great city but the Holy Spirit forbade him. Paul, therefore, turned to the north into Phrygia and Galatia where he and his companions preached and founded churches. It seems that Paul planned to go from this region into Bithynia but again they were hindered by the Holy Spirit. The only course left open now was to go westward. Thus Paul, Silas and Timothy found themselves at Troas on the shore of the Aegean Sea. They found lodging and stayed in this city for some time.

Troas was an illustrious and historic city where the influence of the West was strong. Unable to understand all that was taking place these missionaries were on the eve of momentous events. They had not planned this part of their journey, but were later to see in it the leading of the Holy Spirit. There are certain points in history where one may stop and consider the course of events. Suppose Paul and his companions had been allowed to enter Bithynia and pursue their intended course. They probably would have continued eastward and ultimately might have taken the gospel as far east as India. Had their plans materialized we might have had a different course for all Christian history. It could be that India and China would have been Christianized while Europe and all Western nations would remain pagan. But the Holy Spirit intervened and turned the course of these apostles to the West — to Greece and Rome and other European peoples.

While in Troas one night Paul received a vision. A man of Macedonia stood and called him to come into that land and help them. This vision was so real that Paul took it to be the voice of God to him so they arranged to cross the sea to the continent of Europe. Next day they sailed and with favorable winds to aid them they made a straight course to Samothrace where they spent the night. Next day they made their way to the port of Neapolis. Apparently it was at Troas that Luke, the fourth member, joined the party. At this point, Luke, the writer of Acts, becomes an eyewitness or a participant in events and thus uses the first person plural in writing. From now on we have the use of the pronoun "we" in the narrative.

6. *In Philippi* (Acts 16:11-40).

The seaport of Neapolis was the natural approach to the important city of Philippi which lay only twelve miles distant. This properous and strategic city was named after Philip II, king of Macedonia, the father of Alexander the Great. A strong Roman colony was established in this rich city. The population was composed of three main elements: (1) the Roman colonists, strong and dominant, (2) the native Macedonians (Greek) and (3) a large group of Orientals, including Jews. Because of the splendid highways and its access to the sea Philippi was the meeting place of the East and West. It thus offered a great opportunity to the apostles.

In this city they had a long and active ministry. With the arrival of the Sabbath, Paul went down to the riverside where there was a Jewish place of prayer. They found assembled here a group of women to whom they preached the gospel. Among them was a notable woman named Lydia, a seller of purple dyes. She was a prominent business woman and an influential person in the city. She was responsive to the message of the apostles and readily became a believer. So genuine was her conversion that she invited the apostles to be guests in her home while they evangelized the city of Philippi. It is worthy of note that the first convert in Europe so far as the record goes was a woman.

In the course of their ministry here they were met by the maiden with a gift of divination. There are several different opinions as to the nature of this case, which we need not attempt to state. Paul healed her and she became a Christian. "We have thus a case parallel to the demoniacs who bore testimony to Jesus. But, whatever the explanation, her masters ceased to make money out of the poor girl's misfortune. They seemed to have organized a regular company that traded with her gift of divination. Paul and Silas had touched the pockets of these men, and they rose in wrath against the new preachers who had interfered with their vested rights."[1] In a rough attack Paul and Silas were dragged before the magistrates. Under the guise of patriotism these businessmen appealed to the populace, aroused them to action and had Paul and Silas publicly flogged and placed in jail.

The story of what took place in the jail that night is familiar to all students of the New Testament. The reader will note that Paul and Silas were not complaining; that they quickly interpreted this happening as the work of the Lord; that they won the jailer and his family and baptized them that night; that the jailer after his conversion extended every courtesy to the apostles. The magistrates were eager to get rid of these strange prisoners. These officers were in a predicament because they had publicly flogged two Roman citizens. Paul was independent, however, and forced the officers to appear in person and bring them out. They then politely asked the apostles to leave the city. Paul and Silas went to the house of Lydia "and when they had seen the brethren, they comforted them and departed." They left Timothy and Luke in Philippi with the church which was now established there.

7. *In Thessalonica* (Acts 17:1-9).

Paul and Silas left Philippi, passed through Amphipolis and Appolonia and came to the old city of Thessalonica for their next work. It was the capital of Macedonia and a very important city where many Roman officials lived. There was also a large colony of Jews who had established their synagogues. For three successive Sabbath days Paul preached in the synagogue and was successful in winning many Jews and Greeks to the Christian faith. The jealousy of the Jews was aroused and trouble ensued. These Jews gathered a company of the rabble of the city and "set the city in an uproar." They attacked the house of Jason, thinking that Paul and Silas were there. They brought Jason and others before the authorities and charged them with being members of a dangerous sect. The ruler required bond of Jason and his friends and released them. It was now apparent that the people were so excited and opposition was so strong that the disciples could not accomplish more here at this time. The brethren thus sent Paul and Silas away. The apostles however, had established a strong church here which Paul later referred to as "a sounding-board to echo forth the gospel to all the region around both in Macedonia and Achaia." (I Thessalonians 1:7-8.)

8. *In Berea* (Acts 17:10-14).

At first they were kindly received in Berea where it appeared they might have a fruitful ministry. The Bereans heard the apostles and then studied their scriptures to see if these men had preached the truth. Many Jews and Greeks believed the message and became Christians. Word of this successful ministry soon reached the Jews in Thessalonica.

Fired by anger they sent men down to drive the apostles out of Berea. In the meantime, Timothy had joined Paul and Silas in Berea. These Jews stirred up the people so that Paul, the leader, had to leave here also. Timothy and Silas remained at Berea, but Paul was conducted by gracious friends down to the sea and on to Athens. When these friends were ready to return to Berea, Paul told them to give the commandment to Silas and Timothy that "they should come to him with all speed." He went to Athens, not to evangelize the city at this time, but to wait for further news from Macedonia.

### 9. *In Athens* (Acts 17:15-34).

As Paul found himself in this great city he must have felt terribly alone. His companions were back in Macedonia and he must wait for further developments there. "He had no thought of preaching there, since Macedonia was his field and he was waiting anxiously for his recall thither. It proved, however, that the seeming interruption of his purpose was in truth a providential dispensation, the constraint of an unseen Hand conducting him to a larger ministry. Athens, pre-eminent in literature, art, and philosophy, was pre-eminent also in religion. She rivalled Rome in her hospitality to alien cults. The beautiful city was crowded with temples, shrines, altars, and images, which met the Apostle's eye at every turn as he strayed in street and market-place yearning wistfully for Macedonia. His soul was stirred. He was touched by the pity of it all, and one spectacle especially moved him — an altar bearing the inscription 'To an Unknown God.' Such altars were common in the Greek world, but this was the first he had encountered, and it spoke to him of the heathen heart's yearning after the Living and True God. He could not resist the mute appeal. He knew the blessed secret which would satisfy that blind desire, and he must proclaim it."[2]

At length he could resist no longer the urge to teach the truth and he began to reason both with the Jews in their synagogues and with others he met in the market-place. As he proclaimed the message, the people were intrigued by it. Being the home of philosophers it was but natural that they should want to hear more fully of this strange teaching which this learned Jew was proclaiming. Apparently the Stoics and Epicureans, the two leading schools of thought who held opposing views of what made life worth-while, carried Paul to their central place for debate, the Areopagus, to expound more fully his teaching. "It is, however, an inspiring moment when he stands on Mars

Hill, facing the noble temple of Minerva on the Acropolis, with members of the Council present along with Epicurean and Stoic philosophers, to speak about Jesus of Nazareth in the midst of Greek culture. We have seen Paul in various trying situations before. He has not yet met one that called for more resource and readiness."[3] They would listen attentively and Paul would use the occasion to the fullest. Employing their altar to "an Unknown God" as a point of contact, he claimed that his God was the maker of heaven and earth and that from him came life and strength. He continued to preach, dealing with the necessity for repentance and faith in Christ. They heard him attentively until he spoke of the resurrection from the dead. This was too much. The sermon ended abruptly. It appeared that he had failed — indeed he seems to have felt this himself. He had been faithful and he would go on with his preaching even if the philosophers didn't accept it. "Paul was not driven out of Athens; he was laughed out." But it was not a complete failure. "But certain men clave unto him, and believed; among who also was Dionysius, the Areopagite, and a woman named Damaris, and others with them."

### 10. In Corinth (Acts 18:1-17).

Paul was now through at Athens. Writing later to the church in Corinth he tells of his disappointment and yet of his determination to remain true to his message as he left Athens to go to Corinth. The city to which he now went was not far distant. It was the commercial and political capital of the province of Achaia. It was on a narrow isthmus, was a great trading center and was noted also for its wickedness. It was known for its "sudden wealth and false culture." On reaching Corinth Paul found it necessary to resort to his old trade of tent-making in order to earn a livelihood. It was thus that he met Aquila, also a tentmaker, and his wife, Priscilla. He lived with them and on every Sabbath went to the synagogue and "reasoned and persuaded Jews and Greeks." In this experience in Corinth one catches the spirit of this great apostle to the Gentiles. He was desparately in earnest; he never gave up. Making new friends, earning his living by honest labor, speaking and teaching wherever he had opportunity, he carried on faithfully.

He was eagerly awaiting the arrival of Silas and Timothy from Macedonia. When they finally came he was filled with great joy for he knew now that his church at Thessalonica was standing fast in the Lord. He devoted himself with fresh enthusiasm to his work in Corinth. His labors were so effective that resistance broke out among the Jews. This evidently was so severe that he felt he could accomplish nothing more among them. "He shook out his raiment and said unto them, Your blood be on your own heads: I am clean: From henceforth I will go unto the Gentiles."

He went to the house of Titus Justus adjacent to the synagogue. "Crispus, the ruler of the synagogue believed in the Lord with all his house; and many of the Corinthians hearing believed, and were baptized." To encourage Paul in his work he received a vision at night assuring him of protection and guidance. He remained here for eighteen months "teaching the word of God among them."

There came a change in the government when Gallio came to be the Roman proconsul of the province. The Jews seized upon this as an opportunity for driving Paul out of the city. He was brought before Gallio where the Jews accused him of "persuading men to worship God contrary to the law." Paul started to defend himself but Gallio cut him short with the statement that this case was of a religious nature and hence, "I am not minded to be a judge of these matters." Court was dismissed and the Jews were driven out. They had failed in their purpose. "The result of Gallio's refusal to punish Paul was to give him and his preaching a standing before Roman law that it had not had heretofore, a very important matter. It was a virtual edict of religious freedom for Christian preachers as a sect of the Jews at any rate, for Gallio did not go into the differences between Paul and the Jews."[4]

Paul had now been in Corinth approximately two years. (A.D. 51-52.) A great deal had been accomplished in this wicked city. But it was now time for him to turn homeward. Before tracing his journey back to Jerusalem and Antioch to close his second missionary campaign, we must give consideration to one other important aspect of his work in Corinth. It was here that he wrote the first of his epistles or letters.

## 11. The Pauline Epistles.

We shall see that Paul did some of his most effective and important work through his epistles. He did an unbelievable amount of work in person. But he did a great deal also for both individuals and churches by sending letters to them. We cannot over-estimate the value of these epistles, not only for what they did in the immediate situation that called them forth, but as the authoritative statement of Christian doctrine. They are our greatest theological treasures.

The epistles of Paul are generally placed in four groups according to time and general content.

(1) I and II Thessalonians — A.D. 52-53, dealing with the second coming of Christ.

(2) I and II Corinthians, Galatians, Romans — A.D. 55-58, dealing with Paul's important doctrine of Justification by Faith.

(3) Philippians, Philemon, Colossians and Ephesians — A.D. 60-63, dealing with the person of Christ.

(4) I Timothy, Titus, II Timothy — A.D. 65-67, dealing with the problems of churches and pastors.

*12. Purpose and Style.*

While we rank the epistles of Paul among the greatest of all writings we should remember that he did not write these letters with the notion that they would some time be recognized as great literature. Each letter was written to meet the needs in a specific situation. They won recognition by their merit.

In these writings he was specific, personal and practical. The style is peculiarly his own. In them we see the dynamic, human Paul speaking. "He talks; he yields to the inspiration of the moment; and if his similes and allegories miss fire now and then in print, he made them effectual *viva voce*. Like good talkers, he indicates an idea and leaves you to develop it — and to get it fitted into what he said last and what he is going to say next — if he quite knows so long ahead. His arguments on paper, like some of those in the early chapters of Romans, are not equal to passages where he does not argue at all. In the epistle to the Galatians, his argument is a series of explosions, and every one of them tells; it is all cumulative. It is not easy reading; it is not strictly art; but it is all personality. Whatever his argument is, powerful as it is in Galatians, it is not that that you chiefly remember when he is done. You have been with a man of genius; you have swept with him from peak to peak, vision to vision; you have tried to keep pace with his moods and his subjects, indicated in the amazing vocabulary, the striking metaphors, the compressed word-pictures, popular phrase, Septuagint echo, terms of his own (which he does not always use to mean the same thing — a bad habit which common people often regret in men of genius); you have consorted with a man of elemental force, revelled in all the colours of God with him, mixed them (no doubt), wondered why he was not a poet and why he was so much more than any poet; and all the time you have been growing to love more and more the greatest human being that ever followed Jesus Christ and had Christ living in him. You and he together have been adding to your experience of Christ in every tangled sentence and involved paragraph; and you end (as Paul would have wished you to end) with the feeling that Christ is all and in all."[5]

*13. The General Pattern.*

A study of all the letters of Paul will show that in each of these he followed a general pattern. The framework of these was very much the same in every case. These epistles usually contain some five or six main points.

(1) The salutation or superscription, usually including the names of those with Paul at the time.

(2) An expression of thanksgiving for the good qualities exhibited by those to whom he is writing.

(3) The general theme, or the purpose of the letter.

(4) A practical section in which the truth which he has expounded is applied.

(5) Personal messages to various individuals.

(6) The closing words and benediction.

*14. Some Problems of Early New Testament Churches.*

We are accustomed to think of these early churches as ideal organizations without serious problems and difficulties such as modern churches have. In some way we feel that we should like to have churches exactly like these first ones. Unfortunately, however, these first organizations were not without serious problems and handicaps. In fact they had to work against terrific odds and had to overcome many obstacles which modern churches do not have. It may be helpful to enumerate some of the handicaps under which they were forced to work.

(1) They had no church buildings. It was not until the second century that Christians were able to have their own buildings for assembly and worship. In the beginning the group was forced to meet in the home of some member or sympathetic friend, as with Philemon in Colossae. Oftentimes they met in caves, or out in open places, or perhaps in a rented hall.

(2) Sunday was not a legal holiday. The members had to work on the day of worship and hence the time for worship was usually early in the morning, or at night after the day's work was done.

(3) They had none of the aids of worship such as we now have. They did not have Bibles for general use. In fact they had no New

Testament as such until the second century. They had no hymn books and no literature such as we are accustomed to use.

(4) They had no trained workers or leaders. They were dependent upon a few untrained teachers and preachers except when favored by the visits of men like Paul, Timothy, Silas and others.

(5) They had no denominational organization to furnish fellowship, or general direction of their work.

(6) Their membership was made up of a mixture of races and included all classes from slaves to the wealthy and aristocratic believers. This naturally caused misunderstandings and friction.

(7) They were surrounded by all the influences and practices of a superstitious, pagan people. Many of these superstitious beliefs, such as wearing of a charm to ward off evil spirits, vitally affected religious life. Even after becoming Christians it took some time for the people to divest themselves of these pagan beliefs.

When we consider all the problems which these early churches faced we can understand something of their magnificent achievements in developing great organizations which survived despite dangers and became centers of strength.

*15. I Thessalonians.*

We have seen that Paul left Macedonia when the Jews had stirred up such opposition that he could not work effectively there, and went to Athens to wait for the trouble to die down. He left Silas and Timothy in Thessalonica with instructions to report to him later. Paul left Athens after a short time and began his work in Corinth. Silas and Timothy came down from Macedonia to visit him in Corinth. They brought news that the church there was making progress despite all the opposition but that they were beset by many problems, chief of which was some difference of opinion on the second coming of Christ. In order to clear up these misunderstandings and to give further help on other matters he wrote the first letter to the Thessalonians from Corinth, probably late in A.D. 52 or early in 53. "Its purpose was: (1) To send affectionate greetings, (2) to console them in their afflictions, (3) to correct their mistaken views of Christ's second coming, (4) to exhort them to proper living as against certain immoral tendencies."[6]

*16. II Thessalonians.*

This first letter was delivered to the Thessalonians and served to encourage and comfort them. It appears however, that it did not clear up the various misunderstandings about the second coming of Christ. Some of them understood Paul to teach that Jesus was to return immediately. In view of this immediate return some of the Christians felt there was no need to continue working. This idea would be fatal to the church and community. Paul, therefore, wrote a second letter, probably in A.D. 53, to clear up this false notion and to exhort all Christians to work diligently since no one knew the day of the second coming of Christ. It is a brief letter, very practical in nature, and contains a severe rebuke to mischief-makers.

### 17. The Homeward Journey (Acts 18:18-21).

It was now A.D. 53 and Paul had been gone from his home-base three years. He was eager to get back to Syrian Antioch to learn of conditions there and to get news from other churches where he had worked.

Apparently Paul left Silas and Timothy at Corinth. It may be, as some think, that they then returned to Macedonia. At any rate, Paul left Corinth accompanied only by Aquila and Priscilla. Going through the port of Cenchreae they came to Ephesus, where Aquila and Priscilla remained. In Ephesus Paul went into the synagogue and reasoned with the Jews. Evidently they gave him a sympathetic hearing since they besought him to remain a longer time with them, but he insisted on resuming his journey, but promised them that he would come to them at a later time. We have no details of the voyage to Caesarea on the coast of Palestine except the statement of his arrival.

### 18. Arrival in Antioch (Acts 18:22).

Again Luke gives no details of Paul's experiences. The statement "he went up and saluted the church" is generally understood to mean that he went up to Jerusalem for a brief visit to the church there, though this may not be true. He then hurried to Antioch from whence he and Silas had gone three years earlier on this extended campaign among the Gentiles. He would spend some time here among friends and would report to the church the victories which the gospel had won among the Gentiles in the far west.

[1]Robertson, *Epochs in the Life of Paul*, p. 150.
[2]Smith, *Life and Letters of St. Paul*, pp. 142-143.
[3]Robertson, *Epochs in the Life of Paul*, p. 160.
[4]Ibid., p. 166.
[5]Glover, T. R., *Paul of Tarsus*, pp. 196-197.
[6]Tidwell, *The Bible, Book by Book*, p. 185.

*Chapter V*

## THE THIRD CAMPAIGN

1. Survey of the Campaign. 2. Paul, Teacher of Churches. 3. Pauline Theology. 4. Paul as a Statesman. 5. Back in Galatia. 6. A New Apostle. 7. Ephesus, the Heart of Asia. 8. Paul in Ephesus. 9. The First Letter to Corinth. 10. Paul in Macedonia Again. 11. Second Letter to Corinth. 12. Paul in Illyricum. 13. In Corinth Again. 14. Letter to the Galatians. 15. Letter to the Romans. 16. The Journey Homeward.

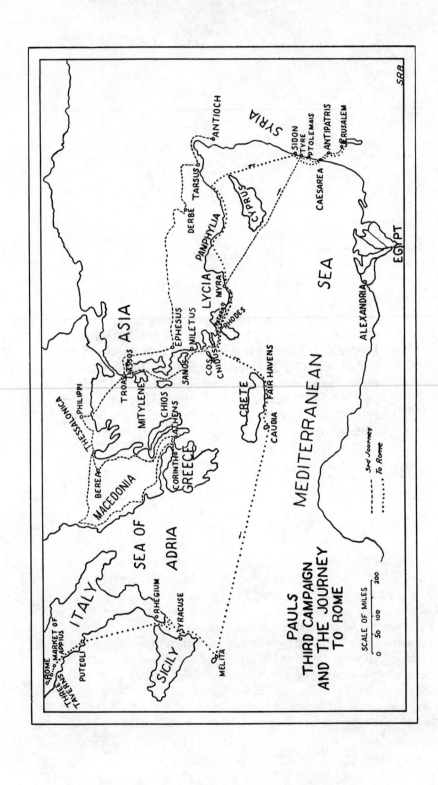

PAULS
THIRD CAMPAIGN
AND THE JOURNEY
TO ROME

SCALE OF MILES

0    50   100        200

3rd Journey - - - - -

To Rome · · · · · · · ·

SRB

## CHAPTER V

# The Third Campaign

*1. Survey of the Campaign.*

It appears that Paul did not stay in Antioch long after the completion of his second campaign. No doubt word had come to him of the serious work the Judaizers had done in the churches of Galatia during the past two years, 52-53 A.D. We see him now starting out on another long, hard campaign where he will find many foes with whom to contend.

This campaign was, with the exception of his long sojourn in Ephesus and his visit to Illyricum, mainly spent in places where he had previously worked. He went overland from Antioch to Cilicia, Phyrigia and Galatia. He moved from here to Ephesus, the capital of Asia, for a long stay. Leaving Ephesus he went back through Macedonia, on to Illyricum and then to Corinth where the campaign was considered finished. From here he returned to Macedonia, thence to Troas, to Miletus and thence to Tyre, Caesarea and finally to Jerusalem. This was his longest campaign. The dates are 53-57 or 54-58 A.D. He had a large number of helpers during this period, no one of whom was with him all the time. Aquila and Priscilla, Timothy, Luke, Titus, Erastus, Gaius, Aristarchus, Apollos, Tertius, Lucius, Sopater, Phoebe, Jason, Tychicus, Trophimus and perhaps others, appear at different points in the campaign.

*2. Paul, Teacher of Churches.*

In the two previous campaigns, the apostles devoted the major part of their efforts to winning new converts to the Christian faith. In this third campaign, Paul was forced to give much of his time to other matters. He wanted these Gentile churches to have a part in relieving the economic distress of the saints in Jerusalem. The need there was great and Paul knew that a generous contribution from the Gentile churches would have a helpful effect in bringing the Jewish and Gentile Christians to a better understanding of each other. Consequently he planned to raise money from these churches on this third journey. Another situation had developed which caused Paul to devote much time to teaching and explaining the doctrines of Christ. The Judaizers had been among these Gentile churches and had spread many false teachings. In fact these Gentile Christians had been most seriously upset and were turning away from the Christian faith. Paul had been attacked by his enemies and must defend himself and his apostleship. In addition to these difficulties, some of the churches had become involved in doctrinal controversies and had serious differences of opinion among themselves. In view of all these facts, Paul was forced to become the teacher of the churches, the great theologian to expound and interpret the Christian faith. He did this both in oral discussions and in the writing of letters. The four letters written on this campaign are his great doctrinal epistles. They incorporate his profoundest thought as a theologian and as a philosopher. These four great epistles "are the crushing and terrible blows with which the mighty combatant openly answered the court intrigues of his enemies. The contest is in reality a drama, which grows larger and more complicated as it advances from Galatia to Rome."[1] Because these epistles contain the chief teachings of Paul it may be helpful to summarize briefly the main doctrines of Pauline theology.

### 3. Pauline Theology.

Unquestionably Paul is the greatest interpreter of the gospel of Jesus Christ. Indeed, he was the first real interpreter. It was his responsibility to systematize and expound Christianity as a way of life, as a system of theological thought.

What are the chief elements in Pauline theology? Most Christians are familiar with these teachings, perhaps not knowing that Paul is the one thinker who arranged these teachings into a system of theology.

(1) He holds that man has failed to attain a righteousness of his own, and thereby failed to merit the favor of God, indeed he has exposed himself to the wrath of God. All men — both the Gentile and the Jew — have failed in this. In Adam all fell, and human nature was too weak to attain righteousness of itself. In this the law could not help.

(2) "Man's extremity was God's opportunity." In the failure of man to save himself, God now provided a way of attaining salvation. This righteousness of God was wholly of God's grace and love. Man did nothing to provide it. He doesn't deserve it but it is his because of the love of God for men. This is "the righteousness of God, by the faith of Jesus Christ, unto all and upon all who believe." Those who accept this righteousness of God enter into peace and favor with God. "Being justified by faith, we have peace with God through our Lord Jesus Christ, by whom also we have access by faith into this grace wherein we stand, and rejoice in hope of the glory of God." This

salvation is available to all men. It is to be appropriated wholly by faith; man needs only to accept it as the free gift of God.

(3) Jesus Christ is the "Second Adam." The choice of Adam in the Garden of Eden brought all men into condemnation. Jesus Christ is the new Adam, the new head of humanity, the one who relieves us from the bondage imposed by the first Adam. "As by one man's disobedience many were made sinners, so by the obedience of one shall many be made righteous." One who accepts this righteousness of God and thereby becomes a child of God still has a fleshly nature and must keep this sinful nature under subjection. He must, by the grace of God, conquer sin. But the victory is assured. Sin shall be conquered. "Neither death, nor life, nor angels, nor principalities, nor powers, nor things present, nor things to come, nor height, nor depth, nor any other creature shall be able to separate us from the love of God which is in Christ Jesus, our Lord."

(4) Christ is the center and the glory of this redemptive plan of God. "But it is in its conception of Christ that Paul's gospel wears its imperishable crown. The Evangelists sketched in a hundred traits of simple and affecting beauty the fashion of the earthly life of the man Christ Jesus, and in these the model of human conduct will always have to be sought; but to Paul was reserved the task of making known, in its heights and depths, the work which the Son of God accomplished as the Saviour of the race. He scarcely ever refers to the incidents of Christ's earthly life, although here and there he betrays that he knew them well. To him Christ was ever the glorius Being, shining with the splendor of heaven, who appeared to him on the way to Damascus, and the Saviour who caught him up into the heavenly peace and joy of a new life. When the Church of Christ thinks of her Head as the deliverer of the soul from sin and death, as a spiritualizing presence ever with her and working in every believer, and as the Lord over all things who will come again without sin unto salvation, it is in forms of thought given her by the Holy Ghost through the instrumentality of this apostle."[2]

### 4. Paul as a Statesman.

In this third campaign we shall see the matchless skill of Paul as a Christian statesman. He is beset by problems of all sorts; he faces situations which would have broken the spirit of a weaker man. His chief burden was the welfare of his churches. "He has now taken the whole world into his vision, and, wherever the body of Christ suffers, Paul suffers. (II Cor. 11:29.) His horizon has broadened till it compasses the whole Roman Empire. At Ephesus he will fight the opposition of Jews and the rage of the silversmiths who are losing the trade in their shrines; he will throw his soul into the solution of the troubles at Corinth; he will superintend the collections for the poor saints in Jerusalem, a collection that has included Galatia, Asia, Achaia and Macedonia in its scope before he leaves Ephesus; he is planning for a trip to Macedonia, Achaia, Jerusalem, Rome. At Troas Corinth will still be a burden as will be the case in Macedonia. In Corinth he yearns after Galatia, where the Judaizers have been playing havoc; after Jerusalem, where the opposition has crystallized against him; after Rome, where he has not yet been and where the Judaizers have gone on ahead of him; after Spain that great Western empire ripe for the gospel of Christ. (Rom. 15:28.) His sweep of sympathy is that of the Christian statesman who loves the whole world."[3]

5. *Back in Galatia* (Acts 18:23).

We have no way of knowing how long Paul remained in Antioch before setting forth on his third campaign. We may assume that he would take time for some rest after the arduous journey of three years which he had completed. Smith in *The Life and Letters of St. Paul* holds that he spent June and a part of July in Antioch between the second and third campaigns. The exact route which he followed in visiting these regions is not certainly known. Some hold that he followed the course of the second campaign: Derbe, Lystra, Iconium and Antioch. Others insist that he touched towns further north like Ancyra and Pessinus where he may have worked in his second tour. Whichever way he went, his program of work would be the same.

6. *A New Apostle* (Acts 18:24-28).

In this connection we are introduced to a very brilliant young man who evidently occupied a place of prominence in the church at Corinth. Apollos of Alexandria was a scholarly man and an eloquent speaker. For some reason he had learned only a part of the story of Jesus. He was, however, unacquainted with the latter part of the career of Jesus and knew nothing of the death, resurrection and ascension of Jesus, and the coming of the Holy Spirit on the day of Pentecost. In other words, he knew about Jesus only what John the Baptist had taught. He was in Ephesus before Paul reached there on his third campaign. While in Ephesus he met Aquila and Priscilla who "took him unto them, and expounded unto him the way of God more accurately." This brilliant young preacher who was already recognized as an influential teacher since he spoke "boldly in the synagogue," seems to have had a humble spirit and was willing to learn from those who knew more than he. When he was fully instructed by this devout man and wife, and had received letters of introduction from them to the brethren in the church at Corinth, he went on to Corinth. He had a notable ministry in this great city for "he helped them much that had believed through grace; for he powerfully confuted the Jews, and that publicly, showing by the scriptures that Jesus was the Christ."

### 7. Ephesus, the Heart of Asia.

For nearly three years Paul lived and worked in Ephesus, the capital of Asia. This was his longest ministry in one place, and this great city with its strategic situation and leadership furnished Paul an opportunity for the use of all his faculties as a preacher of the gospel and as a Christian statesman. Oftentimes he had dreamed of work in this city and hitherto had postponed entering the city until he could remain long enough to undertake the work on a worthy scale.

Ephesus was not only the capital of the Province of Asia but was the leading city of all Asia Minor. Here was the seat of the imperial proconsul and the center of the Asiarchate, the union of the chief cities of the province. Her fortunate geographical position with her fine seaport which accomodated vast trading enterprises made the city a great commercial center. Sooner or later every important person in Asia came to Ephesus. The city boasted also of notable achievements in literature and art. Her principal glory however, was the temple of Artemis or Diana. This vast and magnificent structure was one of the seven wonders of the ancient world. The walls and pillars were of gleaming marble while the interior was decorated with ivory and the finest woods. The imposing columns numbering one hundred and sixty-seven, each erected by a king, were sixty feet high. The structure was four hundred twenty-five feet long and two hundred twenty feet wide. The building was finished only after two hundred and twenty years of labor. This costly and magnificent temple was the gift of the whole population of Asia and was their pride and glory. The chief treasure in the temple was the image of the goddess — "A pedestal surmounted by a bust which was studded with breasts symbolizing fecundity." The cherished tradition was that this image had fallen from heaven. This temple was a real economic asset to the city. Large numbers of worshipers who made pilgrimages to the temple usually purchased some souvenir of their visit. To meet this demand silversmiths manufactured and sold small silver models of the temple. This proved to be a very lucrative business. The worship which centered around the temple was vile and licentious. Oriental magic in its worst form was practiced here.

Such was the situation into which Paul entered. He was wise enough to proceed cautiously and to use all his intelligence in supplanting the worship of Diana with faith in Jesus Christ the Son of God.

### 8. *Paul in Ephesus* (Acts 19:1-20:1, 18-35).

Paul began his work in Ephesus by giving fuller instruction to a group of Christians who did not know the complete story of Christ. Indeed, they seem to have been altogether ignorant of Jesus and the Holy Spirit, and repentance. Paul started at the beginning and gave them thorough instruction which they seem to have accepted readily. Afterwards this company of "about twelve men" was baptized.

His next step was to enter the synagogue and preach to the Jews. Details of his ministry in the synagogue are not given, except that he continued here for three months and was forced out by the opposition of the Jews. It was the same story; many believed, but others "were hardened and disobedient." One can imagine Paul at his best in this ministry as he "reasoned and persuaded as to the things concerning the kingdom of God." The historical references do not tell much of the hardships which he suffered in Ephesus, but in his correspondence he alludes to persecution which must have been severe.

With the synagogue closed to him Paul "separated the disciples" and rented the lecture hall which belonged to the rhetorician Tyrannus. The owner used the hall part of the day for his own lectures but Paul could use it for the remainder of the day. It appears that Paul's hours were from 11:00 A.M. to 4:00 P.M. In this hall he lectured daily for a period of approximately two years. Since Paul had no means of support he worked at his trade of tent-making during the morning and preached and taught in the afternoons.

This ministry proved to be most effective, "all they that dwelt in Asia heard the word of the Lord, both Jews and Greeks." "It is an evidence of the hold which the Gospel had taken on the city, and the conquest of Ephesus proved a far-reaching triumph. She was the metropolis of Asia, and tidings of her gracious visitation quickly spread through the Province. Paul remained within her gates, but his message traveled where his voice had never been heard, and churches grew up which had never seen his face, not alone that little group in the Lycus valley — at Colossae, Laodicea, and Hierapolis — which he had occasion to counsel by letter some seven years later when he was a prisoner at Rome, but those at Smyrna, Pergamos, Thyatira, Sardis, and Philadelphia which St. John addresses in the Book of Revelation, and those at Magnesia, Tralles and Miletus which St. Ignatius afterwards addressed. His companions, especially Timothy and Titus, would be active in this missionary enterprise, and Ephesian converts like Erastus would bear their part; but the work was doubtless done chiefly by representatives of the various cities, like Epaphras and Philemon of Colossae and Nympha of Laodicea, who visited Ephesus, and there heard the Gospel from his lips and carried it home."[4]

In Acts 19:11-20 Luke gives an interesting account of the miracles Paul was able to work at Ephesus. This city was the home of Eastern magic and was filled with superstition. The charlatans who lived here claimed to be able to avert misfortune by the use of magic charms and incantations. Paul's use of miracles thus classed him as a magical person in the eyes of the people. Dispite this misrepresentation Paul's work was effective in getting the attention of the people and winning the devotion of a number. The sincerity of those who believed is demonstrated by their burning publicly their papyri or books on magic.

Another incident demonstrated the effectiveness of Paul's ministry in Ephesus. With an increasing number of people accepting the Christian faith the number who worshiped Diana gradually decreased, and the followers of Diana became genuinely concerned. The suspicion and fear of the populace expressed itself in a serious riot in which Paul almost lost his life. Their grievance, while ostensibly religious, was really commercial. The lucrative business which these manufacturers of the silver models of the temple had developed was so seriously curtailed that they became alarmed and incensed. Demetrius, one of the more prominent silversmiths who employed a number of workmen, led in the public protest. His impassioned appeal fired the assembly and resulted in a wild mob scene. Demetrius led the parade through the streets in their search for Paul. Since Paul happened to be out of reach at the time they seized two of Paul's helpers, Gaius and Aristarchus, and dragged them to the theater. Paul learned of this and was eager to go to the rescue of his friends but was restrained by friends and officials. In the meantime the crowd in the theater became so violent that the town clerk appeared and quieted them after an uproar of more than two hours. The mob was finally dispersed, but this demonstration had made an end to the effectiveness of Paul's work in Ephesus. The people would not forget the man who was responsible for their financial losses and who had proved such an effective agent against their cherished national institution. Paul was no longer able to remain here since his life was daily endangered. His dwelling place was attacked and he was eagerly sought by his enemies. This was a bitter experience for him, but the only way to escape with his life was to retire from the city. Thus it was that after a ministry of some three fruitful years in the city he fled. Sympathetic friends helped him, with Timothy, Tychicus, Trophimus, Aristarchus and Gaius, down to the sea where they took ship and sailed for Macedonia.

### 9. The First Letter to Corinth.

Having summarized the work of Paul in Ephesus during these three years we shall now give consideration to some experiences of his which, while they are not recorded in Acts, are of great significance. These experiences were concerned with his interest in the church at Corinth, not far distant, which he had established on his second campaign. Serious difficulties had beset this church during these three or four years since he had been with them. Members of the church naturally knew of Paul's presence in Ephesus, so messengers, official and unofficial, brought news of these difficulties to Paul. Early in his stay in Ephesus he had written a letter to the Corinthian church concerning a case of gross immorality among them (I Cor. 5:9) though this letter either has been lost or is incorporated in the two letters (I & II Cor.). After this the household of Chloe had reported to Paul the division existing in the church. A committee of Stephanas, Fortunatus and Achaicus had come to him with a letter from the Corinthian church concerning various problems which existed in the church. Even before this Paul had sent Timothy to set things in order, but seemingly this was not accomplished. So in the spring of A.D. 56 or 57 Paul wrote the letter which we now call I Corinthians, to this church. There were serious problems that needed immediate and vigorous attention.

1. There were four factions among them. There was a Paul party, an Apollos party, a group who claimed Peter (who had not been there) as their ideal, and another group who called themselves the Christ party.

2. In this prosperous and wicked city gross immorality had invaded the church.

3. Certain groups at variance with each other were going to civil courts to get their differences arbitrated.

4. There were many other questions which troubled them: marriage, eating meats that had been sacrificed to idols, and some serious questions about Paul's right to claim apostleship like Peter, headdress for women, the real meaning of the Lord's supper, the matter of spiritual gifts and finally, the question of the resurrection of believers. Certainly if ever a church was in difficulties this one was. Most of these questions were stirred up by the Judaizers whose motive was to discredit Paul and destroy his works. With rare insight, with great power and sincere love Paul wrote this letter to help his church.

The scope of this book will not permit any attempt to analyze or expound this remarkable letter. It is very practical in nature and yet contains some of the greatest passages in the New Testament. The most famous treatise on Christian love ever written is chapter 13 of this letter. Chapter 15 is a masterful argument for the resurrection of the believer in Christ.

*10. Paul in Macedonia Again* (Acts 20:1; II Cor. 2:12-13, 7:5-7, 13-14).

The first letter to the Corinthian church was written before the riot led by Demetrius. As already stated, Paul had sent Timothy to Corinth but when he returned and reported his failure to settle the questions in Corinth Paul then dispatched Titus to Corinth to do what he could to help them. He then sent Timothy and Erastus on to Macedonia. Paul had instructed Titus to come from Corinth to Troas where he would join him. At that time he had expected to remain in Ephesus some months longer. However, the insurrection led by Demetrius made it neccessary for him to depart much earlier than he anticipated. Upon leaving Ephesus Paul went immediately to Troas but was so far ahead of schedule that he had to wait some time for Titus. This stay at Troas was exceedingly trying for him. He was physically exhausted after his strenuous years in Ephesus. He was bitterly disappointed over the turn of events in Ephesus. He was sorely troubled over the problems in Corinth. In addition to these problems he seems to have been seized with a serious illness. He finally decided not to wait for Titus to arrive but left Troas and pushed on to Macedonia. He would find Luke, Timothy, Erastus and Lydia at Philippi. They would comfort him in his deep distress. At length Titus came to Philippi and brought to Paul good news of the improved situation in Corinth.

*11. Second Letter to Corinth.*

Some scholars hold that Paul had sent from Ephesus a very sharp letter to Corinth by Titus, and that this letter was much more effective than I Corinthians. Be that as it may, Titus could now give a better report on conditions there. This would bring great relief and comfort to Paul. Titus had accomplished a good work. Paul is filled with joy and no longer regrets any harsh words he had spoken to them, since they had repented.

When Titus joined Paul in Philippi with the good news from Corinth it was in the fall or early winter of the year A.D. 56. Paul was eager now to write to Corinth again primarily to express his great joy at their repentance and their purpose to do better. He had passed through "a crisis in his soul" and wanted to share with them the benefits of this season of travail. (Chapters 1-7.) He wanted also to urge upon them the necessity of doing a worthy part in the collection he was taking for the needy saints in Jerusalem. (Chapters 8-9.) Finally he felt the necessity of rebuking those who were still stubborn and unrepentant. (Chapters 10-13.) Each of these three sections of the epistle stands to itself in a sense, yet all three concur and harmonize with the general situation.

This magnificent letter, which we call II Corinthians, was dispatched by Paul at once to Corinth. It is the least systematic of all his writings and is filled with emotion. In it Paul displays grief, indignation, and great joy. It is very personal in nature and reveals the inner feelings of Paul as do none of his other writings. The first section (1-7), dealing with tribulation and the Christian's comfort is a rich and glorious affirmation of the hope of all Christians in trouble or sorrow. The second section is still the finest argument for the Christian's stewardship of money. The third section contains Paul's fiery denunciation of those who questioned his apostleship and who sought only to disrupt the church. "This Epistle vibrates with passion and power."

*12. Paul in Illyricum* (Romans 15:19).

Luke's record in Acts is very brief at this point. He tells almost nothing of Paul's visit to Troas, his experiences at Philippi (Macedonia) and of his visit to Corinth after the sending of II Corinthians. In his letter to Rome, which he wrote a few months later in Corinth, he declares that he has fully preached the gospel "from Jerusalem, and round about even unto Illyricum." This being true it would appear that the only time in his career when he could have gone to Illyricum, the region west of Macedonia, was after he left Macedonia to go to Corinth on his third campaign. Not all scholars agree on this but there are good reasons for holding that Paul, after sending II Corinthians on to Corinth by Titus and two other messengers, went over to Illyricum for a ministry of two or three months to give this epistle an opportunity to effect its purpose in the church at Corinth.

### 13. In Corinth Again (Acts 20:2-3).

Paul with several companions, Sopater, Aristarchus, Secundus, Gaius, Tychicus and Trophimus, finally arrived in Corinth where he remained for three months. He was graciously received and was hospitably entertained in the home of a good friend. He probably did no extensive missionary work on this visit but spent his time in dealing with individuals, counselling with the church leaders and strengthening the church there. His very presence was a benediction to the Christians. One of Paul's chief labors at this time was his purpose to raise a worthy offering from the Corinthian Christians for the church at Jerusalem. His stay here gave him the opportunity to do a most important work in the sending of two of his greatest letters to the churches. It was during this period that he wrote the Epistle to the Galatians, and the greatest of all his letters, the Epistle to Rome.

### 14. Letter to the Galatians.

We are placing the time for the writing of the letter to the Galatians at this point in the career of Paul. Some scholars insist that this letter was written from Antioch of Syria just before Paul began his third campaign in the summer of A.D. 53. Others believe that it was written during his three years stay in Ephesus. (A.D. 53-56.) In the light of all the facts, however, it seems best to consider Corinth in A.D. 57 as the most likely place and date for the writing of the epistle.

It is one of the most vigorous and impassioned of all Paul's letters. It deals with matters which he regarded as of utmost importance. It was called forth by the activities of the Judaizers. These unscrupulous opponents had been at work among the Galatian churches during the absence of Paul and were so vigorous in their efforts that they were threatening the very life of these churches. They had discredited Paul among many of these Christians and had succeeded in persuading many others in these churches to turn away from Christianity and to return to Judaism. Paul wrote this "blazing little epistle" to defend his apostleship, to win his converts back to their allegiance to Christ, and to expound the doctrine of "justification by faith."

He begins the letter by asserting that he was a true apostle and as such had apostolic authority. In order to do this he reviews that part of his career involving his conversion and his call to his mission to the Gentiles. He passionately defends the doctrine of justification by faith.

His great argument (3:1-5:12) deals with justification by faith. Going back to Abraham who "believed God and it was reckoned to him for righteousness," he proved his thesis that "the righteous shall live by faith." The Law was only a pedagogue (a guide to lead students to school) which leads men to Christ. Christ is our teacher and "we are all the children of God, through faith, in Jesus Christ."

The closing section (5:13-6:18) makes a powerful plea for the ethical and moral realization of our salvation. While "we are called for freedom" we are not to use our "freedom as an occasion for the flesh." We are to walk by the spirit and not after the flesh. In closing he vigorously denounces any false gospel and pleads for loyalty to Christ who saves us by faith.

*15. Letter to the Romans.*

While on this visit to Corinth Paul wrote his Epistle to the Romans. Traditionally this letter has been regarded as a direct letter to the Christians at Rome. Many scholars however, regard it as a sort of circular letter which Paul intended for other groups of believers as well as the Romans. Since we are not primarily concerned with problems of criticism in this book, and since the value of the epistle is in no way affected by this critical problem, we need not be concerned about this question.

For many years Paul had cherished a great desire to visit Rome and work with the Christians there. As he had seen his dream for the evangelization of Greece at least partially accomplished he had now set his eyes on Italy and Spain. He hoped to come to them soon, but at present this was not possible. He regarded his authority as an apostle sufficient ground for expressing his interest in the Roman Christians and in writing them to deal with the important doctrine of justification by faith. While at Corinth shortly before he was to start his journey homeward via Jerusalem he wrote this, the greatest of all his epistles. "Thus it was that the great theologian apostle came to address to Roman Christians his most elaborate treatise and his most logical and cogent piece of theological statement. This *statement of the Christian doctrine of righteousness* more than any other Scripture has constituted the norm for Christian orthodoxy through the centuries. It has been the touchstone for re-establishing our theology after every decline of vigor and defection in thinking."[5]

The content or argument of the letter may be summarized in five stages. (Carver, *Why They Wrote the New Testament*, pp. 91-95.) Paul shows that there is a universal and an imperative need for God to supply a righteousness for man. (1:18-3:20.) Man has naturally gone away from God and has incurred the wrath of God. He proves the truth of this assertion both for Gentiles and Jews. He concludes with the statement, "All have sinned and come short of the glory of God."

In view of man's need and his utter helplessness the apostle then sets forth "a righteousness of God" provided by God without man's effort. It is the gift of God to be appropriated by faith. It is free to all men who may be "justified freely by his grace through the redemption that is in Christ Jesus, whom God set forward as a mercy seat through faith in his blood." This part of Paul's argument (3:21-4:25) represents some of his most convincing logic.

In chapters five to eight we have the third stage of his presentation. This section deals with the two consequences for the individual believer in being accepted of God on this basis. First, it gives him absolute security, hence he can have no fear of his complete redemption. Following this Paul raises the question of the place of sin in the life of the believer. He gives three answers: First, "The redeemed man is committed to the complete conquest of sin; second, man can be delivered from all the conflict of sin only by Jesus Christ, his Lord; third, that man who endeavors with the help of God to conquer sin finds himself supported by the Holy Spirit in the grip of the eternal purpose of God. Therefore sin is to be fully and completely overcome in realizing perfectly the purpose of God."

In the next section (9-11) Paul deals with the salvation of the Jew. He concludes with the assertion that for the Jew and all others Christ is the only hope.

The last stage of his presentation is concerned with how this righteousness operates in society. (12-16.) In chapter twelve he urges a life completely dedicated to the will of God. Chapter thirteen is concerned with the duties of a Christian as a citizen. In chapter fourteen he deals with the vexing question of ceremonies and traditions for the Christian. In this he urges self-denial on behalf of others. Chapter fifteen is devoted almost wholly to personal matters. Chapter sixteen is filled with salutations to a very large number of Christians whom Paul apparently knew. The book closes with a majestic doxology. "Now to him that is able to establish you according to my gospel and the preaching of Jesus Christ according to the revelation of the mystery which hath been kept in silence through times eternal, but now is manifested, and by the scriptures of the prophets, according to the commandment of the eternal God, is made known unto all the nations unto obedience of faith: to the only wise God, through Jesus Christ, to whom be the glory forever. Amen."

*16. The Journey Homeward* (Acts 20:3-21:16).

Having dispatched this letter to Rome by Phoebe, a faithful Christian, Paul was eager to get started back to Jerusalem and Antioch. He had been gone for four years and naturally he was concerned with the condition of the churches where he had begun his work. Then, too, he was eager to get to Jerusalem to take the offering which he had collected during this campaign and he wanted to be there for the Passover. As he planned to leave Corinth he had hope of returning to the West as soon as he could complete his visit to Jerusalem and Antioch. Already he was dreaming of taking the gospel to Rome and ever farther west. He found that a ship was now ready to sail from Corinth or Cenchreae and he engaged pasasge for himself and his party. However, he learned on the very eve of departure that the Jews had been making plans to murder him as soon as the ship was out from the port. The other members of his company embarked on the ship but Paul and Luke remained behind and quietly took the overland route back through Macedonia. This was a long, tedious journey which required several months. At length however, he and Luke sailed from Neapolis and four days later reached the city of Troas where his companions who had sailed from Cenchreae awaited him.

At Troas Paul and his party remained for seven days. Luke tells of Paul meeting with the Christians there on the first day of the week —a custom already observed and soon to result in our Sunday as the day for worship. Paul discoursed with them at length, "prolonged his speech till midnight" and one of their number, Eutychus, who sat in the window went to sleep and fell from this third story window to the ground. His friends rushed to him only to find that the fall had killed him. Paul then restored him to life.

The next day Paul walked alone from Troas to Assos where he and his companions boarded a ship which took them through the Grecian Archepelago stopping at Mitylene, passing Chios, touching at Samos and finally reaching Miletus. Paul had purposely avoided going to Ephesus since he was in a hurry to reach Jerusalem and did not have time to spare for the long visit at Ephesus which the church there would demand. Consequently he sent word ahead to the elders of the Ephesian church to meet him at Miletus. Here at Miletus Paul delivered an address which Luke has preserved. (Acts 20:17-35.) It is a deeply moving discourse which stirred all his hearers. He spoke of his work at Ephesus, urged these fellow ministers to be faithful and then opened his heart to them as he recited the fears which had already beset him. It might mean his death, but he must go to Jerusalem and be faithful to his mission no matter what the cost. When he had finished speaking, he knelt and prayed with these brethren who wept with him as they realized that they might never see him again.

Paul's journey took him by Cos and Rhodes, to Patara where they took another ship for the trip to the Phoenician coast. They finally landed at Tyre where he met with some of the brethren who again warned him of the danger that lay ahead of him. They stopped next at Ptolemais and then set sail for Caesarea, the port for Jerusalem. At Caesarea he was vigorously warned by his brethren of the fate that awaited him in Jerusalem. Again Paul insisted on going on to Jerusalem. "Bonds and death had no terror for him."

From Caesarea he and his party, now augmented by Mnason and a number of other Christians, departed going up to Jerusalem. Paul came to Jerusalem conscious of impending disaster. He knew that his enemies were determined to get him in their power. He did not know how his friends would receive him, but he did know that he could trust himself in the hands of God. He was completing his third great campaign for the Gentiles. He had won his fight for them so far and he was ready to face whatever might come now.

[1]Sabatier, *The Apostle Paul*, p. 136.
[2]Stalker, James, *Life of St. Paul*, p. 56.
[3]Robertson, *Epochs in the Life of Paul*, pp. 173-174.
[4]Smith, *The Life and Letters of St. Paul*, pp. 233-234.
[5]Carver, *Why They Wrote the New Testament*, p. 91.

*Chapter VI*

THE YEARS IN PRISON

1. Paul in Jerusalem. 2. Effort To Avoid Trouble. 3. Assault From Asian Jews. 4. Before the Sanhedrin. 5. Saved From Jerusalem. 6. Purpose of Paul's Imprisonment. 7. Before Felix. 8. Before Festus. 9. Sailing for Rome. 10. The Shipwreck. 11. On the Island of Melita. 12. To Rome. 13. Roman Imprisonment. 14. Close of Acts. 15. The Prison Epistles. 16. Letter to the Philippians. 17. Letter to Philemon. 18. Letter to the Colossians. 19. Letter to the Ephesians.

## CHAPTER VI

# The Years in Prison

### *1. Paul in Jerusalem* (Acts 21:17-20).

Paul had hoped to reach Jerusalem by the time of the observance of the annual Passover feast. This had been rendered impossible, however, by the change in his plans of departure from Corinth because of the plot to kill him on board the ship. The route which he took up through Macedonia had delayed him. When he and his party finally reached Jerusalem it was fifty days later; they came into the city on the eve of the Day of Pentecost. Luke tells us that upon their arrival the leading brethren received them heartily. After one day Paul, Luke and Trophimus made a formal call on James, the distinguished leader of the church. The elders of the church were present for the conference and Paul reported at length, "rehearsed one by one," the things which God had wrought among the Gentiles through his ministry. The entire company of leaders was deeply impressed by what had been accomplished and they glorified God. It was probably on this occasion that Paul turned over to these leaders the "collection" which he so faithfully collected during these four years of work among the Gentile churches. When he had finished his report, James or one of the leaders told Paul of the situation which had recently developed in Jerusalem.

### *2. Effort To Avoid Trouble* (Acts 21:20-26).

These leaders informed Paul that the Judaizers had circulated the report that he had taught that the Jewish Christians should forsake all the customs of their fathers (the Law of Moses) and live exactly like the Gentiles. Of course, this was not true. Paul had insisted that circumcision was not essential in a Gentile's becoming a Christian, but he had not urged Jewish Christians to renounce their Jewish customs. Paul himself had kept up the Jewish ceremonial observances. But, at any rate, the feeling against Paul was strong and dangerous. In view of this situation the brethren suggested to him that he pay the charges for the sacrifices of four men who had a vow, and that he purify himself with these four in the temple so that men might see him actually worshiping in the temple. This should prove to all that he had not taught what his enemies claimed. This proposal was not actually wrong, nor inconsistent, though Paul regarded Jesus as the one great sacrifice for sin. The proposal was an effort to prevent trouble. Paul therefore did as they proposed and apparently this satisfied the Jewish Christians.

3. *Assault From Asian Jews* (Acts 21:27-22:29).

However, the proposal resulted in trouble for Paul. There were Jews in Jerusalem from Ephesus who hated Paul because of his successful ministry in Ephesus. They happened to see Paul in the temple one day near the end of the feast. They knew that Trophimus, a Gentile Christian from Ephesus, was with Paul in the city. It was not lawful for a Gentile to enter the Jewish part of the temple. They did not see Trophimus in the temple, since Paul would never have taken him there, but it was possible to circulate the report and claim that Paul had taken him there. This suited their evil purpose so they immediately spread this false report. This malicious charge was all that was needed to give the hatred of the Jews an occasion to burst loose. Almost immediately the city was in an uproar, a mob had formed and Paul was seized and dragged out of the temple. Thus it was on a false charge that Paul was delivered into the hands of his enemies. This involved him in complications which kept him in prison for five long years!

As the wild mob was about to kill Paul, the chief captain of the band hearing "that all Jerusalem was in confusion" hurried to the scene. He was greatly puzzled about all this; indeed, he seems never to have understood this case. He proceeded to have Paul bound with two chains, thinking he was the notorious Egyptian bandit. He was astonished that Paul could speak Greek but gave him permission to stand on the stairway to address the crowd, which he did, using the Hebrew language. In bold words Paul made his defense to this assembly. He began by reviewing his career to show that he was a loyal Jew. They listened until he reached the point where he was called to preach the gospel to the Gentiles. At the word Gentile, the crowd went wild and demanded his death immediately. They were preparing to kill him when the chief captain intervened and took Paul inside to talk with him. The chief captain permitted him to be bound ready for scourging in order that he might learn what was the cause of all this riotous behavior. As they bound Paul he asked the centurion if it "was lawful to scourge a man that is a Roman, and uncondemned." This was reported to the chief captain who inquired of him if it were true that he was a Roman citizen. Upon Paul's word the Roman officers were frightened because they had already violated the law. Paul thus barely escaped with his life.

*4. Before the Sanhedrin* (Acts 22:30-23:11).

Many times Paul had brought Christians before the Sanhedrin for trial. He was now to face this tribunal himself. The chief captain on the next day in order that he might "know the certainty whereof he was accused by the Jews" had Paul brought before the council. He was brought before them without a charge. He knew this group and "looked steadfastly on the council" probably to see if he could find a friend among them. He knew well enough that he did not have much chance before them but ventured the statement that he had "lived before God in all good conscience until this day." The high-priest, Ananias, ordered one who stood by to smite Paul on the mouth. This unpardonable insult angered Paul and he bitterly denounced Ananias. For this he apologized, since he did not really know at the time that Ananias was the high-priest.

At this point Paul did a thing for which he has sometimes been criticized. He knew that the council was part Pharisees and part Sadducees and that they were bitter enemies. He then cried out, "Brethren, I am a Pharisee, a son of Pharisees." There arose forthwith such a discussion and clamor between these two groups that the session could not be held. The chief captain "fearing lest Paul should be torn in pieces by them" ordered the soldiers to rescue him from the warring members and bring him into the castle. Again he had escaped death. The chief captain was still worse confused.

Paul was still held as a prisoner and the following night received a visitation of the Lord who said to him, "Be of good cheer; for as thou has testified concerning me at Jerusalem, so must thou bear witness also at Rome." He needed this assurance. He could now be assured that he would be spared to get to Rome though he little knew how long it would take or in what way this was to occur.

*5. Saved From Jerusalem* (Acts 23:12-33).

These Jews having been outwitted by Paul in the Sanhedrin were now desparately determined to kill him. "They bound themselves under a curse, saying that they would neither eat nor drink till they had killed Paul." These forty desperate men then informed the council of their vow, asked them to request another trial of the chief captain so he might "judge the case more exactly." Their plot was to slay Paul as he was being conducted to the trial.

Paul's life was spared by another unexpected intervention. Luke tells in graphic style how Paul's nephew, the son of his sister, heard of this plot and then reported it to him, and how he asked one of the centurions to conduct the boy to the chief captain. The lad then told of the plot, and the chief captain charged the boy not to tell anyone else. He then ordered two hundred soldiers, two hundred spearmen and seventy horsemen to take Paul that night to Caesarea. He sent a letter explaining the case to Felix at Caesarea. Upon his arrival in Caesarea, Paul was received by Felix and was placed in Herod's palace. Once more he had been rescued from death. We do not know whether these forty Jews kept their vow or not. At least Paul was safe from his Jerusalem conspirators. Mercifully perhaps he did not know that he should be confined in Caesarea for two years and must wait still three more years before being free again.

6. *Purpose of Paul's Imprisonment.*

Every thoughtful student will ask, Why should this sore trial come to Paul at this time? He was in the midst of his campaign of winning the Roman empire. The way was open; many inviting opportunities beckoned him; hungry hearts in the far west were awaiting his message. Why should five long years of prison life be his portion when there were so many things he was eager to do? We cannot answer these questions fully. Surely Paul did not understand it at the time and probably was somewhat fretful and impatient. "It was a mysterious providence which thus arrested his energies and condemned the ardent worker to inactivity. Yet we can see now the reason for it. Paul was needing rest. After twenty years of incessant evangelization he required leisure to garner the harvest of experience. During all that time he had been preaching that view of the gospel which at the beginning of his Christian career he had thought out, under the influence of the revealing Spirit, in the solitudes of Arabia. But he had now reached a stage when, with leisure to think, he might penetrate into more recondite regions of the truth as it is in Jesus. And it was so important that he should have this leisure that, in order to secure it, God even permitted him to be shut up in prison."[1]

At any rate, just before his release five years later in Rome he was reconciled to the wisdom of it. He wrote to the Philippians and boldly asserted this judgment: "Now I would have you know, brethren, that the things which happened unto me have fallen out rather unto the progress of the gospel."

7. *Before Felix* (Acts 23:34-24:27).

The procurator at Caesarea at this time was Antonius Felix. He was a freedman who obtained his office by political favor, was disdained by other officials and was despised by the Jews. His administration was notoriously bad. As Tacitus said, "He exercised the perogative of a king, with all cruelty and lust, in the spirit of a slave." He was married three times, his last wife being a Jewish princess Drusilla, the daughter of Agrippa I, whom he persuaded to leave her husband in order to become his wife. His term of office was one of maladministration, turmoil and terror. He was finally recalled by Nero in A.D. 59.

Paul was forced to appear for trial before this Roman appointee. His accusers, who turned out to be not the Asian Jews, but Jews from Jerusalem, came up for the trial. They were led by a Roman lawyer, Tertullus, whom they had employed. Tertullus began his address with profuse and unmerited praise of Felix and then finally preferred two definite charges against Paul: he was a member of the sect of Nazarenes, and he had profaned the temple. Paul had no lawyer, but with real skill he presented his own case. He disproved the charge that he had profaned the temple. He then admitted freely that he was a Christian and insisted that this was the "true Judaism." Paul won his case and should have been released. But Felix feared these Jewish leaders and postponed his decision and kept him in prison.

Some days later Felix, accompanied by his wife, Drusilla, sent for Paul "and heard him concerning the faith in Christ Jesus." He spoke with great fervor and persuasion and "as he reasoned of righteousness, and self-control, and the judgment to come, Felix was terrified and answered, Go thy way for this time; and when I have a convenient season I will call thee unto me." This was a courageous thing for Paul to do since Felix had not yet rendered his decision. His greed for money made him postpone his decision in the hope that "money would be given him of Paul." He even sent for Paul frequently, expecting that a substantial bribe would be offered him for his release. But Paul remained in prison two long years.

8. *Before Festus* (Acts 25-26).

When Felix was recalled he was succeeded by Porcius Festus. Apparently Festus was a much better man than Felix, but he occupied a most difficult position. These powerful Jews were determined to push the case against Paul. Festus took up the case at once. He went immediately to Jerusalem and in conference with the Jews heard their demand that Paul be returned to Jerusalem for trial. They were still planning to way-lay him enroute and kill him as they had plotted two years earlier in Jerusalem. Festus, however, refused their request and gave them permission to send their deputation back to Caesarea to prosecute the case. Thus Paul was tried a second time in Caesarea, this time before Festus. He was arraigned on the charges of heresy, sacrilege and treason, which he repudiated. It was a question of Jewish custom and law and since Festus was unacquainted with these matters he suggested that the case be referred to the Sanhedrin in Jerusalem with himself as assessor. Paul knew what this would mean; he would have no chance before this tribunal in Jerusalem. He would never consent to this arrangement. He was a Roman citizen and had the right to enter a protest and appeal the case to the Emperor. He, therefore, cried "I appeal to Caesar." This unexpected development took Festus by surprise, but he knew it was a valid appeal. So he had to give his judgment: "You have appealed to Caesar: to Caesar you will go."

This turn in the case left Festus in an embarrassing position. He had no real charge against Paul, and to send a case from his court to the emperor without a sound charge would be a serious reflection on Festus. Herod Agrippa II and his sister, Bernice, were visiting Festus at this time. They would need to be entertained and this amazing man in prison would provide an interesting diversion for the guests; furthermore since they were familiar with Jewish customs Festus hoped that they would help him prepare a "brief" of the case which could be sent with Paul to Rome. A state occasion of great pomp was arranged and Paul was brought in to speak before the assembly, presided over by Agrippa. His address was long and persuasive. He reviewed his experiences and then preached Jesus Christ with a view to winning the governor to Christ. Festus, Agrippa and the others apparently were moved by the eloquent words of Paul. But they made no decision. After Paul was dismissed they privately agreed that "this man doeth nothing worthy of death." But he was not released. So far as we know Festus got no help in formulating the charges against Paul to be sent to the emperor.

9. *Sailing for Rome* (Acts 27:1-8).

Luke was with Paul and describes with great vividness their experiences on the way to Rome. He writes in the first person plural and gives a wealth of detail which is of great value, not only to those interested in Paul's work, but to all who are interested in nautical life in this century.

Paul and a number of other prisoners were placed in the hands of Julius of the Augustan band for the journey. It would be necessary to use several ships for the voyage, transferring at a number of ports. The first ship carrying a large number of soldiers and prisoners was a freighter bound for Adrymittium near Troas. Julius was kind to Paul, allowing Luke and Aristarchus to be with him, and permitting others to visit with him. They reached Myra on the coast of Pamphylia where they changed ships. They "sailed slowly" on this ship for many days and finally with great difficulty they came to a little port on the southern shore of Crete, called Fair Havens. It was now October and the autumnal equinox was about due. Because of the winter storms travel on the sea was extremely hazardous from early November till early in February. The crew of the ship did not want to spend the winter at Fair Havens but were anxious to get to the better harbor of Phoenix, about fifty miles west. A council was held to decide what should be done. Paul who was an experienced sea traveler, was invited to the council where he argued against the proposal that they slip out of the harbor of Fair Havens, stay close to shore and try to get into Phoenix for the winter. Julius, however, approved the plan, being tempted by the good prospects "when the south wind blew softly."

*10. The Shipwreck* (Acts 27:9-44).

The student should read carefully Luke's classic description of the disastrous storm and shipwreck which came shortly after the ship had left Fair Havens. Luke gives in detail and with precision the steps taken by which the lives of all were saved in the most remarkable record of a shipwreck in existence and the most imposing account of ancient ships. When every means had been employed to save the ship and it appeared altogether hopeless Paul received a visit from an angel who assured him that all would be spared. Note that Paul soon came to be the leading figure on the ship, that all the others did his bidding, that he saved the prisoners from the trickery of the soldiers. At last the ship went to pieces on the rocks but every life on board was spared.

*11. On the Island of Melita* (Acts 28:1-10).

The land on which they came was the island of Melita (Malta). They were received with kindness by the inhabitants of the island who built a fire by which they could warm themselves. As Paul assisted the natives in gathering wood for the fire he was bitten by a poisonous viper. To the amazement of all the islanders he suffered no ill effects from the bite and the people came to look upon him as a god. Publius, the chief man of the island, received and entertained Paul and Luke courteously for three days. The father of Publius "was sick of a fever and dysentery" and Paul healed him. This was the beginning of a fruitful ministry of healing and teaching on the island. For three months he and the other prisoners remained here.

### 12. To Rome (Acts 28:11-25).

With the arrival of spring a ship bound for Rome was ready to sail. On this ship the last stage of the sea voyage was made. They spent three days in Syracuse (Sicily), one day at Rhegium and after two more days sailing, arrived at Puteoli. Evidently Paul had been able to send word of the arrival of the ship to the Christians at Rome for they were met before they reached the city by brethren who came to greet Paul. From Puteoli they went overland to Rome using the famous Appian Way, parts of which can still be seen today. One can imagine the feelings of Paul as he approached the famous city. He had often planned to come to Rome, but had been "hindered hitherto." At last he was in the imperial city, but as a prisoner. He had planned to come as a free man with all the liberties of a Roman citizen. He felt keenly the humiliation of his chains, but he would not grieve nor indulge in self-pity. He would find countless opportunities for work and he would use all of these as far as possible.

### 13. Roman Imprisonment (Acts 28:26-31).

After this long and tempestuous journey from Caesarea, Julius brought his prisoners at last to Rome. Upon arriving in the city, he took all these except Paul to the prisoner's quarters on the Caelian Hill and turned them over to the commander. For some reason, possibly because of the letter of Festus, or more probable, the good behavior of Paul on the journey, he was given special privileges. He was allowed to live outside the prisoner's quarters apparently in the home of some Christian. He was by no means free since he was chained to a guard at all times. He could receive friends and certainly Luke and Aristarchus were allowed to visit him freely.

After resting three days, Paul called together the chief Jews, as his custom was, and reported to them fully concerning his situation, the charges against him and the reason for his appeal to Caesar. These Jewish leaders assured Paul that they had received no letter from Judea concerning him. They expressed their desire to hear him fully concerning this "sect," the Christians. Accordingly, a date was set for all the Jews of Rome who were interested to come to Paul's lodging On the appointed day a very large number gathered to hear him expound his faith in Christ. From morning until evening he explained the scriptural testimonies to the Messiahship of Jesus. Some were persuaded to believe; others rejected his words and they fell into a bitter controversy among themselves. When Paul saw how bitterly they opposed his message, he announced that henceforth he should leave the Jews alone and devote himself to winning the Gentiles in Rome.

Paul had hoped to have a speedy hearing in the court of the emperor, but again he was destined to disappointment. For six years the notorious Nero had been emperor in the imperial city. At first Nero gave promise of becoming an able emperor, but he soon revealed his true character. In A.D. 59, the year Paul left Caesarea for Rome, Nero had Agrippina, his mother, assassinated. This was the beginning of a reign of terror that "invested the name of Nero with lurid horror and unrivalled infamy." One disgraceful episode followed another and Nero being occupied had no time to give to the trial of a Jew from one of the provinces. At length two full years passed and Paul still waited for a hearing.

This tedious delay must have been a sore test of Paul's patience. How easy for a man to grow bitter and indulge in self-pity! But Paul was too big a man and too devout a Christian to behave that way. Instead, he busied himself making use of all the opportunities afforded him in this great city. In truth, these two years proved to be among the most fruitful of all his career. He rented a house where he could be free to do his work, "and received all that went in unto him, preaching the kingdom of God, and teaching the things concerning the Lord Jesus Christ with all boldness, none forbidding him."

### 14. Close of Acts.

The book of Acts closes with the words just quoted. In the book Luke has traced the career of Paul from the time of his conversion in A.D. 33 to his experiences in Rome while awaiting his trial (60-62). This seems to be an abrupt ending, an unfinished story. Why does the book conclude so abruptly? Many scholars believe that Luke had in mind the writing of a third "volume" to complete the story with which he has dealt in the gospel of Luke and Acts. If this third volume was ever written, we have no record of it. At any rate, the book of Acts closes with Paul in prison in Rome.

### 15. The Prison Epistles.

These two years in prison at Rome were marked by intense activity. In addition to all his work in dealing with the Christians of the city and in winning others to Christ, he found time to write four epistles. From this period we have his letters to the Philippians, Ephesians, Colossians, and to Philemon. These, like all his other letters, were written to meet the needs of a particular situation. Each of these is different, and at the same time there runs through each of them the same general idea — the deity and the humanity of Jesus. We cannot be sure of the exact order in which these were written, but this is of no particular consequence.

## 16. Letter to the Philippians.

One of the sources of greatest encouragement to Paul in these dark days of imprisonment in Rome was the sympathetic concern of some of his churches for him. The church at Philippi was not only one of the best of these but was composed of Christians who deeply and genuinely loved Paul. In return Paul loved them with an abiding affection. He referred to them as his "joy and crown." The members of this church knew of his imprisonment at Caesarea and later learned of his shipwreck and his final arrival in Rome. They knew that he was in need of friends and of the assurance of their love. Accordingly, they made up a generous offering among themselves and sent one of their ministers, Epaphroditus, to take this gift with the assurance of their affection to their beloved leader in Rome. Some think that Paul had sent Luke and Aristarchus to visit some of these churches while he himself awaited trial in Rome. In the meantime Timothy had come to be with Paul so that he was not alone. Epaphroditus came with his gift and joined Timothy in his service to Paul. In the sultry autumn in Rome Epaphroditus became seriously ill. His convalescence was prolonged and when he was finally able to travel he was eager to get back to Philippi. His return home afforded Paul an opportunity to send a letter of appreciation to the church at Philippi.

This is the most informal, intimate and revealing of all Paul's epistles. It is a spontaneous expression of love and gratitude. In it the great apostle opens up his heart and reveals his joy and gratitude for these fellow Christians. Though it was written from prison amid depressing circumstances it rings with joy, confidence, faith and hope. "He was full of joy in his work, even with all its disappointments, afflictions, and hindrances. No where else may we better learn how to triumph in Christ over all our ills, and keep on with the work of the Lord. Nowhere else does the noble apostle open wider the door unto the inner sanctuary of his soul and permit us to see him completely dedicated to God, who separated him from birth and called him as a medium for revealing his Son to the world; so Paul feels that for him to live is Christ."[2]

In this book Paul expresses most eloquently his interpretation of Christ. The student should read carefully these two great passages. (2:5-11, and 3:8-14.)

### 17. Letter to Philemon.

In many respects this little epistle is the most unique of all Paul's letters. It is the story of Paul reuniting two of his converts. To understand it one must have the background. During Paul's years at Ephesus he became acquainted with leading men from all the province of Asia. Among these was a wealthy and influential man from the city of Colossae, some one hundred miles east of Ephesus. This man, Philemon by name, became a Christian under the ministry of Paul and became a leader of the Christians of his community. His home served as the meeting place of these Christians.

Philemon had at least one slave, perhaps many more. This young slave named Onesimus, like all slaves, yearned for freedom and planned to escape. He made a successful get-away and probably took with him some money which belonged to his master. Feeling that he could hide himself in the crowds of a great city, he made his way to Rome. We do not know how long he had been there when he came in contact with Paul, nor do we know the circumstances of their meeting. We do know that Paul met him, that he won him to Christ and then insisted that Onesimus must return to his master at Colossae. Naturally he would hesitate, perhaps even refuse, to do this. Paul insisted on his doing it as his Christian duty and promised him if he would return he would assist him by writing a letter to Philemon on his behalf. At last Onesimus consented to go back and Paul sent with him this beautiful little epistle to Philemon. In this letter he pleads with his friend Philemon to receive back his slave Onesimus no longer as a slave but as a brother. "He is to be loved and treated as Paul would be (17) and Paul hints that Philemon will set him free (21). He gave a new conception of love for a slave that has set all slaves free in Christendom and will ultimately shake off all shackles everywhere."[3]

### 18. Letter to the Colossians.

The church at Colossae, a city in the rich Lycus valley, east of Ephesus, grew up as a result of Paul's three years' ministry in the capital of Asia. So far as we know, Paul never visited this church though he was acquainted with its leaders and had a very vital interest in its welfare and progress. While Paul was in prison at Rome, he learned of the false teachings which were being propagated in the churches of the province of Asia. The churches at Colossae and Ephesus seem to have been deply affected by this false teaching and he was concerned about them.

"The main source of all their false teaching lay in an old eastern dogma, that all matter is evil and its source also evil. If this were true, God, who is in no wise evil, could not have created matter. And since our bodies are matter, they are evil and God could not have created them. From the notion that our bodies are evil two extremes of error arose: (1) That only by various ascetic practices, whereby we punish the body, can we hope to save it. (2:20-23.) (2) That since the body is evil, none of its deeds are to be accounted for. License was, therefore, granted to evil conduct, and evil passions were indulged at pleasure. (3:5-8.)

"In seeking to avoid this difficulty they formulated two other false doctrines. (1) An esoteric and exclusive theory which was a doctrine of secrets and initiation. (2:2, 3, 8.) By this doctrine they declared that the remedy for man's condition was known to only a few, and to learn this secret one must be initiated into their company. (2) That since God could not have been creator of these sinful bodies, they could not, therefore, come to Him for blessing, and so they formulated, in their theory, a series of intermediary beings and Aeons, such as angels, that must have created us and whom we must worship (2:18), especially as a means of finally reaching God.

"All these false theories conspired to limit the nature and authority of Jesus Christ, and to limit the sufficiency of redemption in Him. (2:9-10.) They are called by the one name, Gnosticism, and present four aspects of error in this book. (1) Philosophic, 2:3, 4, 8. (2) Ritualistic, or Judaistic, 2:11, 14, 16-17. (3) Visionary, or angel-worship, 1:16, 2:10, 15, 18. (4) Ascetic practices, 2:20-23."[4]

This letter follows the usual pattern of Paul's epistles in that he develops his main thesis or doctrinal teaching in the first part and then makes very practical applications of this truth to every-day living in the second half of the letter. The latter part of the last chapter contains numerous personal references. Among the brethren mentioned is John Mark to whom Paul refers, along with several others, as "having been a comfort to me." Mark has learned his lesson and appears now to have been fully restored to the confidence of Paul.

*19. Letter to the Ephesians.*

The letter to the Ephesians was a general or circular letter. The two oldest manuscripts have no name for the epistle. Customarily Paul included many personal greetings in his letters but this one contains none.

In the opinion of many competent scholars the letter to the Ephesians is the profoundest of all Paul's writings. "During the years of his imprisonment Paul's mind and heart followed the principles of grace and purpose, with which he had been dealing throughout his ministry, until he reached depths and heights of insight which transcend all other ranges of philosophy. He came to an interpretation of the cosmic and historical meaning of the Christ and his church which make them all-comprehensive. He wrote while in Rome a document that for sheer boldness of thought places it in the realm of highest metaphysics; that for depth and spiritual daring it is the greatest paper ever inscribed by the hand of man; for fervor and reverence it is a work of deepest devotion; for practical righteousness it is a plea for Christian ethics unsurpassable. The epistle to the Ephesians is the supreme work of God's written Word, the most comprehensive statement of the origin, nature, purpose, and goal of God's high calling in Christ Jesus."[5]

This epistle has been called an exposition of the doctrine of the Christian calling, with the obligations which it places on all who have accepted the call. In chapter one Paul discusses this calling from the divine side. The latter part of this chapter contains the apostle's prayer for the people of Christ. Chapter two is concerned with the experience by which men who are spiritually dead may be "created in Christ Jesus for good works." In this discussion we have some of the noblest and most profound statements to be found in all Christian literature. In chapter three Paul speaks of God's ideal (mystery) in Christ which once was hid but is now to be proclaimed to all the world. This "mystery" or secret is that "all peoples make up a common heritage of God, are fellow members of the body of Christ, and equal sharers of God's promise in Christ Jesus by means of the Gospel." The latter half of the epistle, beginning with chapter four is a powerful plea that all Christians shall walk worthily of such a high calling. In this section there are many profound and familiar statements of great practical significance. The epistle closes with the prayer that "grace may be with all them that love our Lord Jesus Christ with a love incorruptible."

[1]Stalker, James, *Life of St. Paul*, pp. 129-130.
[2]Carver, W. O., *Why They Wrote the New Testament*, p. 62.
[3]Robertson, *Epochs in the Life of Paul*, pp. 278-279.
[4]Tidwell, J. B., *The Bible Book by Book*, p. 183.
[5]Carver, W. O., *Why They Wrote the New Testament*, pp. 95-96.

*Chapter VII*

## THE LAST YEARS OF PAUL

1. The Historical Problem. 2. Reasons for His Release. 3. The Trial at Rome. 4. Further Travels of Paul. 5. In Asia Again. 6. Mission to Spain. 7. To Crete. 8. The Burning of Rome. 9. Last Visit in Asia. 10. First Letter to Timothy. 11. Titus. 12. Paul's Arrest. 13. In the Mamertine Dungeon. 14. The First Stage of His Trial. 15. Second Letter to Timothy. 16. Paul's Last Days. 17. The Martyrdom of Paul.

# The Last Years of Paul

*1. The Historical Problem.*

As we have previously noted, the book of Acts, which is the historical book of the New Testament, closes somewhat abruptly leaving Paul a prisoner in Rome awaiting trial. Since we have no further record in the New Testament the natural inference is that he was condemned and executed. Until comparatively recent years the majority of scholars assumed that this was the case. Today however, there has come to be a strong feeling among New Testament students that Paul was released from imprisonment in Rome in A.D. 62 or 63 and that he had a further ministry of some five years before he was finally condemned and executed in Rome.

*2. Reasons for His Release.*

There are good reasons for concluding that Paul's first imprisonment in Rome was terminated by his release which gave him several years for further work. The grounds for such a conclusion may be stated briefly.

(1) The pastoral Epistles (I Timothy, Titus, and II Timothy) furnish strong evidence. To begin with, it is all but unanimously agreed that Paul was the author of these three epistles. Apparently no other could have written these letters. This being true there is no possible place in the career of Paul up to the time of his first trial in Rome when he could have written them. This is true of I Timothy since at the time of its writing Paul was at liberty and had just recently been in Ephesus. In the case of the letter to Titus, Paul had just completed an extended visit to Crete with Titus. This certainly could not have happened before his first Roman visit. The same argument applies in the case of II Timothy. In this epistle the apostle has the conviction that he was soon to be executed and he was eager for Timothy, who was at Ephesus at the time, to come to him at once. All three of these Pauline epistles make it necessary to conclude that Paul had a period of service after his first Roman trial.

(2) Paul's own testimony in Philemon, written while on his first visit to Rome, probably in A.D. 62, indicates that he expected to be released. He bade Philemon expect his immediate arrival in Colossae and prepare for his entertainment while there.

(3) Traditions of the early Christians indicate, and actually assert that he was released. Clemens Romans asserts that Paul later visited the "boundary of the West" which is generally interpreted as a visit to Spain. The Muratorian Canon assumes that Paul's release and visit to Spain are well known facts. We may quote the generally accepted statement of Theodore of Mopsuestia: "After his two years stay at Rome he departed, and is seen to have preached to many the Doctrine of piety. On the second occasion, however, he visited Rome, and while he stayed there it happened that by the sentence of Nero he suffered capital punishment for the preaching of piety."

In view of these facts it is reasonable to assume that Paul was released after two years imprisonment in Rome and was free to continue his mission for several years afterwards.

### 3. The Trial at Rome.

In the light of this argument one naturally asks, What happened at the trial of Paul? The simple fact is we do not know. There are several theories about it. Some believe that he was never called for formal trial. If Festus sent any official charge or brief of the case to Rome this was probably lost when the ship was wrecked and everything on board went under water. It may be that any charges which reached Roman authorities were so vague and insubstantial that they would not merit a hearing before the court. Nero was notoriously dilatory with provincial cases and it is possible that the case was postponed again and again until finally it was thrown out. Still others believe that a trial was held, that Paul was acquitted and was released to go as a free man to continue his work.

### 4. Further Travels of Paul.

Without the aid of a reliable historical record it is, of course, impossible to follow all the experiences of Paul from A.D. 62-67. However from the frequent allusions made in the three pastoral epistles and by the aid of tradition it is possible to reconstruct the general outline of his career during these years. Naturally there are differences of opinion in following this general course of travels. It is probable that he passed from West to East and back several times during this time. We may be sure that he was in Ephesus at least once, in Macedonia probably more than once, that he visited the island of Crete with Titus on a missionary campaign, and that he finally got into Spain and probably into ancient Gaul (France). For our purposes in this study it will not be necessary to devote much time to the consideration of the details connected with these years.

## 5. In Asia Again.

It is generally agreed that Paul was deeply concerned over developments in Asia during his absence and since he was so eager to get back there he would probably return as soon as possible after his release in Rome. References in his letters to the Philippians and to Philemon indicate that he was expecting to see them soon. We may assume, therefore, that he hurried to Colossae and Ephesus where he would spend some time in refuting the subtle arguments of the Gnostics who evidently had made considerable progress in disturbing the Christians in these areas. We may assume also that he would go to his beloved church at Philippi for at least one visit.

## 6. Mission to Spain.

The argument for his visit to Spain and Gaul is "merely inferential," but there seem to be good reasons for holding that he did go there and had a successful ministry. Dr. David Smith in his *Life and Letters of St. Paul* (pp. 612-613) argues that his mission to the West, Spain and Gaul, extended from the spring of 64 to 66. But we have no positive proof of this.

## 7. To Crete.

The island of Crete, which lay south of Greece in the Mediterranean, was one place which, up to this point, had not been touched by the labors of any missionary. This densely populated island is said to have boasted of one hundred famous cities. These people had a bad reputation; their proclivity to falsehood was proverbial. They appear also to have been known for their trickiness and deception. Wine was produced in abundance and the people, both men and women, had the reputation of being heavy drinkers. They seem also to have been in alliance with pirates who preyed upon the ships sailing the Mediterranean. On the island were quite a number of Jews, some of whom occupied places of leadership. This island offered, therefore, a great opportunity for missionary work. It may be assumed that Paul had long since included it in his plans for the evangelization of the Roman empire.

We have no record of his work there, though most scholars agree that he spent some time there with Titus. The work on Crete appears to have been successful and offered encouragement for yet greater accomplishments. Consequently when it became necessary for Paul to leave the island for other work he left Titus to continue his ministry among the Cretans.

### 8. The Burning of Rome.

Rome had several tyrannical and corrupt emperors but Nero was the worst. He was immoral, vicious, selfish and despotically cruel. He came to the throne in A.D. 54 and ruled for fourteen years. He incurred the animosity of all, including the Senate who publicly condemned him. In disappointment and self-pity he took his own life. He will go down in history as one of the most despicable men ever to rule over a people. He was "a man who in a bad world had attained the eminence of being the very worst and meanest being in it — a man stained with every crime, the murderer of his own mother, of his wives and of his best benefactors; a man whose whole being was so steeped in every namable and unamable vice that body and soul of him were, as some one said at the time, nothing but a compound of mud and blood."[1]

Historians are generally agreed that it was Nero who burned the city of Rome. He labored under the delusion that he was a genius in music and that his compositions would become immortal if only he had sufficient inspiration. Feeling that a great conflagration would provide the inspiration he had the city set on fire. It is said that he sat on an elevated porch overlooking the city and attempted to play the violin as he watched the city burn. This fire broke out on July 19 in the year 64 and raged for six days. Much to the surprise of Nero there was a violent reaction among the people and he hastened to attach the blame for this on the Christians. Immediately thereafter serious persecution broke out against these Christian people. It took real courage to be a Christian now as they were granted no protection by the law. These Neronian persecutions were unspeakably horrible. Christian men and women were burned, were cast to wild beasts in the amphitheatre to entertain the populace. "Nero lent his gardens for the purpose of exhibiting the tortures of the wretched victims, and at night he illuminated his grounds by the flames of burning Christians."[2]

The change brought about by the burning of Rome affected Paul materially. He was the recognized leader of this sect and as such would be in constant danger. No doubt he refrained from any plan to visit the imperial city for some time after the burning of the city. Indeed, since his leadership was known throughout the empire, he was facing danger all the time.

### 9. Last Visit in Asia.

Paul planned to spend the winter of 66-67 at Nicopolis. Since there were no less than nine cities in the empire by this name at the time there are various views as to which one is meant. However, it seems reasonable to suppose that he meant the city by this name in Cilicia which was not far distant from Tarsus. While he planned to get some rest from his constant and heavy burdens at this place it is not likely that he was inactive. This is the territory in which he did his first real missionary work in establishing churches in Syria-Cilicia and he would have many calls from these Christians. It was not far from Antioch which claimed so much of his labors and devotion. He would have a happy and busy winter in the midst of these friends of many years.

In the spring of 67 he felt impelled to go again to the West. From allusions in Titus and II Timothy it would appear that Luke was with him, and also Titus and Tychicus. He was eager to get to Rome but he would visit some of his churches enroute. He spent a brief time at Ephesus and then hurried on to Troas. He would go then to Macedonia and on to Corinth from where he would take ship for Rome. According to this schedule of travel he would reach Rome the latter part of the summer in A.D. 67.

### 10. First Letter to Timothy.

While scholars are agreed that Paul wrote the three pastoral epistles during these years between his two sojourns in Rome we know but little of the circumstances under which I Timothy and Titus were written. Scholars are agreed that his second letter to Timothy was written from Rome just shortly before his death. Fortunately the value of these letters does not depend on a knowledge of the time and place of their writing.

Timothy was a native of Lystra and became a Christian on the occasion of Paul's first visit there in A.D. 48. His father was a Gentile and his mother a devout Jewess. He showed such promise as a genuine Christian and as a leader that Paul took him as a helper on his second campaign. From this time on he occupied a large place in the activities of Paul and his churches. Paul was strongly attached to him and spoke of him as his "true child in the faith." He later served as pastor at Ephesus at the time when the Gnostic heresy was causing such deep concern. In addition to this heresy he had other serious problems and difficulties to deal with in the Ephesian church. Paul had made an extended visit to the church and had given great help to Timothy in his work there. After his visit he wrote this letter back to him in order to give more detailed counsel in meeting his problems as a young pastor.

He urges young Timothy to stay with his work at the Ephesian church in order to combat the growing heresy of Gnosticism and other false teachings there. "Paul had fought the Judaizers throughout the strength of his manhood and had won freedom in Christ for all men. Now in his old age he still has to battle against the strange medley of philosophy, Essenism, heathenism and Christianity under the guise of Gnosticism. His hope is the young ministers who are to carry the work on after him."[3]

Since there were certain ecclesiastical problems also at Ephesus with which Timothy needed some help Paul gives some detailed instruction on such questions as the qualifications of bishops and deacons, and counsel in certain social problems which had arisen in the church here. This letter reveals Paul's great concern, not only for his friend Timothy, but also for his church at Ephesus.

*11. Titus.*

We do not know a great deal about the work of Titus. He was a Gentile and was with Paul on one of his trips to Jerusalem. He proved his worth as a real misionary, especially in his work on the island of Crete.

The circumstances under which the Epistle to Titus was written are not altogether clear. We may be sure that it was written to him after Paul had worked with him in Crete. He sent the letter back to the young missionary to give him further instructions for the work which he had undertaken there. But the date of the letter and the place from where it was written are not certainly known.

It is a very practical letter and is rich in spiritual emphasis. Paul states the qualifications of the presbyters which were to be selected there and offers suggestions for dealing with some false teachers which appeared to be troublesome. He speaks rather sharply of the tricky and unreliable character of the natives of Crete. He counsels Titus to use caution and wisdom in dealing with certain troublesome social problems which were threatening the peace of the church. In closing Paul urges Titus to avoid foolish and fruitless arguments and be faithful to his chief task.

*12. Paul's Arrest.*

It is held by some that Paul reached Rome unmolested and after being there some time was apprehended and arrested. Other scholars believe that he was arrested somewhere else and was taken to Rome as a prisoner. There is no way of deciding which is right. The charges on which he was taken to Rome the first time were never such as to result in conviction. New charges would be made this time. Now it is not a question of his loyalty to the Jewish faith but of his relation to the Roman government. It would be easy because of his leadership of the Christians to imagine many questionable practices and to implicate him in the burning of the city. This time Paul was not to face the Sanhedrin whose practices he knew, nor even some provincial governor; he would be brought before high authorities in the capital of the empire.

### 13. In the the Mamertine Dungeon.

The comparative freedom which he had enjoyed during his first experience in Rome was denied him now. It was probably the Mamertine dungeon, a cold, desolate and wretched prison reserved for desperate criminals, that would be his lodging place. Previously he could go among his friends and have them visit him; now he was incarcerated in this dreary and uncomfortable place of confinement.

His lot was made the harder by the desertion of most of his friends. The public temper was such that it took real courage to be a Christian. We are told that one of these, Demas, forsook him, "having loved this present world." Others of his good friends were away from the city for good reasons. Crescens had gone to Galatia, Titus to Dalmatia, Tychicus to Ephesus, Timothy, Priscilla and Acquila had gone to the East on a mission. We are glad, however, that at least one man, Onesiphorus, was in the city and was loyal to Paul at all costs. Paul appreciatively speaks of him, "for he oft refreshed me and was not ashamed of my chain; but when he was in Rome, he sought me diligently and found me." (II Timothy 1:16f.)

### 14. The First Stage of His Trial.

Paul's second letter to Timothy, the last of his writings, was written from this prison not long before his death. From it we get our only information about these dreary days. When the letter was written the first stage of his trial had already passed. Probably this was on the less serious charge, and he was then awaiting the real trial. There were some there to accuse him for he asserts that "Alexander the coppersmith did me much evil." Since Paul was internationally known there was a large crowd present for the trial. Evidently many whom he expected to stay with him failed to appear for he says that "all forsook me."

He adds quickly however, "but the Lord stood by me and strengthened me." It appears that he was acquitted on the first charge. But there were other more serious charges to come.

In this letter he requests Timothy to bring his warm cloak which he had left at the home of Carpus in Troas. In this damp, cold dungeon he needs it. He appears to be lonely and adds, "only Luke is with me." The beloved physician deserves this tribute paid by his devoted friend and companion. Paul urges Timothy to come to him as quickly as possible. We do not know whether Timothy got there before the death sentence was imposed or not. Paul gives us one little statement which completes the story of John Mark. He speaks of him as one who could be counted on in this time of trial. Mark has learned his lesson, has demonstrated his true worth, and has won the praise of the great apostle whom he had foolishly deserted on the first campaign. It is high praise to be linked with Timothy as a staunch and loyal comrade of the greatest of all the servants of Christ.

Another touching note is found in this last of Paul's epistles. He had left his books or parchments at Troas and in his loneliness now he yearns for them. He loved his books and found great comfort and stimulus in them.

### 15. Second Letter to Timothy.

This epistle from which we have just quoted was sent to Timothy either in the fall of 67 or early in the spring of 68, since the death of Paul occurred either late in 67 or early in 68. This letter which gives us valuable light on Paul's experiences just before his death, is not altogether devoted to his personal situation. He is still deeply interested in the work of Timothy and all others who were teaching the way of life. He gives many choice bits of counsel to the young minister, urging him to be a good soldier and to bear his hardships manfully. He advises him to train up other young men who will be able to train still others. Christianity is a teaching religion and must be propagated by faithful, persistent and continuous teaching. He speaks freely of the evil days and false teachers and entreats Timothy to be faithful to the trust committed to him.

### 16. Paul's Last Days.

Among the last words written by the great soldier of the cross are the oft-quoted statements, sometimes called Paul's "Swan Song." "For I am already being offered, and the time of my departure is come. I have fought the good fight, I have finished the course, I have kept the faith: henceforth there is laid up for me the crown of righteousness, which the Lord, the righteous judge, shall give to me at that day; and not to me only, but also to all them that have loved his appearing." (II Timothy 4:6-8.) This is no vain boast; it is said in great humility and yet with satisfaction. Looking back over more than thirty years of service to the Lord, who called him on the Damascus road, he has no regrets. He would do it all again. He has suffered more than most men; it has cost him much; but he has gained more than he has lost. The long, hard fight is over now. He is not afraid of the outcome. The Lord, his righteous judge, loves him and will take him home. This is the song of triumph of a great warrior who is soon to lose his life but who has won his cause. "Paul still has interest in earthly affairs, but his heart is in the hills on high. He looks away to the mountains. His feet are growing restless and the sun is setting in the west. Jesus is beckoning to him and he will go."[4]

## 17. The Martydom of Paul.

We have no details on the condemnation of Paul by the Roman court. It probably came quickly. If he were accused of complicity in the burning of the city the judgment would be rendered at once. Since he was a Roman citizen he would not be burned nor cast to the lions; he would be beheaded. At last the sentence of death was pronounced and the great apostle was taken out to the place of execution where he lost his life and gained his crown. "He was led out of the city with a crowd of the lowest rabble at his heels. The fatal spot was reached; he knelt beside the block; the headsman's axe gleamed in the sun and fell; and the head of the apostle of the world rolled down in the dust.

"So sin did its uttermost and its worst. Yet how poor and empty was its triumph! The blow of the axe only smote off the lock of the prison and let the spirit go forth to its home and to its crown. The city falsely called eternal dismissed him with execration from her gates; but ten thousand times ten thousand welcomed him in the same hour at the gates of the city which is really eternal. Even on earth Paul could not die. He lives among us to-day with a life a hundredfold more influential than that which throbbed in his brain whilst the earthly form which made him visible still lingered on the earth. Wherever the feet of them who publish the glad tidings go forth beautiful upon the mountains, he walks by their side as an inspirer and a guide; in ten thousand churches every Sabbath and a thousand thousand hearths every day his eloquent lips still teach that gospel of which he was never ashamed; and, wherever there are human souls searching for the white flower of holiness or climbing the difficult heights of self-denial, there he whose life was so pure, whose devotion to Christ was so entire, and whose pursuit of a single purpose was so unceasing, is welcomed as the best of friends."[5]

[1]Stalker, *Life of St. Paul,* pp. 142-143.
[2]Foakes-Jackson, *Rise of Gentile Christianity,* p. 50.
[3]Robertson, *Studies in the New Testament,* p. 223.
[4]Robertson, *Epochs in the Life of Paul,* p. 314.
[5]Stalker, *Life of St. Paul,* pp. 143-144.

*Chapter VIII*

## COMPLETING THE STORY

# Completing the Story

## *1. Resume.*

It may be helpful to introduce this closing chapter in our studies by a brief resume. Jesus was born in 5 or 4 B.C. and the last book of the New Testament was finished shortly before A.D. 100. The twenty-seven books of the New Testament consist of the four Gospels, the book of Acts, thirteen epistles of Paul, and eight general epistles, and finally the Apocalypse or the book of Revelation.

In our studies up to this point we have dealt with the Gospels, the book of Acts and the Pauline letters. The actual historical record ends with the close of the book of Acts about A.D. 62. In this book Luke's purpose was to deal mainly with the work of Paul. The first twelve chapters tell the general story, while the remaining chapters (13-28) are devoted to the experiences of Paul, the great apostle. In carrying out this plan it was necessary for him to drop out of his narrative the experiences of those whose work he had treated in the early chapters. For example, after recording the story of the separation of Paul and Barnabas on the eve of the second campaign, he makes no further mention of Barnabas. So it was with Peter, James, John and many others.

## *2. Purpose of This Chapter.*

It is our purpose in this closing chapter to deal briefly with the nine books (James, Jude, I Peter, II Peter, the three epistles of John, Hebrews and the Revelation) which we have not considered in our studies up to this point. We have some facts about the later work of James, Peter and John. As we consider their books we shall give a brief resume of their activities in the second half of the first Christian century.

## *3. The Catholic or General Epistles.*

Seven of these nine books — excluding Hebrews and Revelation — are often called Catholic epistles. The term *Catholic* has no connection with the Catholic church. The term simply means general letters because for the most part they are addressed to general groups of readers or churches and not to specific groups as, for example, Paul's epistle to the Romans. This classification is general and must not be pressed too far. The content of these epistles is not as personal as in the letters of Paul.

The fact that we can best appreciate a book or letter only when we know something of the writer, the recipient, the purpose, and the situation out of which the book came into being, applies to each of these books. Of necessity the treatment of these must be brief.

*4. Epistle of James.*

This little epistle of five chapters was probably among the very first books in the New Testament to be written. Some believe it was written as early as A.D. 40, others think 50 is the proper date, while still others place it around 60. However, we believe there are good reasons for accepting an early date.

There are various opinions also as to the authorship of the letter. There are three persons named James in the New Testament and each of these is believed by some to have been the author. One of these three was James, the brother of Jesus. In view of all the facts it seems probable that he was the writer of this epistle. Certainly this James occupied a very prominent place in the life of the early church. He was the natural brother (half-brother) of Jesus and grew up with him in the home at Nazareth. However, he did not become a Christian until after the resurrection of Jesus. When the apostles were scattered abroad from Jerusalem, James came to be the natural leader of the strong church there. According to tradition he was known as "The Righteous," and was so constant in prayer that his knees became like those of a camel.

The letter was written to Jews everywhere and particularly to Jewish Christians. In style it is abrupt, changing frequently from one subject to another. It is very practical in nature. It is concerned primarily with the conduct or behavior of Christians. It appears to have been called forth by a problem among the early Jewish Christians. These converts had been thoroughly grounded in the observance of the endless rules and regulations of Jewish religion in the first century. Upon learning that they were "saved not by works of righteousness which we do ourselves," but by the free grace of God in Jesus Christ they relaxed and became idle and restless. James vigorously insisted that their faith should result in the very greatest of works, "Faith without works is dead." The author in warnings, denunciations and exhortations deals with all the practical questions of their social and religious life.

The book has but little emphasis on doctrine or theology. The name of Jesus is mentioned only twice; the word gospel is not mentioned at all. There is no reference to redemption, the incarnation, nor the resurrection. It emphasizes Christian behavior. It deals with the Christian attitude toward trials and the Word of God. There are stern warnings against empty professions of faith, undue deference to the rich, profuse and foolish speech, pride, greed and contentions. The book closes with a series of urgent exhortations.

5. *Epistle of Jude.*

Jude, the author of the little epistle which bears his name, was a brother of Jesus, though he modestly refers to himself as a "servant of Jesus Christ and a brother of James." The book is brief and direct. It was written probably around A.D. 65 and there is no way of telling the destination of it. Its chief purpose was to strengthen the faith and the courage of Christians who had grown weak and were about to give up their faith. It was brought forth in the emergency created by certain ungodly men who had crept in privily "turning the grace of our God into lasciviousness, and denying our only Master and Lord, Jesus Christ." In vigorous language he urges Christians to "contend earnestly for the faith" and to "build themselves upon their most holy faith."

6. *The Book of Hebrews.*

The epistle to the Hebrews is one of the most eloquent and majestic books in the entire Bible. Because of its literary beauty and the quality of its contents it is also one of the most familiar to readers of the New Testament.

And yet there are many things about the book which are unknown to scholars. We do not know its author, its destination, its date nor the place where it was written. The book itself furnishes no clue for determining any of these.

In the King James Version it is ascribed to Paul. This ascription, however, carries no authority except the opinion of some early scholar. Competent students of the epistle and of Paul are almost unanimous in their judgment that Paul is not the author. Many other names are suggested as the author — Apollos, Barnabas, Luke, Timothy, Priscilla, Clement, Silas, and others. The simple truth is we do not know who wrote it. Origen says that only God knows who wrote it — and some cne has added "He has not told."

Many dates for its composition are likewise given. In view of all the facts it seems reasonable to place it in 69 A.D. just before the destruction of Jerusalem by Titus in 70 A.D. There is doubt also about its destination or the readers for whom it was intended. It was addressed

to a local church, which must be regarded as a Jewish church because of
the nature of the contents of the epistle. But which church we do not
know, though many hold that the Jerusalem church was the logical one.

From the standpoint of literary style the book ranks high. It is
composed of compact and unanswerable argument in stately and
eloquent language. "The book begins like a treatise, proceeds like a
sermon, and concludes like a letter." The occasion which called forth
this letter was the increasing tendency among these Jewish Christians
to turn away from their faith in Christianity and return to the old,
well-established religion of their fathers. As this new faith emerged and
gradually became a religion wholly independent from Judaism, the
Jews developed a "counter crusade to recover Jews from Christianity
and restore them to the Jewish fold." The strategy of these crusaders
was to ridicule Christianity as a new faith without a revealed law,
without a temple or a priesthood or a covenant with God. The appeal
was for the Jews to abandon this barren, new religion and come back
to the faith held by their forefathers for so many centuries. The issue
resolved itself into a comparison of what each of these two faiths had
to offer; it was Judaism or Christianity. It would appear that many
were turning back to Judaism and the Christians were losing in the
contest.

Then some eloquent and able Christian was led to present the claims
of the Christian faith and to show the infinite superiority of his faith
over that of Judaism. This writer shows that Jesus is the real glory of
Christianity and that he lifts it above Judaism at every point. His
masterful argument is easy to follow.

The writer begins by asserting that Christianity is superior to the
Jewish faith (Judaism) because Jesus through whom it was inaugurated
was far superior to those who were the messengers of Judaism (1:1-
4:13). Jesus is superior to the prophets, to angels and even to Moses.
Jesus is the Son of God and it was through him God spoke in
inaugurating Christianity. So Jesus was God's agent in creation.
Throughout the book Jesus, "the express image of his (God's) person,"
is held to be above all others in the plan of God in revealing himself
to men.

The author argues convincingly that in every respect Jesus is far
superior to the messengers of the Old Testament. However, the main
portion of his book is devoted to the superiority of Jesus over the
priesthood of Judaism. He shows that "Jesus is like Melchizedek and
so superior to Aaron" (4:14-7:28), works under a better covenant of

grace (8:1-13), works in a better sanctuary which is in heaven (9:1-12), offers a better sacrifice which is his own blood (9:13-10:18), and gives us better promises for the fulfillment of his task (10:19-12:3). Hence this epistle deserves to be called the Epistle of the Priesthood of Christ."[1]

There are many eloquent passages in this remarkable book. The student should read again such passages as 1:1-3, 2:1-3, 4:12-16, 10:19-25, 11:1-40, 12:1-3, 13:20-21. This book has a literary flavor which indicates that the author was a man of culture. "It points to the fact that the Epistle to the Hebrews, with its more definitely artistic, more literary language, constituted an epoch in the history of the new religion. Christianity is beginning to lay hands on the instruments of culture; the literary and theological period has begun."[2]

### 7. Later Work of Peter.

It is unnecessary to give even a brief survey of the remarkable career of the apostle Peter up to the point where he drops out of the New Testament narrative around A.D. 50. Suffice it to say that he was among the first and greatest of the disciples, that he was one of the three so intimately associated with Jesus, and that he naturally assumed a place of leadership in the church after the ascension of Jesus. In the important period of its early expansion he was unquestionably its greatest figure. After Paul came into the picture Peter was associated with him on several occasions. The last historical mention of him is in connection with the great council in Jerusalem A.D. 50.

Of the events in Peter's career after the Jerusalem conference we are in almost total ignorance. From brief allusions in the epistles we may safely assume that he continued his work chiefly as a missionary to the Jews of the Dispersion and that he was in Asia on a mission accompanied by his wife (I Cor. 9:5). Beyond this we have nothing on which to build. In his first epistle (5:13) he speaks of being in Babylon. This reference is interpreted by some to be literal; in other words a part, at least, of his later years were spent in this proverbially wicked city in the East. Others insist, however, that this is figurative language which refers to the city of Rome. This is possible but by no means certain. "But certainly Peter was not in Rome during Paul's first Roman imprisonment, nor during the second unless after the writing of the second letter to Timothy or unless Paul studiously avoided mentioning him, which is not likely. There is every argument against the idea that Peter founded the church at Rome and remained there till his death. He may have labored a while in Rome. On the whole it is more than probable that he did visit Rome. That is all we can say."[3]

One of the legends concerning his death is that he was involved in the Neronian persecutions and was condemned to crucifixion but at his own request was crucified head downward because he felt he was not worthy to die like his Lord. But there is no historical foundation for this story.

### 8. *The Epistles of Peter.*

Two brief books of the New Testament bear the name of Peter. There is reasonable unanimity of opinion as to the authorship of I Peter. There is considerable question among scholars as to who wrote the second letter.

(1) *I Peter* — There are sufficiently good reasons for concluding that Peter was the author of this epistle though this conclusion is not unanimously accepted. In the letter Peter writes as if he were in Babylon at the time (5:13). On the whole this would seem to mean that he was in Rome since "Babylon" was often used as a mystical allusion to the city of Rome. The bearer of this letter to its destination was Silas, or Silvanus, the companion of Paul on his second campaign. The letter was addressed to the Christians of Pontus, Galatia, Cappadocia, Asia and Bithynia. A glance at the map will show that these regions constituted the northern part of what was known as Asia Minor. The churches in this area were founded as the result of the work of Paul, though Peter writes to them in a tone of authority. From the references to the sufferings which these Christians were enduring we may assume they were involved in the organized persecutions of Nero. This would place the date of this letter around A.D. 65.

The epistle was intended to hearten these disciples by the example of Christ. The author calls attention to the "inheritance incorruptible and that fadeth not away" which was theirs. They were not promised immunity from hardships but consolation and assurance. The loss of worldly goods is of small consequence in view of the riches of their inheritance in Christ. In their sufferings they will find great blessing and distinct spiritual values. "If, when ye do well and suffer, ye bear it patiently this is grace before God. For hereunto were ye called; because Christ also suffered for you, leaving you an example, that ye should follow in his steps."

The letter has many valuable suggestions for practical Christian living. Christians are to keep their hearts in right relation toward God and man. This involves all social, family and spiritual relations. They are to learn the true values of life through their sufferings. The Christian will find many words of comfort and grace in this letter written by one who himself in suffering had tasted of the riches of God's grace.

(2) *II Peter* — While many scholars do not accept the Petrine authorship of this little letter there are many reputable authorities who feel that there are sufficient grounds for following the traditional view of Petrine authorship. Assuming the epistle is genuine the date of its writing would be around A.D. 67 or 68, probably not long before Peter's death. The letter is addressed to the same readers as I Peter.

The letter is intensely practical in nature. The writer is concerned that his readers shall resist the false teachings, probably Gnosticism, to which they were being subjected. He reminds them of their rich inheritance in Christ and of his privilege in exhorting them to be steadfast. The reading of this vigorous letter would kindle anew their courage and would inspire them "to grow in the grace and knowledge of our Lord and Saviour Jesus Christ."

Despite the fact that this is a brief letter whose authorship may not be beyond question it is worthy of serious study. "Though its authorship has been debated by competent scholars and unquestioned Christians it has stood the test of use by generations. It speaks about matters which were once dangerous to the Christian faith, and are dangerous still. It calls attention to the subtle ways by which the Christian heritage may be sabotaged by the infiltration of those who denature the faith of its normative historical content. It warns about the devastating effects of divorcing the gospel from ethics. And it exalts the lordship of Jesus Christ in all its majesty and power."[4]

### 9. *Later Work of John the Apostle.*

The reader will recall that John was one of the foremost disciples of Jesus during his earthly life. Probably because of his great modesty he has not been given credit for all that he did both before and after the resurrection of Jesus. Peter took the lead in the early church but John was always there to support and strengthen his work. In the book of Acts he is referred to a number of times. The last mention of his work in this historical record is in connection with his mission from Jerusalem up to Samaria to investigate the work of Philip there (Acts 8:14). He drops out of the record at that point, not because he was inactive but because Luke is giving his attention to the larger work of evangelizing the Gentiles. We know, however, that he was in the great conference at Jerusalem in A.D. 50 and shared in the honor and responsibility of this momentous occasion.

John was a man of genius as all his work testifies, but he was not a man of the schools with scholastic training. Several allusions to his fiery temper and the nickname, "Sons of Thunder" given to him and James, indicates that he was impetuous and hot-headed. He was closely associated with Jesus and probably was able to understand the mind and spirit of Jesus better than any of the other disciples. Certainly he loved Jesus and in turn was loved by him. He was philosophically minded and had a sensitive spiritual temperament which enabled him to understand the moods of Jesus better than the others. He was the disciple who leaned on the bosom of Jesus at the supper. He followed Jesus to his trial and was able to get Peter admitted to the inner court that night. As Jesus died on the cross he tenderly committed his mother to the care of John.

The later years of John are veiled in obscurity so far as any historical record is concerned. However, from allusions in his writings and from reliable tradition we are able to know something of his last years. Irenaeus, Polycrates of Ephesus and Clement of Alexandria are trustworthy sources of authority for the statement of his last years. According to this tradition he went to Ephesus and spent his closing years in missionary activity in Asia. In the terrible persecutions inflicted upon Christians by Domitian (A.D. 81-96) John being a leader, was banished to the isle of Patmos where he remained for some time. He was later allowed to return to Ephesus where he died probably after A.D. 98. One of the traditions is that he, like Peter, died a martyr's death. According to this story he was submerged in a vat of boiling oil.

### 10. The Epistles of John.

Traditionally it has been held that five of the books of the New Testament were written by the Apostle John. These are the gospel which bears his name, three epistles, and the Revelation.

(1) *I John* — There is no way of determining certainly the details of the writing of this epistle. Perhaps the majority of recognized scholars are of the opinion that John wrote this letter from Ephesus about 80-85 A.D. It seems to have been intended for churches in Asia Minor where John spent the last forty or more years of his life. As the recognized leader of Christians in the area he would be well acquainted with the members of these chuches. This was at the time when

Gnosticism was making real inroads in the thinking of Christians. This was quite an involved and subtle philosophy which would cut the tap-root of the Christian faith. It was a mixture of Oriental and Greek philosophy with some Christian doctrines. It was a complicated system of thought; in fact, there were several schools of thinking among those who belonged to this cult.

The heart of their teaching centered around the person of Christ. They denied the humanity of Jesus, the fact that he existed in the flesh. John wrote this epistle to refute this contention of the Gnostics. He goes immediately to the matter in the very first statement: "That which was from the beginning, which we have heard, which we have seen with our eyes, which we have looked upon, and our hands have handled, of the Word of life" (1:1).

While the letter is a powerful refutation of Gnosticism it is a warm, rich treatise on the reality and the rewards of Christian living. Those who are genuine disciples of Christ will live in light, will live a life of righteousness and love and will walk by faith. Christians will be known by their love, and their faith will overcome the world.

(2) *II John* — This is a very brief letter addressed to an "elect lady and her children," which is understood by some to refer to a church and its members or, as is more likely, to a devout Christian lady and her own children. It may be that John had been entertained in her home or had come to know her family in some other way. In the epistle he exalts love as the chief virtue. The true Christian will make progress by accepting Jesus Christ seriously and by following his teachings.

(3) *III John* — This brief letter is addressed to Gaius, probably the one who lived in Corinth and was associated with Paul in his work there. Certain missionaries had come to this church with a letter from John but were forbidden to speak and receive an offering in their work by a leader of the church, Diotrephes, "who loveth to have the pre-eminence." Gaius received and entertained these visitors in his home and joined with other like-minded Christians in supporting their work with a generous offering. Diotrephes led in a movement to exclude Gaius and his friends from the church because of their missionary generosity.

When these facts were made known to John he wrote a letter to Gaius to commend him for his action. He promised to come later to deal with Diotrephes. In the letter he encouraged the Christians to give even more generously to the work of preaching the gospel of Christ. "If thou shalt bring them on their way worthily of God thou shalt do well." Such hospitable support constitutes a worthy part of the whole enterprise of Christian missions.

### 11. The Revelation.

Because of its nature this book proves to be fascinating to many readers, and easily leads to gross misrepresentation. The limits of space will not permit even the briefest mention of all the strange and fantastic interpretations based on the book. Frankly there is much in the book which we may not understand, but the general purpose and value of the book can be easily discerned.

It was written by John while he was in exile on the island of Patmos. The Domitian persecutions were very severe and John as a Christian leader was banished from the mainland and sent to the bleak little island in the sea, presumably between A.D. 90-95. While on this island he received the visions related in the book and was commanded to write these in a book. These visions were meant to cheer the hard-pressed Christians in Asia who were sorely persecuted in the bitter effort of Domitian to stamp out Christianity which was already threatening the existence of the Roman empire. These seven churches of Asia were in the very center of the persecutions and they needed cheer and encouragement as they faced sufferings of such severity.

The book is an apocalypse, that is a revelation or "unveiling." Many oppressed peoples have learned to communicate in cryptograms. John used figures, symbols, cryptic phrases, and words which, when their enemies read them would seem but the meaningless jargon of a defeated old preacher. But to the Christians these symbols and figures and visions had significance and meaning. So these words of the aged apostle would easily pass by the Roman authorities into the hands of these believers who would read and understand what John was saying to them.

We may readily admit that these symbols and visions are not understandable to us. For this reason there have been so many strange and fallacious interpretations of them. However, the central truth of each of the seven visions is easily discerned. We get into endless difficulties when we seek to know the detailed meaning of all the pictures, beasts, horns, trumpets, horses, trees, seas, stars and so on.

The book is made up of seven visions and their messages. The first vision is that of the triumphant, living Lord who moves among his churches with the assurance that he is the first and last, the living one who has the keys of death and of Hades (1:10-3:22).

The second vision (4:1-8:1) is the vision of the slain Lamb controlling the events of history.

The third vision is that of the seven angels with the seven trumpets (8:2-11:19). Calamities and devastation are visited upon unrepentant people, but at last victory comes and men worship God.

In chapters 12-14 we see the seven symbolical figures that represent the great conflict between good and evil. Opposition finally ceases with victory for righteousness.

In chapters 15-16 we have a picture of the seven angels who came to pour the bowls of divine wrath upon the earth.

Chapters 17-19 give the vision of judgment of "the great harlot that sitteth upon many waters." In chapter 20 we are told of the capturing and the binding of Satan.

The seventh vision is a picture of "the consummation of the historical process" (chapters 21-22). Here we see a "new heaven and a new earth," and "the new Jerusalem coming down out of heaven from God." The book closes with the assurance of final victory. "Thus in a series of moving pictures John has seen, and has said to the hearts of the Christians in their persecution, that God is on the throne of the universe and in control of all the forces that make history; that the distinction between good and evil is radical and eternal, and that the conflict between righteousness and wickedness is bitter and persistent; that the living Christ is present in the conflict with his people, in full knowledge and sympathy, in their struggle; and that he dominates every stage of history; that in the long run the forces of righteousness are to win; that the outcome will be a righteous order which the redeeming God will rule in loving presence; that in all this glorious conflict the people of Christ are his witnesses, his representatives on earth, through whom he carries on his saving work and constructs his kingdom."[5]

## 12. Conclusion.

We have now come to the end of the New Testament story. The reader has had an opportunity to acquire a general understanding of the origin and development of the most significant movement in human history. He has had a glimpse of the contents of the most important book in literature. The New Testament contains the historical record of early Christianity; but it contains much more. In it is found the inexhaustible body of eternal truth without which men can not really live. Those who are wise will seek a more perfect comprehension of this truth in order that they may walk in its light, and thus find the fulness of life.

[1]Robertson, A. T., *Word Pictures in the New Testament,* Vol. 5, pp. 327-328.
[2]Deismann, Adolph, *Light from the Ancient East,* pp. 70-71.
[3]Robertson, *Studies in the New Testament,* p. 233.
[4]*Interpreters Bible,* Vol. 12, p. 167.
[5]Carver, W. O., *Why They Wrote the New Testament,* p. 132.

# A BRIEF BIBLIOGRAPHY

Adams, J. McKee: *Our Bible.*
Battenhouse, H. M.: *New Testament History and Literature.*
Blaikie and Matthews: *A Manual of Bible History.*
Carver, W. O.: *The Self-Interpretation of Jesus.*
Carver, W. O.: *Why They Wrote the New Testament.*
Dana, H. E.: *The New Testament World.*
Denny, W. B.: *The Career and Significance of Jesus.*
Edersheim, Alfred: *Life and Times of Jesus the Messiah,* 2 Vols.
Farrar, F. W.: *The Life of Christ.*
Foakes-Jackson: *A Brief Biblical History.*
Glover, T. R.: *The Jesus of History.*
Glover, T. R.: *Paul of Tarsus.*
Glover, T. R.: *The World of the New Testament.*
Maclear, G. F.: *A Classbook of New Testament History.*
Mathews, Shailer: *A History of New Testament Times in Palestine.*
McDaniel, G. W.: *The Supernatural Jesus.*
Morton, H. V.: *In the Steps of Jesus.*
Morton, H. V.: *In the Steps of St. Paul.*
Mould, E. W. K.: *Essentials of Bible History.*
Robertson, A. T.: *A Harmony of the Gospels.*
Robertson, A. T.: *Epochs in the Life of Jesus.*
Robertson, A. T.: *Epochs in the Life of Paul.*
Robertson, A. T.: *John the Loyal.*
Robertson, A. T.: *Studies in the New Testament.*
Shepard, J. W.: *The Christ of the Gospels.*
Smith, David: *The Days of His Flesh.*
Smith, David: *The Life and Letters of St. Paul.*
Smith, George A.: *Historical Geography of the Holy Land.*
Smith, Miles W.: *Upon Whom the Spirit Came.*
Stalker, James: *Life of Christ.*
Stalker, James: *Life of St. Paul.*
Tidwell, J. B.: *The Bible Book by Book.*
Tidwell, J. B.: *The Bible Period by Period.*